"[Josse's] exploration of the philosop contracts, fraud, and finance writ large starts like an itch that won't go away and needs scratching, each vignette and chapter pulling the reader in more deeply into a discussion of the evolution of finance that I now find important and fascinating—thanks to this book."

Steve Clemons
Editor at Large, *The Atlantic*

"A compelling, interdisciplinary journey into the arcane world of finance. Josse takes a dry topic and through modern day stories and historical references deftly educates and entertains. Each topic is intricately analyzed and then all the thoughts are threaded into a coherent and unique perspective and understanding of finance as both a science and reflection of underlying societal norms. I strongly recommend this book to practitioners and students who wish to understand finance in the context of global business and its impact on society."

Bruce R. Magid
Dean International Business School
Brandeis University

"Jeremy Josse's book takes you on a wild ride—from Dinosaurs to Joseph's dream (the one speculator in history that had a direct line to the Almighty) from Macbeth to English ships at the end of the 19th century, from Lehman brothers to Ferraris and from Talmudic scholars to antique map dealers. Faust, Marx and Atlantis (the lost continent) also appear as characters in a slew of entertaining stories and philosophical musings which illustrate financial concepts such as derivatives, contracts, uncertainty, taxes and ownership. Josse has some strong views based on his many years of experience in the market. You may not always agree, but will always be entertained, informed and want to keep on reading."

S.A. Ravid
Professor of Finance,
Sy Syms School of Business, New York

DINOSAUR DERIVATIVES AND OTHER TRADES

JEREMY JOSSE

WILEY

This edition first published 2015
© 2015 Jeremy Josse

Registered office
John Wiley & Sons Ltd, The Atrium, Southern Gate, Chichester, West Sussex, PO19 8SQ,
United Kingdom

For details of our global editorial offices, for customer services and for information about how to
apply for permission to reuse the copyright material in this book please see our website at www
.wiley.com.

Wiley publishes in a variety of print and electronic formats and by print-on-demand. Some material
included with standard print versions of this book may not be included in e-books or in print-
on-demand. If this book refers to media such as a CD or DVD that is not included in the version
you purchased, you may download this material at http://booksupport.wiley.com. For more
information about Wiley products, visit www.wiley.com.

Designations used by companies to distinguish their products are often claimed as trademarks. All
brand names and product names used in this book are trade names, service marks, trademarks or
registered trademarks of their respective owners. The publisher is not associated with any product
or vendor mentioned in this book.

Limit of Liability/Disclaimer of Warranty: While the publisher and author have used their best
efforts in preparing this book, they make no representations or warranties with the respect to the
accuracy or completeness of the contents of this book and specifically disclaim any implied
warranties of merchantability or fitness for a particular purpose. It is sold on the understanding that
the publisher is not engaged in rendering professional services and neither the publisher nor the
author shall be liable for damages arising herefrom. If professional advice or other expert assistance
is required, the services of a competent professional should be sought.

A catalogue record for this book is available from the Library of Congress.

A catalogue record for this book is available from the British Library.

ISBN 978-1-119-01959-6 (paperback)   ISBN 978-1-119-01961-9 (ebk)
ISBN 978-1-119-01963-3 (ebk)   ISBN 978-1-119-01960-2 (obk)

Cover design: Wiley
Front cover image: © Victor Habbick/shutterstock.com
Background overlay: © steveball/shutterstock.com

Set in 11/13pt MinionPro-Regular by Thomson Digital, Noida, India
Printed by Courier Westford

To Muriel

CONTENTS

ABOUT THE AUTHOR

Jeremy Josse has spent the last 20-plus years of his career working as an executive in some of the world's leading financial institutions, including Schroders, Citigroup and Rothschild.

Josse was born in London, England, and earned his BA degree in Philosophy and Economics at Trinity College, Oxford University. He subsequently did a master's degree at University College, London University, in Political Philosophy/Economics, as well as qualifying as a banking attorney.

Josse's earliest thesis work at Oxford and London University related to certain theories of meaning as they pertained to economics. He has published numerous articles on a wide range of financial subjects including the credit crisis, bank restructurings, and financial engineering.

Josse lives with his wife, Muriel, and three boys in New York City.

ACKNOWLEDGMENTS

My first acknowledgment for a book like this really goes to the finance profession itself. It is a very old profession that is at once fascinating and engaging, yet suffers from a perennial existential crisis—what is the point of it all? But for this dichotomy, the book would simply not have been possible. I suppose this particular conflict can be said of many things in life, but it seems to me to be particularly acute in the finance world. I could not have committed (nor continue to commit) myself for so long to this industry if it were not compelling and important. Equally, it would be disingenuous not to recognize the periodic absurdities of the whole undertaking. It is therefore, the very nature of finance itself that engendered the issues touched on in this book—hence I am thankful to the industry for that.

However, my first human acknowledgment must go to Ed Claflin. Ed is nominally referred to as my agent, but he has been much more than that to me. Ed reviewed every word of the book numerous times and there is not a single paragraph that he did not have some impact on. He is also a long-time master of the publishing industry (another puzzling business), a wise old bird and he has carefully advised me on all aspects of the book's production. In the course of this process, Ed has also become a personal friend.

Ed introduced me to the Wiley publishing team and they too have been huge supporters and enablers of this book. First and foremost, I refer to Thomas Hyrkiel, who from the beginning became the book's sponsor and pushed it through all the way from contract to final production. Thomas, like Ed, saw the potential at an early stage and he too has become a friend.

Thomas has been supported by a fine team at Wiley, including Jennie Kitchen, Sam Hartley, Ben Hall, Heather Dunphy, Lucy Valantine and others, all of whom have played their critical role in the production process.

There are also those who made meaningful contributions to the content of the book from a research perspective. In particular, I must thank Craig Zabala of the Concorde Group for multiple reasons. Craig is a fighter, an entrepreneur and a true friend. He provided both financial and practical support for the book. In addition, his leading contributions to our joint research into the shadow banking sector had direct bearing on specific parts of the book. There are others to thank here, including, inter alia: Jeremy Rosen for his insights into the antique laws of usury; Viraj Parekh for taking out some weekend time to research various aspects of the book; Jason Shela for establishing media and PR support for the book; Daniel Perez for his last minute corrections; my friend Ron (whose real name must remain unsaid) for his insight into the tortuous nature of fraud; to Graham Arader for his unique knowledge of the antique map market; and even to some of my old Oxford and London philosophy and economics tutors for helping me to think, at least occasionally, in a curious way.

Finally, there are the thanks to family. Some may think this last type of acknowledgment is the stock sentimentality seen in all book acknowledgments. However you only have to write one of these books to realize the real burden it puts on your family. It is both a time and an emotional burden and they have all borne it with incredible equanimity—my boys, Noam, Yonah and Gabriel, but above all, my ever-patient and supportive wife, my pillar—Muriel.

INTRODUCTION

"Money speaks sense in a language all nations understand."
                                                    —**Aphra Behn** (1640–1689)

"Let us all be happy, and live within our means, even if we have to borrow the money to do it with."
                                                    —**Artemus Ward** (1834–1867)

"Crito, we owe a cock to Aesculapius; please pay it and don't let it pass."
                                                    —**Socrates' last words** (c. 470 BCE–c. 399 BCE)

It is fair to say that finance is a serious matter, whereas riddles are often frivolous. Money, on the other hand, can be very superficial, whereas philosophical puzzles are profound.

Finance is viewed as a dry subject, engaged in by men and women in dark suits who toil away for innumerable hours in large, box-like buildings. What is finance, after all? It's the counting of numbers, isn't it? Or the practical investing of money, providing loans and capital and settling of accounts to ensure proper payments of due bills. Finance, if seen this way, is essentially for the straight shooters. It's a serious occupation reserved for those whose minds are embedded in the settlement of everyday, practical affairs.

It would seem utterly contradictory then, to claim that every aspect of finance involves some philosophical puzzle. How could a subject as "dry" as finance be related to philosophical matters? Philosophy reminds us of the strangest things in life, the paradoxical. Don't philosophers deal with moral purpose? They dwell on those deep contradictions and inconsistencies in humanity that seem inexplicable. Philosophical riddles take us to the heart of ancient Greek thinking or to the most ethereal topics involving logic and semantics. It is a subject that is seemingly mastered by only the least practical of thinkers, those whose minds can wander far from mundane concerns. Surely, we would never imagine that a person contemplating deep philosophical paradoxes could be the same individual who carefully reviews the accruals and payments of a company.

In the conventional view then, the discipline of finance is the polar opposite of philosophical thought.

In this book, I hope to prove to you that this view is profoundly wrong. Not only that—it is a view which shows a fundamental misunderstanding of the business of finance and perhaps, also, a misperception of the essence of philosophy.

Deep within the financial world lie a series of puzzles. Below the apparent formalities of the world of finance, there are quandaries involving the unexplained. There are paradoxes involving hypocrisy, double standards, dilemmas, and contradictions that border on the absurd. These are all the things I am particularly curious about.

Now it's true that some of the most serious financial practitioners do not spend much time contemplating deeper philosophical challenges. But then, the same goes for most of us. I do not spend much time contemplating whether the chair I am sitting in really exists or not. Yet that obscure philosophical problem is always there, every day, whenever I sit in my chair. And so it is with the paradoxes underlying finance.

This book consists of a set of particular stories in the philosophy of finance. If all goes well, I hope these stories will give you an inkling of this world of financial curios. In other words, here are case-by-case studies of some basic concepts in finance that take us deep into the territory of paradox.

The sources of these stories are various. Some are drawn from my own 20-plus years of real-life experience as a financial executive in the banking sector. Others are famous stories or legends of old. A few tales are entirely apocryphal, a way to deal with abstractions by presenting examples. But all, however odd or enigmatic, are intended to give you some perspective on what's going on "inside" the world of finance itself. Each story is, you might say, a thought experiment in the laboratory of the philosophy of finance. Our objective is to journey over the meta-phorical financial rainbow, or perhaps go with Alice and explore the other side of the financial looking glass.

Now, let me also say what this book does not intend to cover. There is already a very large body of mainly academic writing on the so-called philosophy of economics. This writing tends to be technical. Typically, the academic approach covers issues of political philosophy and sociology, demonstrating their impact on economics. (One of the burning issues seems to be the question of whether economics is a science on a par with the natural sciences.) Many of the issues addressed by academicians are couched in very formalistic terms, and their theses are developed through citations of different historical schools of economics, philosophy, or political theory.

This book takes another route. My aim is to show what we actually mean when we're talking about some very basic concepts in finance. Each chapter will begin with the story and then go on to analyze what the story might tell us about that fundamental concept. I agree that our under-standing of these puzzles and questions needs to be informed by some knowledge of the history and substance of philosophy, economics, and social/political theory. But here I have no intention of engaging in some sterile academic exercise in technical or analytical philosophy. Nor am I going to introduce analyses typically found in academic finance journals. The point is to bring out conceptual conundrums and moral dilemmas that touch all of us in the world of real finance.

What I've found is that many people in the finance business do sense these philosophical puzzles whispering in their ears as they go about their daily business. In fact, I suspect that all of us, as we deal with everyday, personal financial concerns, have some sense of the paradoxical soup lying just below the surface. But you can't spend a lot of time mulling over the paradoxes when you have income to produce, investments to make, and bills to pay. Dwelling on conundrums would be seriously distracting if it interfered with settling your accounts.

To put it another way, the problem of the existence (or not) of the chair I am sitting in seems an absurd problem—not only pointless but perhaps even meaningless. Similarly, it might seem like the questions I pose in this book are unrelated to what we would call your real financial life. But anyone confronted with a financial problem will tend to find some of the challenges they have are directly related to the questions I am addressing in this book. If you are facing some financial vexation, you don't necessarily see the issue in overtly philosophical terms, let alone perceive some theoretical paradox at the heart of your problem. Nevertheless, a financial challenge often leaves us with an uneasy sense of tension or even frustration. We have to recognize that certain assumptions are being made or that many financial concerns involve some form of moral inconsistency.

One of the most basic questions in the philosophy of finance is what we ultimately mean by "value." So, that's where this book begins. What does it mean to say an asset has value? Indeed, why does anything have any economic value? And if we ascribe a value to a certain asset, what does that say about our attitudes? How does our valuation of assets affect our behavior and morality? Knotty questions. So the first chapter deals with the peculiar story of an option to buy . . . an extinct dinosaur. What would you do if you were attending a live auction to buy or sell such an option (for "value")? Under what circumstances would people pay good money for a dinosaur derivative?

Then I want to move on to the anxiety we feel when confronting a financial problem—a feeling that results from what we call "doubt" or "risk." We can never be quite sure whether things may, or may not, turn out in the way contemplated when undertaking a particular financial exercise, or calculation, or plan, or investment.

A better word than "doubt" is "uncertainty." And this is where finance and philosophy really converge. Volumes have been written, in the great pantheon of philosophy, on the question of how we can be certain of anything. (My "chair problem," for instance: how can I really be certain my chair exists, even though I can feel it supporting my backside?) In finance we are plagued with uncertainty, and it's no abstraction. While philosophers and academicians may write at length on the topic of certainty without disrupting the general ebb and flow of goods and services, those actually involved in finance know all too well how uncertainty creates real-life events, including catastrophic economic collapses affecting whole societies worldwide.

Of course, in finance most questions about uncertainty have to do with the *future*. We're concerned about managing the risk associated with uncertainty, or beating others by using our predictive capabilities. So the second chapter will analyze this concept through a very famous story about "prophecy"—namely, the story of Joseph from the book of Genesis. Here was a man (prophet) who apparently predicted firstly seven good years, then seven bad years in the Egyptian economy. But Joseph's predictions were quite unique for he was not "uncertain" about this economic future. According to the story, God had already informed Joseph what the outcomes would be.

By looking at Joseph's ability to circumvent doubt over the future, and seeing the way he used his privileged economic knowledge, we glean some insights into the nature of "uncertainty" and "certainty" itself. As we all know, there are in practice, limits to human foresight.

Next, the "contract"—perhaps the most basic building block in finance. What, really, are contracts? Why do business people so often argue and dispute their terms? In the third chapter, I will describe an old English legal case in the law of contract, just to give you a sense of what a contract may really be. This, in turn, opens a window on some very curious, logical puzzles concerning what it actually means to follow the terms—or "rules"—of a contract. Far from being set in stone, the rules in a contract can almost always be interpreted in such a way that any pattern of behavior (any pattern *whatsoever*) can be shown to be in conformity with those rules. No wonder then that hugely divergent interpretations of the terms of a contract can arise. When you mix that insight with good old human self-interest, it goes a long way toward explaining why the business world spends its time litigating, lying, and fighting over the terms of many business deals.

"Financial instruments" are themselves a form of contract. So we look next at the concept of a financial instrument itself. In Chapter 4 I tell an antique tale about some of the earliest forms of financial contracts and the old prohibitions on usury. All financial instruments are merely peculiar interpretations of contracts, or reconfigurations of contracts, to achieve certain ends. They are invariably a form of "legal fiction." And yet, though quite artificial in design, they can sometimes produce important economic benefits.

Another peculiar philosophical question in finance concerns the very nature of "financial innovation," the topic of Chapter 5. Why is financial innovation important and yet also potentially so dangerous and open to human distortion? Financial innovation is, in effect, the invention or discovery of new financial instruments and contracts. But when a new financial product is developed, or a new theory in finance is advanced, is that really the equivalent of a scientific discovery or a new invention? It certainly doesn't feel like that. Perhaps it is more like the development of a new theory in mathematics, though that doesn't seem quite right either. This is an issue that has manifested itself throughout economic history and even (as we shall see) in the growth of the American railway system in the 19th century. Meanwhile, it has still more direct relevance to us today. I will argue it gives us a concrete insight into one of the often neglected causes of the 2007/8 credit crisis.

Then, on to another core concept (Chapter 6): what really is an "ownership right?" This is a question that moral and political philosophers have brooded over for centuries. I'm going to approach it from a slightly skewed angle by considering the story of Faust and his pact with the Devil. Faust was a trader himself: he traded certain moral rights for material rights. So, what are these material rights? What, for example, does it mean to own a stock? And what would happen if we too could enter into a Faustian-style pact? Suppose we could trade, say, our political right to vote for rights to more money? Could it be that, in fact, we all do something like that in our everyday business activities? Do we trade away certain rights for cash?

We must, of course, also ask "What is money?" While we know that money is just a means of exchange, today's electronic money has taken on a form that makes it uniquely incorporeal and replicable. In Chapter 7 I tell the strange story of a computer hacker who succeeds in breaking into the accounts of the major banks of a nation. What I want to imagine, however, is not a case of theft. Rather, what would happen if our hacker took nothing at all from anyone's accounts? Suppose that instead, he *filled* everyone's accounts with large quantities of electronic money. Should we consider him a great philanthropist? So it would seem. Instead, we will find that his largesse is more damaging than if he had stolen in the first place. Nor is this purely imaginary. What I wish to portray is a picture of our modern (IT-based) money supply and inflation. This story also gives some perspective on the latest financial buzzword, "quantitative easing."

Let's then touch on the whole issue of distributive justice. Huge profits can be made in lucky (or clever?) financial dealings—so how should these profits, and indeed all our finite resources, be shared among a nation? How do we manage wealth inequalities? This is a very hot issue today post the credit crisis and I want to analyze it via the question of "What is taxation?" However, my focus will not be taxation as it is today, but taxation as it might (perhaps) have been in the lost city of Atlantis. Tracking the political economics of that mythical land may give us some insights into today's polarized debate on taxation policy and wealth re-distribution.

In Chapter 9 it's time to shift to the darker side and look at finance when it goes wrong. In order to address the question of "What is fraud?" I will tell a true tale of a brazen fraudster who destroyed multiple financial businesses. (The saga is from my own personal experience—though fortunately, I was a mere spectator, not a participant.) What is the nature of a fraudster? Often, we tend to imagine a "normal" individual who has gone astray or fallen on hard times. But there are those who are way beyond that. I'm going to pose the strong possibility that there really are white-collar "psychopaths." These are people who do stuff that most of us would never do, and they do it consistently. For this select demographic, I question whether any sort of financial regulation will ever provide a foolproof barrier against wrongdoing. In fact too much regulation may make the fraudster's life easier, not harder.

Which then brings us to the nature of "financial regulation" itself—addressed in Chapter 10. Truth to tell, much of the Western financial world is what I would call "regulated to death." People might not agree whether this is a good or bad thing, but certainly in the U.S. we have one of the most complex bodies of financial regulation in history. With so many rules, how can we see which rules are effective and which unhelpful? The story I tell in this chapter focuses on one of the last remaining vestiges of a truly unregulated financial environment—the Fine Art market. This is the sole remaining Wild West frontier. In this truly bizarre landscape of financial freedom, I see the upside of an unregulated market but also the dubious practices and double dealing inherent in the business. This is a unique world where anything is possible: pigs fly, there are two moons, and nothing is kosher. We really do need effective market and financial regulation, but is modern financial regulation, with its micro-managing tendencies, undermining its own purpose and efficacy?

Finally, there is the "end game" in finance, which is at heart another conundrum; "What is bankruptcy?" Here again I will dip into my own financial practice and tell a tale of one of the most curious modern financial restructurings I have ever witnessed. This all-too-true story concerns the bankruptcy and reconstruction of a large asset finance business that had became mind-numbingly complex. Once this firm entered a period of distress, it revealed such a circular array of financial flows that it was hard even to contemplate a rational resolution. So why are financial institutions so vulnerable to collapse and how does "debt" feed that vulnerability? And to what extent is modern financial complexity so overwhelming that it exceeds our human capacity to manage large, inter-related (and international) financial institutions?

When all is said and done, we'll see that perhaps it all comes down to a curious computer game or simulation. I'll touch on that at the very end. And childlike though it is, it seems, nevertheless, to capture many of the themes of this book. For the more we think on the core financial concepts in this book, the more we will see they are all (or mostly) linked by a single chain of thought and causality. It is a conceptual chain that I think, runs through much of the abiding preoccupations within the money world today.

And here we arrive at the heart of the conundrum. Far from being the pursuit of dark-suited professionals in box-like towers, finance is, after all, a living and breathing subject that we all contend with in our daily lives. True, the great adventures in finance take us on journeys to lands filled with curious trades and unlikely forms of commerce. Yet what we ultimately find is that none of us can escape the philosophical and social riddles that are embedded in all our financial practices. As it turns out, the puzzles are not hidden away in distant rooms of commerce or financial ivory towers. Instead they are woven into the very fabric of ordinary social life.

WHAT IS VALUE?

Dinosaur Derivatives

"A man who knows the price of everything and the value of nothing."
—Definition of a cynic, by **Oscar Wilde** (1854–1900)

I want to begin our travels with a tale told to me some years ago by a close friend. To maintain the anonymity of my friend I shall just call him Karl. Karl's strange story relates to an auction he once attended at a very elite auction house (which shall also remain unnamed) in a relatively unknown street in downtown Manhattan. The auction occurred at a time of great financial uncertainty. And Karl, as it happened, had never previously attended an auction at this establishment.

The auction was held in a beautiful room furnished with a variety of antiques. The ambience was stately grandeur—oak paneling throughout, some fine Colonial-style windows and a preciously carved cornice. Most striking, in Karl's view, was a long painting in a rich gold frame that occupied one wall. It was an oil painting, in mock Renaissance style, showing a scene depicting . . . a herd of dinosaurs. They were of many types—a large group of scaled Stegosaurs drinking water from a small lake; or a lone Diplodocus in the background, its long neck stretched to reach the branches of a prehistoric palm tree. In the distance, at the top of the canvas was a Pterodactyl flying over a group of Triceratops. Most curious of all, to Karl, was one small Raptor in the foreground. It seemed to look obliquely out at the audience with a captivating glare. According to Karl, he thought he even heard the Raptor speak in an antique and bestial tongue, saying, "Here we sell the particularly absurd. Come and buy, my friends!"

The layout of the room was typical of a high-class auction room. A dais in front bore the podium where the auctioneer would stand. Behind the dais, on the back wall, was a large electronic screen that remained dark as participants entered the room. Arrayed in front of the dais were rows of chairs.

Flanking one wall were desks with telephones. Before the bidding commenced, agents positioned themselves at the desks ready to place and receive calls.

Karl was among the first to arrive. As he waited patiently, the room gradually filled. A lady entered who, it soon became apparent, was the auctioneer. She took her place behind the podium and in short order the auction was under way.

Yet never had such a strange auction been held. In some 10,000 years of bartering and trading, never had there been anything quite like this. Try as he might, Karl could not recall any episode of human commerce, from the first loans in Mesopotamia to the ancient bazaars of Arabia and the Silk Road, when there had been an auction so defying the premises of economic rationality. Who could have imagined that trade would come to this?

For as Karl soon learned, the assets being auctioned—hinted at in the dinosaur painting—were many derivations removed from physical reality.

The first item being sold, just as one example, was no less than an option to buy a Megalodon. (In small print on the auction list, it did state that the option could be exercised only in the event that a Megalodon "should become available.") For the benefit of the uninitiated, the listing also noted that a Megalodon was a prehistoric shark that had become extinct many millions of years previously.

A number of clauses were added to clarify the terms of the sale of the option. The clauses stated that the option was robust and universally applicable across most world jurisdictions. Wherever this Megalodon might be found, the option would give a legally binding right to the holder to call for the beast.

In fact, however, it mattered very little whether the Megalodon ever materialized. The term on the option was many centuries long and investors had been actively buying, even trading, the option for some period prior to the auction.

The screen at the back of the chamber now showed a huge, clear image of a Megalodon. The shark was unimaginably large. The screen was dominated by the beast with its mouth gaping open to reveal three rows of white, triangular-shaped teeth. The body of the Megalodon was sleek and grey—somewhat resembling a shark, though more bulbous and massive than any now alive. Its streamlined body seemed perfectly suited for rapid aquatic attack. In fact, it was hard to imagine that a beast with such a voracious aspect and vicious jaws could have lost out in the evolutionary game and become extinct.

Inset at the bottom left-hand corner of the screen was a real picture of a set of fossilized Megalodon teeth. To convey the dimensions of the fossilized jawbone, a museum curator was depicted standing inside the gaping maw, clear evidence that the diameter of the animal's mouth was greater than the height of a human body.

The image on the screen, Karl told me, seemed even to have a three-dimensional quality that no doubt stirred a response in the audience. It was as if the very image of the Megalodon created the strongest incitement to bid. The vivid picture made a profound impression on the audience—and, no doubt, added a compelling impetus to the excitement and marketing appeal of the call option.

Bizarre though it was, the auction of a Megalodon call option came as no great surprise to Karl. The auction house had been promoting it heavily over an extended period of time. Karl was reasonably well-to-do. Hence, he had been specifically targeted by this auction house. He had been told that this offer was only open to an exclusive group of High Net Worth investors.

Judging from the sales literature Karl had received and the calls from reps, Karl had amassed sufficient assets to have recently entered into this exclusive club.

As he soon observed, bidding for the option soon became hot, even aggressive. Bids came in thick and fast from a large pool of speculators. A man in a fedora was quite active. A number of old ladies were perched nervously on the edge of their seats. Another gentleman, standing by a post, seemed to maintain an icy calm. Near the front was a couple bidding in unison, secretly whispering their strategy in each other's ears. There were also hidden bidders, their presence indicated by the ranks manning the desk phones.

In fact, the phone bidders were especially active. Those working the phones, themselves agents of the auction house, conferred furtively with their distant clients. To conceal the exact nature of their conversations, they spoke behind cupped hands. In repeated outbidding, these phone-based investors often topped offers coming from those in the immediate audience. The "big money" seemed to be with the phone buyers. To Karl it seemed obvious that the participants who would never deign to appear on the scene were the ones driving the market. (In our later conversation, Karl told me of his private suspicion that the phone bidders were themselves colluding. In fact, he pondered the question of whether there were any callers at all on the other side of those phones.)

Unsurprisingly, the option eventually went to one such telephone bidder. Since the name was never revealed, the audience had no way to tell whether it was the auction house itself that had won. In any event, the moment the hammer fell, calm descended. What had been a rising frenzy of speculation was brought to an abrupt halt by the auctioneer.

But the bidding was far from over. Soon other assets were presented before the eager audience. There were many curious ones, including even a letter of credit presentable on the coming (or second coming—which ever turns out to be first) of the Messiah.

As the auction continued at a furious pace, Karl found himself beginning to dissociate. Later on, when he confided in me, he told me how he felt all the trade occurring in that room amounted to an intensely refined essence of pure contractual dystopian risk. Sitting there, surrounded by throngs of bidders chasing after obscure bearer notes, negotiable instruments, and oblique rights of all kinds, he began to experience a spinning, unbalanced sensation. (I could relate to this: it's a feeling I've felt in many a business meeting.)

Equally unsettling was the way more people flowed into the auction chamber like flies attracted to the glowing light of the market. There was a sense that something important must be occurring here. Many bodies started to fill the back of the chamber where no seating remained. Some of these new entrants began to buy, but it was obvious to Karl that many had simply come to gawk at this grand enterprise. They looked on in astonishment, but there was also envy in their expressions—as if to say, "If only I could play in this high-stakes game!" The air in the room became stifling. As Karl later explained to me, he began to feel physically oppressed. The mood in the auction rose to a fever pitch. It now seemed like a creeping psycho-pathology had gripped the room. In that chamber the market had taken on its own energy. Amid the clamor of bids, it was as if the collective were giving birth to a deranged new child.

Ultimately, Karl himself was overcome. "What nonsense! What a mania!" he finally called out. He stood up bewildered but then collapsed on the floor. After that everything went black.

Well, that's the story, as Karl recounted it to me. The reader must make his own judgment as to whether the story is true, one of Karl's dreams, or a plain fabrication. Perhaps some readers might feel that such fevered bidding for putative contracts is quite incredible, or highly exaggerated. But I believe it's more likely that all of us have, at some time, witnessed similar occasions when people seemed overwhelmed by financial exuberance or folly. Because, whether the bidding is for Megalodons or for anything else, the dynamics of such an auction house are strikingly familiar to anyone who deals in finance for any length of time.

The fact is, it requires just a handful of features to create a market for an asset. And none of these features has anything to do with the asset itself having what we might call "real" or "intrinsic" value. So let's start by asking how on earth could the market for Megalodon call options ever have begun?

First and foremost, there's the great machine of salesmanship. The dinosaur option itself is born in the office of some real-life brokers. Call them wacky, creative, or unscrupulous, their method is a traditional one. First they conceive of the option structure, then document it, and finally generate some bids. They do this by taking what auctioneers call "bidding off the wall." That is, brokers just start marking up prices or trading between themselves—colluding, you might say. As they begin playing with the supply of the asset, they are not really making money, just getting some notional liquidity going. (For established public securities this can often be illegal—but only for established asset classes.)

Soon after, the brokers start setting a clearing price for the option, with bid and ask spreads. With this tentative beginning, a market in the asset is thus ceded. There is now potential for the option value to go up and down.

Funnily enough, something like this really does happen even with the most legitimate and mainstream of Initial Public Offerings (IPOs). The investment bank that leads the offering is typically given what is known as a "greenshoe right" which allows that bank (legally) to "manipulate" the market in the new stock. In summary, on closing an IPO, the underwriter sells more stock than is actually being offered. This creates a technical "short" in the market. If demand for the new stock in the aftermarket turns out to be low, the underwriter fills the short by buying stock from existing stockholders, thus (artificially) creating at least some base secondary market demand. If, on the other hand, purchase orders in the immediate aftermarket are high, the underwriter "exercises his greenshoe." This allows him to call for more stock from the issuer to fill the demand, hence putting the brakes on an excess rise in the stock price.

This type of "stabilization" (as it is known in the securities business) is in fact considered by the SEC an important function of investment banks—at least for a limited period after an IPO. It is meant to avoid excessive volatility in the newly-issued stock. So, under SEC regulations, there is nothing "wrong" with it, per se. Still, it is a very telling example of how brokers themselves can affect the value of an asset merely by playing with the notional demand and supply of the stock.

So—now a base market for the Megalodon asset has been created, and with that we are off to the races. For then the vast network of intermediation begins to operate. Prospective buyers are encouraged to participate by armies of salespeople present in many advanced capitalist economies. The asset becomes increasingly known. At first, it is offered only to exclusive groups. And I mean *really* exclusive groups—groups that Karl could not even dream of joining. But in time it gets offered to a clientele that, though still exclusive, is drawn from slightly less rarified circles. At this level, Karl might be invited in. Said clients are now gratified—flattered even—to be allowed in to what they see as an exclusive cadre of investors. Eagerly they invest. In time the brokers could step away from the market—although, of course, they never do as they wish always to keep oiling the gears and pouring in the fuel, keeping the engine burning. In time, investors become accustomed to buying and selling at certain established price levels. The asset has "obtained value."

The U.S. legal system fully recognizes these types of investor stratifications. Under current SEC and FINRA rules, certain securities can only be sold to "accredited investors," defined as those having annual incomes of $200,000 or to those whose net worth exceeds one million dollars. Still more exclusive offerings can only be sold to Qualified Institutional Buyers (institutions managing at least $100 million in assets). Now, these rules might seem arbitrary, but do nevertheless have some rationale. By imposing these stratifications, the laws are meant to protect the "non-qualified" from being sold overly risky securities. The rules don't always work. But when (if) they do, they are important mechanisms for protecting those with limited means, from buying assets exactly like dinosaur derivatives. "Non-sophisticated" investors really shouldn't be buying assets whose value is, we might say, highly elusive or heavily driven by speculative demand. But the cautionary intention of the rules comes with a backlash directed by the all-too-human emotions of envy and desire. If you do make it into one of these specialized investor buckets—well, what a privilege! All the more enticing is the prospect of playing in a game restricted to an elite.

So our asset has by now attained some perceived value in the market. But then a second, powerful financial force comes into play. It's called "liquidity," which is the notion that someone else will always buy or accept the option for value at a later stage. In fact it is recognized by financial commentators that investors often buy an asset only because they are confident someone else might buy it (hopefully, at a higher price) in the near future. The immense herd of brokers and salespeople have now upped their game still further: they are industrializing the exchangeability of the Megalodon option. And this in turn brings us to another notion—the "greater fool theory." Namely, that in any chain of transactions when an asset value is rising there is always (usually) a "greater fool" who will bid even higher. Of course, this can never be an endless chain. Eventually some buyer gets caught out acquiring the asset at the end of the chain before the price falls.

It's a sequence eloquently described by Charles Kindleberger and Robert Aliber in their seminal study of financial crises, *Manias, Panics and Crashes.* Among other crises, the book analyzes the phenomenal surge in the price of gold that occurred in the 1970s. "At some stage," they concluded, "in the late 1970s, investors were extrapolating from the increase in the market price of gold from Monday to Tuesday to project the market price on Friday; they purchased gold on Wednesday in anticipation that they could sell at a higher price on Friday. The 'greater fool theory' was at work, some of these buyers may have realized that the increase in price was a bubble and anticipated that they would be able to sell at a profit before the bubble imploded."[1]

Actually, liquidity also goes to the concept of managing the "uncertain" future. In the next chapter, we'll take a look at this concept—the Genesis story of how Joseph made a killing in a market where God apparently removed the element of uncertainty entirely. But for most of us in finance, uncertainty is a constant, and hence "risk" is always an element in decision making. Liquidity does not remove the element of risk—far from it. But it signals something to an investor. Liquidity says to the investor, "Even if this investment does not turn out how I thought it would—that is, no Megalodon actually appears— well, I can still exit the asset."

There is an element of trust embedded in liquidity: "I will pay value for this asset now because I trust another will take it from me, for value, in the future." And indeed this is not fundamentally different from the trust we hold in a dollar bill. After all when we are given a dollar for our work or our goods, we blithely trust that we will be able to exchange that dollar—that is exchange it in the not-too-distant future, for the goods or services provided by others.

Interestingly, also, mainstream financial theory recognizes pure "liquidity" as something that has value in and of itself. There are many analyses showing the increased value of a stock that is listed with an *active market* versus a private, "illiquid" stock (not offered on any market). The former is commonly identified as having a "liquidity premium." In fact, just adding liquidity can increase a stock's value by as much as 20 or 30% over a private (illiquid) stock that is identical in every other way.[2] These liquidity premia are regularly used in professional valuation work by investment banks, accountants, and the like. In other words, investors and traders recognize that there is additional value in something purely because it is exchangeable, and they are willing to pay a premium . . . even at risk of ending up greater fools for doing so.

But now we come to the next factor. We have arrived at the curves in the road where "greed" and "fear" create rapid acceleration and deceleration. With the establishment of the ability for any asset to go up and down in value, the potential arises to make money buying cheap and selling dear (arbitrage). When these factors come into play, there's a new compelling logic behind investing in Megalodon options. How appealing these are to anyone who wishes to speculate! Fear is the quintessential human emotion that arises from financial uncertainty. Greed—well, I think we're familiar with its appetites. In any event, note for now how often greed and fear do generate precisely the type of mania seen among the Megalodon bidders in our story.

And then there is a final piece in the puzzle—that is "habit" or "conditioning." As more people trade in the option, the reality of its value seems to be confirmed daily by the ongoing patterns of behavior of the crowd. Like a religion or a credo, the more often certain ideological concepts are repeated, the more we become conditioned to accept what appears to be an independent truth. Now, instead of "high priests," think "brokers." As brokers repeat their buy/sell mantra to eager investors, they continually promulgate and perpetuate the dinosaur dictum. Repetition of this credo can take the market value of assets to levels that are way, way beyond anything that can be connected with the underlying economic utility of the asset. Sound familiar? Yes, we call these run-ups of the market based on fervid beliefs "asset bubbles" and "market mania." What occurs is a sort of financial religious ecstasy as each new zealot experiences his or her own epiphany.

The 18th-century British philosopher, Hume, spoke a great deal about habit. In Hume's view, much of what we believe is really just a consequence of habitual associations.[3] He noted, for example, that when we say "x event caused y effect," there may be no actual connection between "event x" and "event y." Much as we may feel the need to find the *mysterious nexus* that links x to y, it's really nothing more than our habitual experience of y following x. If the sequence happens repeatedly, we reach for the conclusion that y *is caused* by x. So too, it seems, does the finding of value become a habit. There may be no such thing as real value in our Megalodon options. But what happens when we repeatedly witness one person after another buying the option, then selling it to someone else? The pattern is first established, then repeated, and finally becomes habitual. And so, an established trading practice in the option (a habit) eventually manifests itself in the collective human psyche (the market) as a sense of "value."

So now: everything is in place to lend credence to the Megalodon option story.

Pure fiction?

Well, here I would suggest the reader think of one of the most highly valued commodities on earth. Diamonds. No huge shark ancestor with bared teeth, for sure. An asset that glitters rather than threatens. And one that, unlike a Megalodon, can actually be worn on the finger or be fashionably displayed at social gatherings.

It might seem heresy to suggest that a diamond has very questionable fundamental value. However I wouldn't be the first to say so. For in many respects it shares some characteristics with our grey-skinned predator. Its supply is controlled by the De Beers' cartel. The asset is actively marketed as an exclusive product (by multiple high-end retailers). The market in diamonds is highly liquid, involving thousands of brokers. And the asset is so embedded in the human social consciousness that the acquisition of diamonds—or the longing to acquire them—has become a permanent habit.

I mentioned in passing how Karl's experience occurred during a time of economic recession. In an even more confusing way, an unstable economic environment might actually drive up interest in our nutty Megalodon option. It can do that precisely because the underlying asset may be thought to have some unique value quite detached from economic productivity. This is not dissimilar to the tendency of the market to buy otherwise worthless hunks of gold in inflationary and risk-averse times. In fact, it is not ludicrous to say—based on the working of the gold market—that the greater the fear in the failure of the real economy, the more people are likely to seek out such curious assets. Hope springs eternal, and such assets offer the promise of a future that's more bountiful and—one dreams—more certain and secure than current circumstances.

Strange and distant indicators also influence the value of certain assets. The slightest rumor of a bid for a stock for instance—or the possibility of future changes (say, in central bank policy)—can quite dramatically shift the trajectory of certain assets. And in the case of our crazy option over a Megalodon, there is also a clear parallel to public bid frenzy. While the prospect of discovering an actual Megalodon may seem far-fetched, consider how long hope is sustained in the public imagination, especially if the press feeds the frenzy of speculative rumor. Many generations have sustained the belief that there might be—yes, just *might* be—UFOs hovering around selected sites in the American West, or a Loch Ness creature wriggling in the depths of its Scottish home, or Yetis leaving footprints in the Himalayas. And one rumored siting of a Yeti or a UFO only fuels the (imagined) possibilities of these other alternatives—like finding a live Megalodon. After all, in 1938, a coelacanth (a prehistoric fish believed to have been extinct since the end of the Cretaceous period) was found alive and well in the Chalumna River in the Eastern Cape of South Africa. Who's to say that a Megalodon, larger but perhaps more elusive, might also be found in the great darkness of the Mariana Trench in the deepest part of the world's oceans? Anything is possible. (Actually, anything *is* possible).

So, are we saying that certain features of human behavior and psychology allow real markets to coalesce and attach value to *any* asset . . . whatsoever? Well, maybe, though that view is certainly open to at least one critical objection. The above is all well and good, but this market will only sustain itself if there is real "intrinsic" value in the option to buy a Megalodon. It looks like I'm merely differentiating between what economists call "market value" and "intrinsic value." It would seem obvious that, if the Megalodon is extinct, an option on the beast could never have intrinsic value. Sooner or later, therefore, the market will give up on the asset.

I think actually I am saying more than that, but let's just dig a little deeper into what we really mean by these different notions of value. "Intrinsic value" is typically understood in the financial world as the underlying economic/productive benefit of an asset. More precisely: an asset's intrinsic value is based on and quantified by the future cash flows generated by that asset.

One way of looking at this is to say that if you're dealing with an asset that has intrinsic value, its real worth should be quantifiable within reasonable bands. Put together two assets that each have an intrinsic value of "two" and you end up with a total value of "four." If you find that people are paying five, six, or seven for assets that only add up to four, you're in the midst of a speculative bubble. Or, as one economist put it, "The additional rise above the true capital will only be imaginary."[4]

All commentators on the gap between what I am calling "market value" versus "intrinsic value" are effectively commenting on the whole issue of the "rationality" of markets. The so-called "efficient market theorists" want to say that market value will sooner or later reflect intrinsic value. The gap between the two will simply be arbitraged away. And it is true that economists periodically show how market values can give a much better marker of intrinsic value than individual views. The "wisdom of the crowd," it is sometimes called.

But the efficient market theorists have come under increasing pressure in recent years. The disjunction between market value and intrinsic value is seen by many in regular bouts of "irrational exuberance," which are often used as proof that the efficient market hypothesis is simply wrong. Take the dotcom bubble of the later 1990s and early 2000s. As Frank Partnoy has pointed out in his book, *Infectious Greed*, at that time there was an ever-upward rise of internet stocks increasingly dislocated from the likely future performance of the underlying companies represented by those stocks. As Partnoy puts it, "People overestimated their own skills, overvalued items they owned, were shortsighted, greedy and occasionally even altruistic."[5] And hence certainly some economists, like Andrei Shleifer, have plainly rejected the rational market hypothesis; their ideas now being embodied in the school of "behavioral finance."[6]

Perhaps also there's something of a conceptual flaw with the notion of "intrinsic value." Assessing intrinsic value inevitably requires predictions of future cash flows as well as discount rates. In other words, if you want to know anything's intrinsic value, you still have to speculate on the future. If you're doing that, you are immediately trying to see through the mist of uncertainty. How, you wonder, will my asset *actually* perform in the future? And to get any kind of grip on this, you generally have to turn back to the market price. It is, after all, the market price itself that is the quintessential mechanism in the financial world, for assessing future risks.

Something very much like this happened with the mania for Collateralized Debt Obligations (CDOs) in the 2007/8 credit crisis. These securities represented multiple strings of underlying cash flows from huge and complex baskets of other assets. The underlying cash flows were, in many cases, so complex that no human could calculate or conceive what they were. Hence, the price at which a broker offered you a CDO was the only meaningful benchmark for valuing those securities.

In fact, there are many other assets that really do function in ways that resemble our Megalodon options. Consider the world of currency trading. There, many traders are fundamentally speculating on price movements via "contracts for differences" that have no intrinsic value whatsoever.

A contract for difference ("CfD") allows an investor to make a pure bet on the direction of a financial index. For example, I could buy a CfD to bet on movements in the $/£ rate (the exchanged rate between the British pound and U.S. dollar) without buying either dollars or pounds. The CfD simply allows me either to buy the index ("go long") at a certain level (say $1.70 to £1) or sell the index ("go short") at that level. If I am long and the index goes up, I can then subsequently sell the index to take my profits. If, however, I have bought and the index falls I will be selling at a loss.

The similarity with the dinosaur derivative is pretty clear. The real problem we all have with the dinosaur option is there is no meaningful underlying asset over which the option is taken. But of course this is equally true of the CfD. In the CfD, where the underlying assets are dollars and pounds, neither of those currencies is actually purchased. Money is made purely by virtue of movements in the currency index.

Well, perhaps—though at least, with the CfDs, there is *some* underlying asset that is driving the movement in the currency index. Even if you do not actually buy any dollars or pounds themselves when you buy a CfD, nevertheless you are looking at movements in the underlying value of those currencies to drive the movement of the index on which you are betting. With our dinosaur derivatives there is no movement in the value of dinosaurs at all.

A fair point, but we should remember that currencies themselves have no real value other than as a means of exchange (again, it's the element of trust that allows people to exchange currencies for value). So we can legitimately ask: "Does the $/£ CfD have any solid intrinsic value?"

To make this point even clearer, consider a CfD over a gold index. With that kind of CfD, I am betting solely on the movement of the gold index. Unlike dollar bills or pound notes that I can actually see and touch from time to time, I never actually hold any gold at all. The unseen chunks of gold stored away in underground vaults have no utilitarian benefit, and I am not even buying them, either. I'm only buying a contract whose value is linked to the movement in the value of said blocks of gold. So, a CfD over a gold index? Well, now we have found our real-life dinosaur derivative.

Off the back of the CfD example, we begin to take our analysis to its logical conclusion. It seems we are not really talking about the gap between "market value" and "intrinsic value" after all. Apparently, not only can value be dislocated from intrinsic value, but in fact highly sought-after assets (with significant market value) do not need to have any real economic value whatsoever.

In other words, *of course* powerful behavioral and psychological forces have a material effect on price movements.[7] In fact, let's not even go deeply into the "efficient market hypothesis," for only academic economists could debate for years what is patently obvious to anyone who has spent even one year trading in financial markets. (Among those whom I would classify as "academic economists," I include Alan Greenspan—he apparently only understood the potential irrationality in markets at the ripe old age of 87.[8])

So, if assets like the Megalodon option can have value without any link to fundamental economic benefit, what shall we call this strange, floating type of value—value that seems to come unhinged from anything real and tangible? Well let's look again at the case of gold and of the ongoing value we maintain in currencies (in spite of gold and currencies being in themselves worthless pieces of metal and paper/computer blips). In *The Power of Gold*, Peter Bernstein makes the observation that "all the countries in the world now function with monetary systems convertible into nothing except from one nation's money into another nation's money." Bernstein further speculates that, today, the U.S. dollar is "the glue that holds the system together, as gold did in the past."[9]

At given times, certain assets do act as barometers of definitive value. These assets—such as gold (in the past) or reserve currencies (today)—have value that is quite separate from their intrinsic value. They act as benchmarks. Before Einstein, physicists believed an "ether" existed all around us that provided an absolute framework for space against which each item was positioned. These basic assets are like the ether of 19th-century physics. Because we humans have come to trust these assets, they act as definitive signposts of value. Supported by that broad-based kind of trust, currencies can be continually exchanged for value with other buyers. Though they are also vulnerable markers. They may resemble solid benchmarks, but in fact they are far from it. These benchmarks can plummet or soar in value as human trust waxes and wanes.

So it is with many assets that become, in some fashion, barometers of value. Indeed any asset or piece of paper can become such a barometer. Once trust in exchangeability in an asset is established, intrinsic value just seems to take second place.

I should add that I am not questioning the validity or morality of speculative markets. As in the currency markets, speculation very often provides important liquidity to our system, and this liquidity is critical in providing capital for real economic benefits. But we must see these markets for what they are and remember also that they can therefore be abused. They need to be monitored. As the 18th-century conservative philosopher Edmund Burke said, "It is the nature of all greatness not to be exact; and great trade will always be attended with considerable abuses."[10]

So what are we left with? Well, we might call it "value in itself." It is the value that can exist in an asset just because it *was*, and *is*, exchangeable for *something else* of value. We are left, in other words, with a compelling sense of the philosophical vicious circle. The awareness of this circle may not mean much to a theoretical economist, but it haunts every market trader. As for the average consumer, we confront it daily in our personal choices. When we go to buy some item and wonder whether it is actually worth what the retailer claims it's worth, we are stepping into the world of Megalodon trading. Someone wanted it, so it was valuable, and they wanted it because it was . . . wanted. This is perhaps not a very reassuring way to think about what we own, or buy, or invest in. But like it or not, we have to live with the uncertainty of not knowing what anything is ultimately worth anyway.

I'm sure this is no revelation. We all understand that value is deeply subjective. To say something has value actually means no more than that it is "desired" or "needed" by someone. One assembly of humans may desire gold; another may see beauty in mud. Most psychological studies show that—once people have the basic necessities of food, shelter and their health—happiness does not really increase with more wealth. And in the end it's easy to understand why. Wealth depends on the accumulation of things whose value is subjective and never certain. Value so often performs a cruel vanishing act: melting down or disappearing like some ludicrous financial mirage.

Nonetheless, perhaps our story itself gives us a final handle on the concept of value. Part of the problem with the mania in the auction room was that the bidders had become obsessed with chasing value for its own sake. Karl observed a relatively well-heeled clique of buyers who were, themselves, being herded this way and that by the big-money bids that were phoned in. No one in that insulated auction room really needed to buy Megalodon derivatives, e.g. for food or shelter. Those dinosaur derivatives could only obtain value because—as evidenced by the active trading in that room—there was liquidity and arbitrage opportunity in the asset. Ultimately the main motive for buying the Megalodon options was purely to make more money.

Now, I certainly think it is important for people to make money. And we need the means to make money (i.e., businesses). I also believe there is value in a lot of things well beyond shelter and sustenance. Much can be said for the many objects and experiences that feed or satisfy our aesthetic needs. Money can help us acquire or invest in things that bring unique fulfill-ments. But where value, as a concept, seems to become unhinged is when we invest value in something solely and exclusively because it is a route to making money. When an asset's only value is to generate more value, we begin to believe in Megalodon derivatives. That's when we're in trouble. And we all know this, for it's a truth as old as the world.

When something is valued solely because it begets value, then we have created assets infused with the disease of Midas—assets that one day can be sold for a huge price, and the next day, plummet to zero in a market panic. When that happens, we see human mania and we see the venality of the bidders in the auction room. We see how our society can actually give birth to assets that live in a sort of economic vacuum, devoid of human connection. We have, in other words, created dinosaur derivatives.

WHAT IS UNCERTAINTY?

Joseph's Dreams

"For I dipt into the future, far as human eye could see,
Saw the Vision of the world, and all the wonder that would be;
Saw the heavens fill with commerce, argosies of magic sails,
Pilots of the purple twilight, dropping down with costly bales . . ."
— Locksley Hall by **Tennyson,** (1809–1892)

"It is certain because it is impossible."

— **Tertullian** (c. 160 CE–c. 225 CE)

There is one story in the Old Testament that is of a uniquely economic nature. It is the saga of Joseph, his prophetic dreams, and the seven good years and seven bad years.

You may be familiar with these chapters from the Book of Genesis, but let's summarize the overall story. In so doing, I am not trying to teach a religious lesson, nor am I opining on the veracity of the story. The element that intrigues me most is the story's *financial meaning*. This is a drama which brings out, in the most striking fashion, some antique issues of finance and philosophical uncertainty.

Let's review the situation as it stood in ancient days. Joseph was the second youngest son of Jacob. From an early age Joseph showed precocious talents that triggered the jealousy of Joseph's many brothers. His gifts were so abundant that he was favored by his father, who gave him a particularly fancy (and brightly colored) coat. But his brothers, sick of this arrogant little kid, began to plot against him. Initially they contemplated the unthinkable—killing the boy. Eventually, however, they chose to sell Joseph into slavery in Egypt. The brothers then told their father Jacob, that Joseph was dead, and the loving father spent much of the rest of his life in mourning.

I don't think anyone today would question that the brothers' actions were over the top. However overweening Joseph's pride may have been, he and his father surely did not deserve this. They were (at least at that stage) a somewhat dysfunctional bunch of boys.

After Joseph was sold into slavery, the story picks up in Egypt where the young man endured various challenges and betrayals at the hands of his master Potiphar. Among his many tribulations, Joseph had to deal with the sexual advances of Potiphar's wife. (Joseph was apparently handsome as well as bright.) Eventually, having been framed, Joseph ended up in prison, destitute. But at this low point, something special occurred. Joseph discovered that, among his many talents, he now possessed the most valuable gift of all—the ability to prophesy. What manifested itself was an uncanny talent: Joseph could accurately interpret dreams and understand their meaning as harbingers of things to come.

Joseph recognized his new expertise when, first of all, he interpreted the dreams of two fellow prisoners, the royal cupbearer and the royal baker, and correctly predicted the fate of these prisoners. As such predictions proved accurate, the Pharaoh himself came to hear (from the cupbearer) of Joseph's unique talents. Joseph was then asked to interpret two of the Pharaoh's own dreams.

One of those dreams was a dramatically visual episode in which seven shriveled ears of corn consumed seven fat ears. Another seemed related: the Pharaoh dreamed that seven thin and sickly cows consumed seven fat cows.

Joseph proceeded to interpret the dreams in strictly economic terms. In his view the dreams symbolized periods of boom and then bust. There would, he said, be seven good economic years followed by seven bad economic years. Given this impending 14-year cycle, Joseph recommended that the Egyptian government implement an aggressive savings plan during the good years, building a huge food surplus. That precautionary measure would put Egypt in a good position to manage scarcity during the bad years.

His accurate prophecy of the future, as well as his proposals for managing it, were profoundly influential and resulted in rapid promotion. He was chosen by Pharaoh to be the equivalent of the Egyptian Treasury Secretary. That lofty post gave him the power to oversee transactions throughout the Fertile Crescent.

What then follows in the story are various details associated with the reuniting of Joseph, his (reformed) brothers and ultimately, his father. At the onset of the famine years, Joseph's brothers had to emigrate from Canaan to Egypt to seek food. Joseph challenged the brothers in various ways, mostly to assess whether the siblings, who had wronged him so badly, were capable of reform. Ultimately, the family was once again reunited, though now living in Egypt. Joseph's father, in his old age, at least had the pleasure of welcoming Joseph back into the family fold and—no small achievement—seeing his young star achieve greatness.

But more than the family saga is included in the story. At its conclusion we are told the nature of Joseph's economic policies during the "bad" seven years when—as foretold in the dream—the countryside was wracked with famine. By the end of the good years, the Egyptian state had a huge stockpile of grain and crop holdings. This Joseph used to buy up everything he could. He vastly increased the state's cash reserves as well as buying up land, livestock, and ultimately labor. In fact the story indicates he acquired more or less the whole economy of the then known world. Joseph and the Egyptian state effectively cornered the whole Fertile Crescent. For our purposes, it is this final part of this story that will be the most interesting element of the parable. In its broadest interpretations, it teaches us something quite philosophical about economics.

In the Bible the Joseph story takes up many chapters, and there is a wealth of detail. In fact, no other story in the whole Bible contains quite the same level of specificity. (Indeed, many stories—like the Tower of Babel—are handled in just a few sentences.) While the whole saga can be seen in purely religious terms, with reference to Joseph's prophetic ability and his link to God, everything about this story is (also) related to economic nuances.

For example, let's return to the events surrounding the reuniting of Joseph with his wayward brothers. Genesis Chapter 44 tells us that Joseph's challenges to the brothers were of a distinctly pecuniary nature. He initially gave them all the grain they asked for without accepting the money they were supposed to pay for it. The brothers were horrified. Surely, if they accepted the grain as a gratuity, they were liable to be accused of fraud.

Later, Joseph "framed" his youngest brother Benjamin by planting in his sack a silver goblet, a classic ancient symbol of wealth. That left the brother open to direct charges of being a simple thief. In context, it seems clear that such schemes were used by Joseph to test the integrity of his brothers. Scholars have dwelt at length on the details and meanings of these various tests. Those considerations aside, what strikes me is that many of Joseph's actions involved some form of financial gaming or machination (wise and clever though they may have been).

You can also see the intrinsically economic nature of Joseph's prophecy. It could be argued that Joseph had a choice in how he interpreted the Pharaoh's dreams—and, given the alternatives, he deliberately selected an economic message. In this he had the full compliance of the Pharaoh. But that was either a conscious choice or the only choice that made real sense to the two men. As Biblical scholar Julius Theodor suggests in the *Genesis Rabbah* (a collection of folkloric stories embellishing on the Old Testament), other court wizards and wise men did try explaining the dream in non-economic terms.[1] Some suggested, quite reasonably, that "the seven fat cows mean that you will beget seven daughters; the seven lean cows mean that you will bury seven daughters." Others took the seven full ears of corn to mean that seven principalities would be conquered while the seven thin ears meant principalities would be lost in a rebellion. But Theodor points out that Pharaoh rejected all the alternative interpretations in favor of Joseph's explicitly economic one.

So what is the obvious financial interpretation of this tale?

Once the Pharaoh had accepted Joseph's interpretation as being unambiguous, he had every reason to elevate the interpreter to the position of Treasury Secretary of Egypt (or, as we might call it, the Fund Manager Royal). In essence, prophecy allowed Pharaoh and his newly appointed treasury secretary to overcome that core philosophical problem we touched on in the Introduction—namely the "uncertainty" inherent in finance. For Joseph does not just *guess* the future, Joseph *knows* the future. His gift may come from a special relationship with God, but he exercises that gift so as to fully realize the economic consequences. Joseph can sidestep economic risk entirely by seeing Egypt's future in deterministic terms. The story is not just telling us about economic booms and busts—which, clearly, are as old as the Bible. It is telling us about our (normal) failure to have predictive powers. We simply do not know when recessions are coming. So most people, then as now, cannot prepare for them, or at least cannot foresee in any meaningful way when busts will occur.

What Joseph achieved was an unimaginably powerful financial advantage. And it all came about by removing the most constant inconstant in human affairs—the element of uncertainty.

I touched on this before in the previous chapter, but here I'd like to add a bit of background on the *study* of uncertainty. The whole philosophical discipline of epistemology (the study of "how we know anything") can actually be regarded as the study of uncertainty's bedfellow—that is to say, *certainty*. How can I be *certain* the sun will rise tomorrow? (In philosophy that's called the problem of induction.) How can I be *certain* that my sense experience is not deceiving me? (Enter empirical skepticism.) How can I be *certain* that one plus one always equals two? (Welcome to the philosophy of mathematics.) How can I be *certain* that the theory of relativity is true? (There we have the philosophy of science.) All the greatest philosophers wrote tomes on the subject (from Aristotle, to Augustine, to Descartes, to Hume, to Kant, to Wittgenstein). Philosophy and many of the paradoxes inherent in that subject, generally deals with the search for some foundation for our beliefs and ideas. And what else is "foundation" other than a sense of certainty? Yet invariably we find it very hard to find solid bedrock.

Now, as I've noted, these issues of uncertainty are directly relevant to finance, which is ultimately the *management* of risk. It is the management of tomorrow, the future. Nearly every financial problem has embedded in it a judgment about what might, could, or can happen. And the financial decisions I make all depend on how much confidence I have in my views of future outcomes.

"Risk and time are the opposite sides of the same coin," wrote Peter L. Bernstein in *Against the Gods*, "for if there were no tomorrow there would be no risk. Time transforms risk, and the nature of risk is shaped by the time horizon: the future is the playing field."[2]

None of this comes as fresh news to the investor. After all, why are various types of finance called "speculation"? It's precisely because an investor is taking a bet on what is an uncertain future. Since the future is unknowable (here, cite all the philosophers who stand by that tautology) finance is an exercise in figuring out what is certain and what is not—or, at least, in deciphering what outcomes are more certain than others.

If I invest in a stock, I am taking a view on the direction that stock may go. (I have a view, but there is no certainty.) If I make some financial projections or create a budget, I am taking a view about future cash flows and performance. I can never be certain about the correctness of those judgments. If I make a loan, I am betting on the ability of the borrower to pay back the principal with interest, and indeed the interest rate assigned to my loan, attempts to reflect the possibility of the debtor *not* repaying (since his repayment can never be certain). Even if I am preparing historical accounts, I must make assumptions about accruals, provisions and reserves that require future (and therefore uncertain) judgments.

Casually, we all admit "nothing in life is certain," with just the hint of a shrug. We generally accept this maxim as it applies to our daily lives. In fact those who cannot accept the natural constraints of uncertainty are usually the psychological victims of anxiety or, perhaps, obsessional behaviors. But here's the thing—finance has a particularly close and integral relationship to the certainty/uncertainty paradox. And that is why the story of Joseph is so compelling.

For prophecy (or indeed any view on the future) can create a strange disturbance in the normal continuum of uncertainty, visible even in the behavior of the markets. Prophecy (if ever it were possible) allows men to mold the future and fit it to the prophecy itself, it has a self-referential quality. I might remind the reader of the great story of Macbeth by Shakespeare. There, Macbeth was given a prophecy by the three witches that he would become King of Scotland. As a result, specifically of the prophecy, Macbeth killed Duncan, the then king of Scotland, to assume the throne.[3] But for the prophecy Macbeth may never have done the murder in the first place. And indeed we see exactly the same trend in markets. If market speculators believe an asset may fall in value due to certain expected economic events, selling patterns will commence, bringing down that value, just as a self-fulfilling reflection of a future view.

And Joseph also acted (via his economic policies) on his view of the future. But in Joseph's case he was not "betting" on anything in the ordinary sense. No, Joseph *knew* the future. That certainty about events that were to unfold during the next 14 years put him in a unique position, which raises questions concerning what this story is really about.

Is the Joseph story telling us something about the financial disposition and activities of Joseph himself? Or is it telling us what happens at the intersection of human doubt and economic policy? What we are given is a transparent picture of what happens when knowledge transcends human limitations and enters into an otherworld of religious prophecy.

Before we get to those questions, we should first get to the real economic juice of the tale. One of the important features of the Genesis story—albeit often neglected—is the nature of the economic policies that Joseph decides to adopt during the seven bad years. Let's take a closer look at the impact of his policies.

We know that during the seven good years Joseph chose to run a massive surplus. He saved up grain in great storehouses in anticipation of the troubled times to come. Very judicious. But his policy was aggressive (very aggressive). When the bad times came, he did not moderate the distribution of that surplus with an eye on equality for all. He could, for example, have provided food to those who needed it in Egypt, Israel/Canaan, or Assyria. He might even have "gifted" food where needed. But he chose otherwise. Chapter 47 of Genesis makes it quite clear that Joseph exploited his management of the surplus to the *nth* degree.

Initially he sold crops for cash, and for as much cash as possible. As the famine continued and the needy ran short of money, he began to demand animals and livestock in recompense for grain distribution. He then began to require land exchange for food, and finally the labor of the hungry and needy. The text explains that the whole population was even relocated to new parts of land based on the Pharaoh's dictates—in modern terms, forced labor repatriation. On behalf of the Egyptian monarch, Joseph effectively bought up the whole Fertile Crescent—every single asset—and indentured the whole labor force.

Many Biblical commentators in the Judeo-Christian tradition have struggled with this part of the Joseph story. Why on earth would one of the prophets (supposedly beloved of God) behave in this way? Why was Joseph so apparently greedy? And why would he want to nationalize the whole Egyptian empire? It looks very much like central planning in the extreme. One interpretation could be that Joseph, in fact, was the very opposite of selfish. Perhaps he was an exemplary communist—the first in history. If so, it would be a good example of communism that slipped rapidly into dictatorship, as would happen so many times in later eras.

Of course, with other ranks of Biblical scholars, there's something concerning about the image of Joseph as a precociously inventive communist leader. Seeing him as leader who advocates centralized planning perhaps sits somewhat uncomfortably with the modern religious right.

Some religious as well as liberal commentators do try to provide explanations. For example, some of the traditional Jewish rabbinic sources say that Joseph was actually inflicting a perverse form of punishment on the Egyptian people: he effectively indentured the whole Egyptian people to show them the nature of bondage. A later argument was taken up by the famous medieval Jewish commentator Rabbi Shmuel Ben Meir (c. 1085–c. 1174, also known as the "Rashbam") who argued that the relocating of labor imposed on the Egyptians was punishment similar to that which would be imposed on the Israelites a few hundred years later by Sennacherib, the King of Assyria (described in The Book of Isaiah, Chapter 36). The even more brilliant Jewish rabbinic commentator (Rabbi Shlomo Yitzhaki, "Rashi," 1040–1105) took the position that Joseph made the Egyptians strangers in their own land so they would not object to his own non-Egyptian brothers settling in Egypt (i.e. the Egyptians became aliens like Joseph's brothers). And the 13th-century scholar Nahmanides pointed out that Joseph at least only made everyone "serfs" and not "slaves"—that he was always a man of integrity acting in the interest of the Pharaoh and the Egyptian state.

Clearly, the whole scenario is something that scholars have fretted over for centuries, and though their observations are fascinating, none quite satisfy me. The Egyptians had not (at that point in the Biblical narrative) been particularly bad to the Israelites, so it is hard to see why Joseph would want to be so harsh on them. More significantly, it is clear that Joseph bought up and indentured much of the Fertile Crescent (certainly also all of Canaan and not just Egypt), so his policy was not specifically directed at the Egyptians. It is apparent in the Genesis text that anyone on the Pharaoh's turf who needed food during the seven bad years had to cut a deal with Joseph. After all, Joseph's own brothers were subject to his policies, but *they* did not come to him from Egypt.

As an aside, there is the question of whether the Joseph story corresponds with archeological evidence of changes that occurred at this time. According to some scholars, there is indeed real historical evidence of this restructuring of the Egyptian economy. The British Assyriologist and linguist Rev. Archibald Henry Sayce (1846–1933), who held a chair as Professor of Assyriology at the University of Oxford from 1891 to 1919, claimed that the Joseph story coincides with the disappearance of the old Egyptian nobility (in the Hyksos period). The Hyksos, who came to dominate Egypt at this time, were themselves from Northwest Semitic stock. And Sayce argued that from the time of the Eighteenth Egyptian Dynasty onward, the land, which had previously been held by local proprietors, was owned either by the Pharaoh or the temples. Public granaries apparently also make their appearance at this time, the superintendent of which became a critical Egyptian official. Other archeologists have also noted that it is quite possible for these economic changes to have been effected by a non-Egyptian. There was some element of meritocracy in ancient Egypt, and various precedents exist where foreigners rose to prominent positions. In the time of Akhenaten (14th century BCE) there was a Semitic Egyptian commissioner for Canaan and Syria (called Yanhamu), and a marshal at the court of Merneptah (13th century BCE) called Ben-Ozen, who was from northern Canaan.

So, was Joseph a leader in the concept of central planning, or not? A fair question. But that's not what really interests me most. Concepts of capitalism versus centralized socialism were simply meaningless at this time in history. These notions only gained currency with the industrial revolution, and Joseph was dealing with an essentially agrarian economy. From a broader macro-economic perspective, if he created anything it was not a centralized economy, but probably an early form of feudalism—an economic system which, in fact, remained the norm right up until the Renaissance. Joseph just handed all assets, and rights to all assets, to the King. The Pharaoh then apportioned out, or rented out, assets to those of his landlords (or cronies) who he felt merited special favors.

Instead, what intrigues me is the question of why Joseph would have wanted to implement such policies. And if we turn around and examine this story under the lens of modern financial theory, then add to it a dash of philosophy, well—a completely different portrait of the protagonist is unveiled.

Perhaps what happened to Joseph, after being sold by his brothers, was that he turned into a—financier. He certainly had a good opportunity. He received his training at the feet of one of the greatest Egyptian financiers of all, Potiphar (who, we are told in the story, was one of the most wealthy and influential men in Egypt). His education under Potiphar was conducted in the bustling bazaars of Giza or Luxor or Aswan, the ancient Mediterranean equivalents of Wall Street. To be precise, Joseph became an arbitrageur— that is, he was involved in the business of trying to buy assets cheap and sell them dear.

Unfortunately, all went awry (as so often occurs in the tricky world of finance). Joseph was ultimately framed by Potiphar. He found himself in prison. All, so far, fits the plotline of a typical Wall Street movie. But then something literally miraculous happened. In his prison cell Joseph was given an extraordinary gift in the form of a hot tip allowing him to foresee the financial future. Seven boom years will be followed by a bust. Not "perhaps." Not "maybe." Absolutely: *this* is what's going to happen. In tipping Joseph, God has given him a huge piece of "inside information" that puts Joseph in a very dynamic financial position.

Admittedly, this was no ordinary tip. This was a tip from God himself. That is, one that ought to be taken pretty seriously. In fact, the story means to tell us that a tip from God ("the word of God") is the absolute truth. So Joseph now possesses much more than a "likely scenario" about the future of the Egyptian economy. In his grasp he now holds absolute, incontrovertible knowledge of that future. As indicated above, he *knows* what the future is. Unlike the hordes of financiers who will be born, live, and die during the ensuing millennia, Joseph is a man who has uniquely bankable prophetic powers.

Anyone who knows (really knows) the future enters into a peculiar nether land in terms of financial returns. Investment theory in conventional financial practice is based on the well-known risk/reward relationship. An investor willing to assume greater risk should, at least in theory, be rewarded with higher returns than the investor who operates in lower-risk territory. But what if the risks are zero, yet returns are still available? Well, in general, there is no such thing as zero risk in any endeavor, so this case never arises in ordinary financial dealings. But, for a man who knows (definitively knows) what the future holds, there is no longer risk (at least for that one man and in relation to the events he has foresight over). He would be perfectly rational to bet everything he has on the prophesized outcome, for there is no chance whatsoever of it *not* occurring.

Given this, the true prophet who also makes the career choice of becoming a rational investor can, and will, make vast profit. In fact, profits can be infinite because such a prophet could leverage up and bet the whole universe on his predictions. All perfectly rational. The true prophet can make such a bet because he simply has no chance whatsoever of screwing up.

Now we get a clearer profile of Joseph the financier, the arbitrageur. He demonstrates this very point—the opportunity for infinite profit under circumstances of perfect certainty.

Let's take another brief look at exactly what Joseph was doing in the good and the bad years. In the good years Joseph was not really "saving up" in any conventional sense. Rather, he was going long on grain and crops. He was buying and holding every square cubit of grain he could get his hands on. And it was a one-way street; he was not selling any of it. During the good years, when crops were plentiful, he bought cheap. But he knew (and only *he* knew for certain) that bad times would come. Inevitably when there was a shortage of crops, prices would be driven up.

Sure enough, when bad times came, everyone in the Fertile Crescent was desperate for food. So the price of grain rose with demand. It was a natural consequence of a demand/supply imbalance. And as demand continued to soar, it sucked all the cash out of the economy. Before long, the average breadwinner on the banks of the River Nile was paying for crops "in kind"— and later, when the livestock resource was drained, with land and labor. Ultimately, as noted, these were the only ways to get access to Joseph's stockpile. Having "gone long" on grain in the good times, Joseph then entered into the most pure form of market "short" as times went bad. His prophetic certitude meant he knew he couldn't be wrong. And sure enough he was soon selling an asset so dear that the price of it was the whole economy.

"Given the profits he and Pharaoh made, one might call Joseph the first international arbitrageur," observes Benoit Mandelbrot (the mathematical prodigy and founder of chaos theory) and Richard Hudson in *The (Mis) behavior of Markets*.[4] Of course, Joseph's employer was happy to reap the rewards of his most valuable market player. It's easy also, to conclude that Joseph's original boss (Potiphar) became a happy man too when the deal was done. The sketch of him in Andrew Lloyd Webber and Tim Rice's famous musical, "Joseph and his Amazing Technicolor Dream Coat" seems entirely accurate:

> "He was one of Egypt's millionaires,
> Having made a fortune buying shares,
> In pyramids . . ."

All in all, Pharaoh, Potiphar, and Joseph certainly seemed to do well for themselves (in fact it is understood Joseph ended up marrying Potiphar's daughter).

So does the story just want to tell us that God favors asset managers in a very special way or that arbitrage is really the root to salvation? Given the vast profits that some hedge fund managers make today, one could be forgiven for reaching that conclusion. But then we have to measure that interpretation against many other Biblical statements, "I amassed even silver and gold for myself, and the treasure of kings and the provinces; I provided myself . . . with every human luxury—chests and chests of them . . . Then I looked at all the things that I had done and the energy I had expended; it was clear that it was all futile and a vexation of the spirit—and there is no real profit under the sun."[5]

Or perhaps the story is ultimately telling us less about Joseph himself and more just about the core subject of our chapter—"certainty," economics, and human limitations within the physical world.

No (earthly) man can predict a downturn with certainty, and hence men are always at risk from economic recession. We must somehow manage them in our rather human ways. We mere mortals simply never know the future with certainty. That is just part of the human (physical and mental) condition.

However, our profound story demands that at least we contemplate a man, Joseph, who can indeed foresee times to come without the limitations of human sense and reason. We are required to envisage someone taken beyond the bounds of reality, who entered the realm of "certainty" and who had therefore gone beyond the borders of the mortal world. "The sense of the world must lie outside the world,"[6] explained the 20th-century philosopher Wittgenstein in his analysis of our empirically constrained human experience. Or in other words, really to know (be certain) of the financial future, you have to leave this world, see it "under the aspect of eternity" (Spinoza's phrase) or become one of Isaac Asimov's curious, fictional "Eternals" who were capable of leaving time and space.[7] And Joseph did (apparently) enter this realm of God and the realm of omnipotence and therefore he must have gone beyond "the world as a limited whole."[8] He was therefore able to make not just a hugely valuable arbitrage, but the ultimate trade. He was, in other words, able to own and have dominion over everything.

I'm sure many arbitrageurs sweating it out in today's market would wish to be in Joseph's position. But in worldly affairs, that will never be. Joseph's deal was special. In becoming the one speculator in history who had a direct line to the Almighty, Joseph ceased to be a speculator at all, for he was no longer dealing with the realities of this world (the kind you and I deal with). Profits without end are an alluring concept—metaphorically, the equivalent of thinking you can own the world. Maybe some investors, who perennially call the market right, even have that "Joseph-like" feeling of unique foresight and power. But in truth it is beyond our human reach. To imagine such certainty is to ignore what the Joseph story tells us, that there are peculiar, inviolable boundaries between the physical and mystical worlds.

WHAT IS A CONTRACT?

2,4,6,8 . . .

"All sensible people are selfish, and nature is tugging at every contract to make the terms of it fair."

—Ralph Waldo Emerson (1803–1882)

I magine if you will, that the year is 1887 and you are standing alongside the River Thames in Victorian London. In those days London was very different from today. The Thames was busy both with cargo and military ships—England was, after all, a major commercial power. The environment is pretty much as portrayed in films about the Dickens era, the atmosphere a stew of fog and low-hanging coal smoke. From where you stand at the edge of a pier, you can hear the clanking and banging of the cranes. Dock workers are shouting out in Cockney English. Barrels of wine, lengths of timber, sacks of coffee beans, and iron girders are all being downloaded from arriving ships. You can hear the clop-clop-clop of horses' hooves as they drag away the delivery wagons. Let your imagination run wild enough, and perhaps you'll catch a glimpse, through the dense smog, of Mary Poppins flying past, borne on the breeze by her little umbrella.

But now let's focus on a steamship making her way up the river. She is called *The Moorcock,* and she is heavily laden with cargo. The steamship has a very specific destination—a certain wharf where, if all goes well, she will rest safely for the unloading of precious goods. Follow *The Moorcock* now as her able crew and captain bring her alongside the jetty where this transfer is to take place. All seems to be well. *The Moorcock* arrives at the far extremity of the jetty and ties up to the wharf. In the chill air and lingering fog, the ship begins to discharge its cargo, using a series of cranes, into the local storage facilities.

So far, so good. But behind these smooth maneuverings of a ship and its cargo, there was another form of transaction—specifically, a contract between the owner of *The Moorcock* and the owner of the wharf. It was seemingly mundane, like so many used in everyday business or financial activities. Yet, events were afoot such that this contract was to become symbolic of something much greater. Indeed, what transpired after the docking of *The Moorcock* on that particular day would change the very concept of a contract itself.

Under the terms of this contract, the owner of *The Moorcock* was not charged for the ship being moored alongside the jetty. But the ship owner did pay for the use of the cranes. What the contract covered were the rates to be applied, according to the volume of goods landed and stored at the wharf. Such an arrangement was typical of contracts drawn up in those days.

Now let us leave the contractual arrangements for a moment and return to our seagull's-eye view of *The Moorcock.* Quite suddenly, we hear the ghastly crunch of wood and metal churning against solid rock, a merciless sound like a massive scream. In the ensuing chaos, as the ship's captain helplessly bellows orders and shouting crewmen scurry about, it rapidly becomes apparent what has occurred. The tide is ebbing. *The Moorcock* is no longer buoyed by the murky Thames water. The horrible crunching and grinding that we hear is the sound of a ship running aground as its keel, then its entire hull, impinges on a ridge of unyielding rock that lies beneath a thin layer of mud. As the hull of the ship cracks open, massive damage ensues. Inrushing water wreaks havoc on the valuable cargo that has yet to be unloaded.

As the smooth operation rapidly devolves into a chaotic salvage attempt, the jetty fills with longshoremen working desperately to rescue whatever can be saved. Remaining cargo, some dry, some waterlogged, is pried out of the hold and hoisted from the stricken vessel. That mission accomplished, with the wounded vessel still firmly lodged on the rock in the river, the enraged owner of *The Moorcock* sets out for a heated confrontation with the wharf owner and managers.

Clearly, his outrage seemed justified. *The Moorcock*'s owner had been directed by the wharf owner himself, to tie up his ship at this particular point on the jetty. Surely the owners/managers of the jetty knew the risk of the ship running aground at low tide. Yet this was the precise spot where he had been told to unload. Their crass irresponsibility, argued the ship's owner, was a violation of the contract between them. The owner of the wharf should pay for all damages—not only the ship but also the ruined cargo.

This would have seemed a convincing argument but for one *apparently* logical flaw in the ship owner's reasoning. In point of fact, the contract between the wharf owner and *The Moorcock* owner was quite silent on the issue of what constituted a safe dockage area. The contract was clear about the rights of the ship owner to dock, to use the cranes and storage. It was also clear about the cost structure for the wharf services, noting that there were no charges for docking but only for the crane usage and the volume of goods discharged. In fact, the contract was quite thorough in stating the arrangements made for unloading and storage. But it said nothing at all about the need for the docking ship to be safe at low tide.

As you can imagine, the owner of *The Moorcock* didn't care too much about this lacuna in the contract. As far as he was concerned, it was absurd for the wharf owners to offer docking facilities that were fundamentally dangerous. Being familiar with the range of tides around their property, they must have realized the jetty was not suitable for docking on the ebb tide. In fact, *only* the wharf owners could have known that. It was, *The Moorcock* owner argued, *implicit* in the contract that the docking facilities would not create a material risk of a ship running aground. This was surely an unspoken *assumption* of the contract. Though not stated orally or in writing, this understanding was *embedded* in the contract nevertheless.

Funnily enough, that very evening in a charming 19th-century townhouse only half a mile from the jetty, a young boy was just being tucked into bed by his loving mother. His name was Tarquin. As it happened, his mother always liked to practice a bit of elementary mathematics with her little angel before he slept. (She had great ambitions for her young star.)

"So, my sweet, tell me, suppose I were to give you a series of numbers . . . two, four, six, eight . . . Can you tell me what the next number would be, my little one? I'm sure you know!"

The boy looked deep into his mother's eager eyes. Actually he was a very clever boy—smarter even than his mother realized.

"The next number Mummy . . . the next number is . . . 20!" he said.

The mother looked at him quizzically, slightly disappointed. "Oh, little Tarquin—don't be silly. How could it be 20? How on earth could it be 20? The next number is 10! You just add two to the previous number—don't you?"

"Well, maybe, Mummy," responded Tarquin. "Still, I thought the rule could also have been add two until you get to eight, and then add 12. That rule would still have explained the two, four, six, eight bit, but then, well, then, the next number would have been 20."

The mother, confounded by the answer from her grinning boy, stared at him. Rather than clarifying what he meant, his answer left her even more puzzled than before.

"So I'm not wrong—am I, Mummy?" he probed.

"Well, well—I suppose not. I guess there are multiple interpretations. Oh, I don't know, dear—how silly. I just think that mine makes . . . well, my interpretation is the only one that makes . . . *sense*."

With that, she gave sweet Tarquin a kiss, blew out his candle, and left him to sleep.

Meanwhile, a mere half a mile away, the owner of *The Moorcock* and the owner of the wharf were now shouting and gesticulating at each other on the jetty.

"The contract says you were to provide me with a place to dock my ship for purposes of unloading my cargo," yelled *The Moorcock* owner. "That means a place to dock my ship that is safe, that is stable. The contract must be open to interpretation—and my interpretation is the only one that makes . . . *sense.*"

That's the story. As for the connection between the cute Tarquin and the whole *Moorcock* affair, I will explain more—much more—in this chapter. For the reader's information, the whole story is quite true (certainly about *The Moorcock*). The bedside episode between Tarquin and his mother, I admit, is my own fabrication.

The damages incurred by *The Moorcock* would become the basis for a very famous English legal case in contract law. *The Moorcock* owner and the wharf owner ended up going to court. Indeed, by 1889 the whole matter had proceeded upward to the English Court of Appeal, resulting in a famous ruling by one Lord Justice Bowen.

But before we look at the outcome of that case, I want to step back and discuss two preliminary issues. Firstly, what exactly is a contract? Secondly, what was the nature of Tarquin's little mathematical paradox?

Let's begin with the contract. In some early societies the concept of a contract did not seem to exist at all (at least not in our sense of the word). In the North American Cheyenne tribe, for instance, entering into a contract showed "relatively little of that side of contract which looks to engaging for the future," according to Karl Llewellyn and E. Adamson Hoebel, authors of *The Cheyenne Way*.[1] Rather, it had to do with changing your social status entirely: "Cheyenne practice shows assumptions of office or of marriage obligation was felt as change of status rather than as the incurring of modern-type contractual duties."

Among other ancient societies it was common to give contracts metaphysical meanings. That is to say, while a contract was seen as a bond linking two people together, that bond might be quite ethereal or mystical. The contract existed on some higher, non-physical plane and represented an invisible moral connection between the parties. When we read of, for example, the Biblical covenant between God and the Israelites, we are meant to appreciate an immutable link between man (a physical being) and God (an eternal being without physical form). The bond was manifest in the Ten Commandments that were supposed to have been kept in the Temple in Jerusalem.

Think, also, of the chivalric concept of marriage vows. Such vows, whatever their actual wording, are deemed to be a contract made in the presence of God: they represent a virtually mystical manifestation of the supposedly eternal love between man and wife.

Similarly, there was divine ordination in ancient treaties or agreements between leading governing authorities of the ancient world (say the Egyptians and the Assyrians) or between kings representing principalities, nations, or empires. They, too, were written so as to imply that a deity was present. They were meant to implement a civic or diplomatic order in the world, but manifest in the terms of the agreement was a heavenly intercession confirming that "it was so" because of a higher power.

One of the great jurisprudential thinkers of the 20th century, H.L. Hart, observed, "To some thinkers . . . transactions . . . have appeared mysterious—some have even called them magical—because their effect is to change the legal position of individuals."[2] Indeed, the idea that contracts were originally seen as representing some form of metaphysical or mystical bond is clearly indicated in archeological records. The first ever recorded contracts (typically taken to be the bullae style contracts of ancient Uruk in Mesopotamia) were really vows or promises by individuals who pledged gifts to the gods (in other words, to the temple and its priests). Contracts preserved from ancient Egypt show that the gods were sometimes assumed to be present at the execution of the contract. They, along with other key witnesses (usually priests), gave their blessing to the proceedings.

Today, very few theorists see contracts in those terms. But another more modern view of contracts does invoke a psychological element that is just as immaterial as a spiritual presence. To cite Hart again: "According to one principal theory (the 'will' theory), a contract is essentially a complex psychological fact, something that comes into being when there is a meeting of minds (*consensus ad idem*)."[3] And whilst it is certainly true that parties must 'voluntarily' consent to a contract to make it binding, to see contracts in purely psychological terms is surely somewhat limited.

Meanwhile, in law a contract is typically defined as: an offer, acceptance, and consideration. This certainly captures that a contract involves a set of mutual commitments between one or more people and is a very useful legal characterization of a contract. However, beyond that, this definition only provides criteria to identify when a contract is formally struck or not (rather than telling us what, exactly, constitutes a contract itself).

In most proceedings today, I think we tend to understand contracts in more prosaic terms and look at their ordinary language usage. In general, I think contracts are really blocks of rules fixing the mutual behavioral patterns of two or more parties. They are, in other words, mini legislative codes that provide a regulatory framework for two individuals to work reciprocally together (often, but not always in the context of the exchange of goods or services between the parties). Sometimes the rules engaging one person with another are fairly simple (think of an IOU). Other times, they are immensely complex (think of a multi-party, one-hundred-page syndicated loan facility). But in all cases, a contract encompasses "rules" that in some fashion, try to define certain obligations owed by one party to another. Indeed, that is why great political theorists like Jean-Jacques Rousseau (in *Of The Social Contract, Or Principles of Political Right*, 1762) and in more recent times John Rawls (*A Theory of Justice*, 1971) define all the laws of society and government as a form of "social contract" among the people as a whole or between the people and their government. In this context the terms of the social contract are the laws, government legislation, or "rules of the land."

So contracts are, in a nutshell, rules that bind and determine the mutual behavioral patterns of two or more people. Again, serious political and legal theorists may contest this definition or may consider it an over-simplification. But certainly rules governing the mutual interrelationship of two or more people are at least a critical part of contractual arrangements. For our purposes this type of definition should suffice. So for now let's remember, but park, that definition.

OK, so what about Tarquin's little number puzzle? Well that puzzle is in fact the beginning of a great expanse of particularly curious (and well researched) logical problems in the rules of mathematics and, more broadly, in the concept of rule following. Much work has been done on this problem by one of the most famous living logicians, Saul A. Kripke, who developed these ideas in his analysis of the work of Ludwig Wittgenstein (see *Wittgenstein on Rules and Private Language*[4]). I won't go too deeply into this very heavy work dealing with logic and semantics, but we need to grasp the core of Kripke's seminal ideas.

The fact is, clever Tarquin's response to his mother was spot on. No doubt in a school test, any kid who gave the answer 20 as the next number in the 2, 4, 6, 8 series would be marked as wrong. But, as a matter of pure logic, Tarquin's answer of 20 was as perfectly correct as the answer 10. Whenever people answer this type of question, they are applying an interpretation to the series and inferring from it some rule. One interpretation (the most common) is "add two to the previous number." But another interpretation (equally consistent with the numbers shown in the series) is indeed "add two to the previous number until you get to eight, and then add 12." Of course, the problem is that the interpretative possibilities are endless. Perhaps the rule is, "Add two to the previous number until you get to eight, and then subtract 18." In that case, the next number would be −10. Or, even worse, perhaps the rule is "add two to the previous number until you get to eight and then do a little dance around the classroom." In which case the student, in a perfectly coherent interpretation of the rule embedded in the series, should start a merry jig as his answer to the question. In fact, absolutely any calculation or action (as a matter of pure logic) can be found to be consistent with some or other interpretation of the series 2, 4, 6, 8.

Now the reader may consider this a somewhat absurd analysis (well, like many thought experiments in this book), but bear with me as this is leading to something fairly serious that will bring us back, ultimately, to *The Moorcock* itself. You see, our little paradox above was developed much further by vexing logicians like Mr Kripke. Kripke next began to say, "Imagine you had only previously encountered numbers up to 57 and were now asked, 'What is the answer to the sum 67 + 58?'" Well, most of us would say 125. But unfortunately, as Kripke pointed out, interpreting the above computation as *addition* is only one possibility. Since this is my first computation north of the number 57, it would be equally consistent with all my past computations to suggest the meaning of "+" was (what Kripke called) "quaddition." Quaddition might, for example, be understood as: "Addition *except* where all numbers involved exceed 57 (after which, you are to treat the sign as subtraction)." In this interpretation of the rule "+," if you followed the rule *correctly*, you would come up with an answer of 9.

Actually the problem here is not too dissimilar to the famous philosophical paradox of induction. Just because the sun has risen millions of times in the past doesn't mean I can be certain that tomorrow, after time "t," the sun will rise again. In any event, you can surely see where this is going. From a strictly logical perspective just about any action whatsoever can count as following a rule (even rules that appear fairly clear cut). And if this is true for the apparently black-and-white rules of mathematics, how much more so is it in relation to the intrinsically less clearly defined rules of law, of morality, or, of a contract.

Kripke sums up this grim state of logical affairs by quoting the great Wittgenstein: "This was our paradox: no course of action could be determined by a rule, because every course of action can be made out to accord with the rule. The answer was: if everything can be made out to accord with the rule, then it can also be made out to conflict with it. And so there would be neither accord nor conflict here."[5] More generally, doubts about the determinacy of rule-following are sometimes called "rule skepticism" or even "legal realism." The subject is hotly debated by jurisprudence academics (among others). Legal realists are very exercised by how we determine what counts as the "correct" following of rules (particularly the type of rules we see in contracts or in the law). Like Kripke, they do not believe rule following is akin to a straight deductive inference, but is perhaps determined by community consensus or the opinions of judges. Jerome Frank, a leading American legal realist of the early 20th century, passed judgment himself on the application of legal rules to specific facts. As Frank put it, "Until a Court has passed on some facts, no law on that subject is yet in existence."[6]

All right, enough logic. And you, the reader, may now be saying: that's all very cute (or not . . .), but it is a typical piece of obscurantist semantics, just so many angels dancing on a pinhead? Well, I accept it is a slightly rarified analysis. Unfortunately, like so many philosophical paradoxes, it does ultimately impact the real world. And in this case it impacts (big time) the world of business and financial contracts.

So now, finally, we are back to our poor steamship *The Moorcock*. What was this case really about?

Well, in English commercial law, it now holds stature as one of the seminal precedents determining the principle of "implied terms" in contracts. Because of *The Moorcock* precedent, the courts have to pay attention to terms that are neither written into the contract nor spoken between consenting parties. And the question that comes up repeatedly in contract disputes is, "What terms are *implied* in the contract?" In other words, the rules of the contract are *interpreted* in such a way as to imply that certain incremental terms are actually assumed to be implicit in the contract.

In the ruling of the, no doubt, wise Lord Justice Bowen in the real life *Moorcock* appeal, the justice concluded that *The Moorcock* owner was in the right. The judge argued that the only interpretation of the rules of the docking contract that made sense to him (or were fair to him) were ones that implied obligations on the wharf owner to provide safe docking. And that meant providing wharf space where the water was sufficiently deep irrespective of the tidal flow. Though it was not specifically stated in the contract, the ship owner had the right to expect that his vessel would not be stranded or mauled by running aground during the ebb tide. The judge famously said (in long-winded legalese typical of 19th-century judgments), "The law is raising an *implication* from the *presumed* intention of the parties with the object of giving to the transaction such efficacy as both parties must have intended."

Springing from this ruling, many generations of judges have recognized the principle of "implied terms" in English contract law. Translated from legalese, it basically comes down to this: "OK, guys, I am going to read a whole bunch of stuff into this rule and find one (of potentially an infinite number) of interpretations of the contract that seems fair enough to me. Oh and I can do that because, after all, what's the next number in the series after 2, 4, 6, 8—heck it could even be . . . 2001."

We may think the judge's interpretation was quite fair—although I assure you the owners of the wharf protested that it was nothing of the kind. The contract they held in their hands, they asserted, was a contract that said nothing whatever about low tides. From their point of view, it was clearly the ship owner's obligation to check the tides and take regular depth soundings alongside the wharf.

Furthermore, even if we consider the judge's ruling to be fair or commonsensical, who was he to intervene in the terms of the contract? Surely the whole point of our free market, private right to contract is that we can choose what contracts, and what contract terms, we enter into. Plenty of deals are struck that favor one party over another (e.g. if I buy an asset at an excessive price this is a great deal for the seller at my expense; or by contrast if I manage to buy an asset well below typical market value that's a great deal for me at the seller's expense). As Professor Michael Sandler states, "The mere fact that you and I make a deal is not enough to make it fair."[7] We see that effectively Lord Justice Bowen's judgment was (rightly or wrongly) a direct form of social intervention into the free workings of the market.

But Lord Justice Bowen was not swayed by such arguments. His finding in favor of the ship owner essentially opened the floodgates to much wider interpretations of contracts. The fact is, every rule is open to an infinite number of interpretations. Which is in perfect accord with the thinking of quirky logicians like Kripke and Wittgenstein and their claim that, if you create a rule, any act of any kind can count as being in accordance with that rule. Contracts are just a bunch of rules governing the behavior of two or more parties and hence, contracts are in fact open to endless interpretation.

And indeed today there is a wealth of precedents in the whole Anglo-American legal system showing how contracts should or should not be interpreted. *In re: Motors Liquidation Co.* (a U.S. case in 2011) tells us that apparently the key rule in contract interpretation is to ascertain and "give effect to the expressed *intentions* of the parties." Likewise the famous English case of *Reardon Smith Line Ltd v. Yngvar Hansen-Tangen* outlines various interpretative principles: e.g., that a contract should be interpreted by reference to the meaning conveyed to a reasonable person; or that the meaning of contractual words is not their literal, dictionary meaning, but one that should be understood from the context; etc.

Whether any of these interpretative rules actually make things any clearer or determinate is however a very moot point. After all, a rule as to how you interpret contractual rules is itself, a *rule*. Hence these interpretative rules are themselves open to endless interpretation and so, round and round we go and find ourselves back where we started. Bizarrely, some judges have even tried to establish rules of contractual interpretation to tell us when a contract needs interpretation in the first place—"[a] contract is ambiguous only when the provisions in controversy are reasonably or fairly susceptible of different interpretations or may have two or more different meanings" (*Hamilton Partners v. Highland Capital Management*, 2011). Truly, only judges with their unique verbosity, could think it adds something to tell us that a contract needs interpretation if, and only if, it needs . . . interpretation.

To this then, we only need to add one final, but toxic piece—those men and women who act aggressively in their own self-interest. We then find one of the core realities of contractual disputes in the business world— super-charged monetary motivation to interpret contracts in the way that best serves any given party. It is Kripke's, or little Tarquin's, paradoxical logic itself that feeds the instinct for rival business parties to twist the rules of a contract. And the indeterminate nature of rule application means the possibilities open to hard-nosed businesspeople are endless.

Of course, the signs of contractual paradox in action are all around us, visible daily in our business and financial dealings. We see it even in mundane contracts with service providers or repair shops. One party expects a contract to provide a particular service while the other party thinks it should provide a slight variant on that service, or not so much of the service, or perhaps a completely different service altogether. In other contractual arrangements, a certain amount of time passes, circumstances change, and suddenly one party no longer thinks it appropriate to be bound by prior terms that were agreed upon in the earlier contract. (This is very common in real finance/business activities and indeed, circumstances may genuinely require reinterpretation of a contract.) Or perhaps the contract refers to a partnership arrangement in which, after 20 years or so, one partner falls out with the other. "Let's recognize things have changed now," he says, "so I don't think our partnership agreement rules can be read in the way we used to read them." Given these new circumstances, Partner A goes on to say, "I in fact, interpret the partnership contract such that . . ." and proceeds to screw his partner of 20-plus years and divest him of everything he's worth. (A not-unfamiliar scenario.)

In the finance world I have seen Kripke's paradox particularly active among some of my insurance and reinsurance clients. Insurers are very sensitive to what is known as their "claims ratio"—that is, the ratio of claims paid relative to premiums received. An insurer's claims plus operating expenses can actually be higher than premiums paid, because insurers also earn investment income on their reserves. It is often the investment income that tips an insurer into profit. But either way, clearly more profit will be made if fewer claims have to be paid out in full. As a result, any large insurer has whole departments focused on reducing claim payouts. Much of this is achieved by utilizing the small print in contracts and indeed, applying every possible interpretative twist to a given insurance contract with intent to reduce or void a given claim.

The reader will surely recognize the extraordinary ability of insurers to find reasons not to pay on claims. How many times do we believe something is insured only to find that said item does not quite fit the definition of an "insured item" under a given contract, or the contract does not quite cover the type of accident or incident that occurred in this particular case? Indeed, many consumer lobbying groups specifically target insurers for abusing the interpretative possibilities in insurance contracts as they seek to minimize claim payments.

Note that the American Association of Justice (AAJ) has amply documented many of these insurance tricks. Among the recorded stories: an insurer claiming that a car accident was not in fact an "accident" since it was deliberately caused by one party acting upon an impulse of road rage. Hence, apparently, the relevant claim was not valid since the policy only covered "accidents." In a paper entitled *Tricks of the Trade: How Insurance Companies Deny, Delay, Confuse and Refuse*, the AAJ notes that the Farmers Insurance Group "even ran an employee incentive program 'Quest for Gold' that offered incentives, including $25 gift certificates and pizza parties, to adjusters who met low payment goals." Again there is U.S. case law that supports the AAJ's position—the case of *Banco Multiple Santa Cruz v. Moreno* (2012) tells us insurance contracts should be interpreted based "on the reasonable expectations of the average insured upon reading the policy and employing common speech."

I have also seen Kripke's paradox particularly active in bankruptcy and restructuring situations. I have worked on a good number of bank and finance company restructurings in my career (and more about these in Chapter 11). Suffice to say, when things go wrong, every creditor is eagerly interpreting the terms of his credit/loan agreement or bond to try to push himself as high in the priority ranking as possible. Each creditor will use whatever it takes to suggest they should be prioritized in payments to other creditors.

The International Swap Dealers Association (ISDA) has been particularly successful in this regard in saying that the debts owed pursuant to swap agreements (particular types of derivative contracts) must be understood as having special rights and immunities in the bankruptcy process. These special rights include fairly unlimited enforcement rights against the debtor (such rights being known as a "safe harbor" under U.S. bankruptcy law). ISDA argues for this "safe harbor" for its members' contracts due (they claim) to the potential systemic risk caused by defaulting on massive derivative obligations. Consequently, for example, many of the legal cases surrounding the recent Lehman bankruptcy (which itself involved many thousands of derivative contracts) have focused on interpretation of this "safe harbor"—i.e. to which contracts should it apply and when? In reality special rights and immunities get *interpreted* into certain contracts simply because of the persistency of industry lobbying groups (like ISDA), as opposed to any other concept of justice or fairness.

But outside of finance, there is one industry that has taken the art of exploiting Kripke's paradox to rarefied heights of near genius. That, of course, is the world of contractors. All too often, those referred to as "contractors" are just that—ultimate masters in twisting contractual meaning itself. Virtually anyone who has done work on a house will tell tales of a contract that was supposed to have cost "x" but ultimately cost "$3x$" (apparently this new cost being well within the ambit of the original contract). Many pieces of work, adjustments, extensions that were never contemplated by anyone at the beginning of the contract turn out to be—as the contractor explains—very much part of the "original deal" or "original work spec." And in some cases the delivery of many items in dysfunctional states, incorrectly positioned or not operable at all, is quite consistent with the terms of the original contract. Meanwhile, repairing these faults requires, the contractor explains, a wholly new contract since nothing in the original contract talked about addressing the original "imperfections." (Loan sharks truly look like saints compared to the household contractors who demonstrate extraordinary agility in contract interpretation.)

Of course, there is also the particularly American propensity for endless, detailed legal drafting. It's as if phalanxes of lawyers could finally address the whole "Kripkesque" problem by attempting to create contracts that legislate for every possible situation. As a result of this industrious paperwork, today's U.S. economy is one of the most bureaucratic in the Western world, with commensurate sky-high legal bills (and we'll come back to that in Chapter 10). Such legal exercises are particularly futile. For all the layers of paragraphs and subparagraphs are unable to prevent, in any way, disputes over contracts. And why? As we now understand, it is because every rule, however drafted, is open to infinite interpretation.

And it's all because of an obscure theory in logic, one that most of us would never dream of and yet one which our instinctively self-interested businessperson knows how to exploit. Kripke's logic comes into play quite subconsciously, and yet it is a powerful determinant of human behavior. It seems that when it comes to a contract, capitalist instincts can put all of us on a par with the greatest logicians in history.

WHAT IS A FINANCIAL INSTRUMENT?

A *Legal Fiction*

*"There may always be another reality
to make fiction of the truth we think we've arrived at."*
—A Yard of Sun, **Christopher Fry** (1907–2005)

I am now going to tell you what is, by a long shot, the strangest story in this whole book. It is very brief.

I once journeyed to a far-off land to meet two ancient men in an antique bazaar. One man was tall, and the other short. The tall man took possession of a donkey from the short man for 50 gold pieces. One year later, the short man took possession of the donkey from the tall man in exchange for 60 gold pieces.

That's the story.

Finished. A story of two men trading donkeys. That's it—nothing more. It doesn't seem strange, not strange at all. It appears to be one of the most straightforward, even dull, stories in this book.

But I suppose the core of my ideas is to show the curious (sometimes hidden) puzzles that lie beneath many commercial activities. And in fact, this story is "donkey deep" in strangeness—but it requires a little thought. Or rather it requires a little peeling, for when you do that, the story evaporates entirely.

First and foremost, is this really a story of a trade? It turns out the tall man and the short man were not really trading in donkeys at all, nor did they want to trade in donkeys.

Actually the tall man was making a loan to the short man for one year. He loaned the short man 50 gold pieces. And after one year the short man paid him back the 50 gold pieces plus a high(ish) 20% per annum interest rate, making 60 gold pieces. The donkey was always the short man's donkey and was never sold. It was simply collateral for the loan—held by the tall man for the one year as his security (think of a pawn broker). Then on repayment of the loan (with interest) by the short man, the donkey was returned to its rightful owner. Notice, therefore, how the story never uses the word "trade" or "sale" about the donkey—it just refers to "taking possession" of the donkey.

So the trade was a fiction—a *legal fiction*, a fictional tool that replicated all the cash flow dynamics of a loan.

Of course the whole story is itself a fiction. I made it up—all four sentences being a total fabrication. The fictional story was also a tool, one that I used to elucidate something about finance. It was the fictional story of two men who appeared to be effecting a trade, though the trade, being a loan, was a fiction itself.

So, there it is—the real end of the story. Churchill called Russia a "riddle wrapped in a mystery inside an enigma." But why would I bother creating such a Russian doll, content within content within content, or rather, appearances within appearances within appearances? Well, because so it is with financial instruments. And that's what this chapter is *really* about.

I'm going to argue in this chapter that one of the best ways to understand the nature of financial instruments is to see them as "legal fictions." This does not provide a total picture of said instruments and toward the end of the chapter I will give a broader and more comprehensive definition. But the notion of legal fictions does provide us with some unique (and curious) insights into the workings of financial instruments. It shows, among other things, how powerful the profit motive is and how it manifests itself in the strangest ways—for we will see how men are great creators of fictions that are used to achieve various business objectives. So that's where I want to start.

First of all—what is a "legal fiction" itself? Well, there is a good deal of theorizing about the concept. Broadly, a legal fiction is the assumption of certain facts, or depictions of reality, which are palpably false, yet the use of which allow us to achieve useful objectives (typically moral objectives). One of the most famous legal fictions is the idea that a corporation is a "person." Corporations are clearly not persons. But by allowing the law to treat a corporation as a person, all manner of legal responsibilities and liabilities can be associated with that corporation without said liabilities attaching to the owners (or shareholders) of the corporation. Or— another example of a legal fiction: there's the doctrine of survival. This doctrine holds that if two people die simultaneously or in a situation where it is impossible to know who died first, the older of the two is assumed to pre-decease the younger.

Another example: consider the laws of adoption. In this instance, a child once legally adopted is assumed to be the biological child of the adults who adopt him or her. Clearly that is not really true, but for legal purposes the adopting parents can make all the decisions that relate to the child as if they were the biological parents.

Legal fictions are a very old device going back to Roman law. You can see that one of their specific elements is the depiction of reality in some sort of parallel form, as if in a mirror— appearances within appearances. And yet by describing reality in that way, we get a deeper insight into actual legal, social, and economic relationships.

In fact, we use fictions as a useful tool in many areas of life—not just the law. There is of course the use of fiction in storytelling. That is what we see periodically throughout this book—i.e. I've used (or at least tried to use) fictions as mechanisms to explain certain curious aspects of finance in a tangible and amusing fashion. The fiction casts light on some aspect of reality.

More concretely, we know from modern physics that much of the way we, as humans, see the world is a sort of cognitive fiction. These cognitive distortions are themselves survival tools. I see tables as solid, when in fact they are really made of endless numbers of particles and mainly nothing between those particles. Color is not a feature of an object as we think of it, but the product of photons (emitted by an object) interacting with my eye—these photons themselves apparently being part wave and part particle. Time seems constant, but we know from the theory of special relativity that for those traveling at very high velocities relative to others it materially slows. And so on. We have evolved a commonsense view of the world that helps us function effectively, but modern physics tells us this view is a total fiction.

These fictional tools exist even in mathematics. The square root of a negative number (e.g. $\sqrt{-3}$) does not "really" exist; and yet in mathematics it can be assumed to exist and $\sqrt{-1}$ is defined as "i" for "imaginary" number.[1] The use of imaginary numbers again turns out to be a very useful tool allowing for a whole range of computations that actually have great practical use in engineering, physics and other fields.

But how is all this relevant to financial instruments? Well, bear with me. One of the earliest, but very creative evolutions in financial instruments, actually occurred over quite a stretch of time, from ancient Roman days to the late medieval era. This wave of developments was a response to a particular problem that ancient scholars created—namely, the prohibition on usury.

Sometime during the first millennium BCE there emerged a doctrine saying that it was wrong to charge interest on money that was loaned by one person to another. This was more than a matter of mere disapproval. Lending with interest was morally and legally forbidden. The origins of this proscription were clearly outlined in the Old Testament.[2] The doctrine was more fully developed by Jewish Talmudic scholars. In Roman times, they established the principle in law and wrote at length in defense of their arguments.

We can see where these early scholars were coming from. They recognized the bondage that debts could create and that vulnerable people, in need of cash, could be subjected to egregiously high interest rates. In giving someone a loan, you were not producing anything tangible that provided food, shelter, or service to the other person. And since there was no real product being traded, the scholars argued, why should the lender get the benefit of a profit? Surely if someone needed cash, it should be given to them—we should always be helping people get on their feet/become self-sufficient. To do otherwise was considered usury, and that in turn was regarded as a form of exploitation. So in one respect, this was an enlightened view. Certainly the policy of "no interest" or "no usury" helped protect the unwary borrower from being fleeced.

The policy would have been all well and good, but for one thing. It is not possible to lend money without there being *some cost* to that money. That is to say, all money has a time value. If I am due to get $100 from you in one year, the money you pay to me on that "due date" does not have the same value as $100 that you might give me right now. There's the question of inflation, of course. But more critically is the risk involved. There is always a chance that *I will not actually get* the $100 payment that you promised to make to me in one year. (Remember the "uncertainty" in finance!) So I can't possibly say the $100 one year from now, has the same value as $100 in my hand right now. Interest rates reflect this critical point—namely, the time-based uncertainty as to repayment, which is in itself linked to the credit quality of the person who will be paying me in one year.

Certainly, charging excessive and exploitative interest rates is unnecessary and wrong. (Laws relating to usurious interest rates are still on the books today.) And that is where the ancient laws made sense. But if I do not charge any interest when I give a loan, then this does not mean I have eradicated the cost of that money. That cost is still there. It simply means I (the lender) am bearing the cost myself. By not charging interest, I'm merely making a gift, granting charity (and in fact it is pretty clear the Talmudic scholars recognized this). And that's the crux of the problem: very few people involved in commercial endeavors are willing to go around lending money on the same basis as making a charitable gift. If they lend $100 for one year, they want back cash with at least the same value ($100 of present value). That means the business-like lender must get back in one year, something greater than $100 (the delta being the interest rate). Yet the ancient prohibitions on usury were very clear: no amount of interest whatsoever could be charged by a lender.

It is probable that the intrinsically time-based value of money was only fully understood in late medieval times. In Babylonian loans, for example, the evidence is that the same absolute quantum of interest was applied to the full term of a loan, whatever the period.[3] Many scholars believe Fibonacci's *Liber Abaci* in 1202 was the first clear exposition of the time value of money, interest rates, and discounting to present values. But, in the meantime, Jews, Christians, and Muslims had all adopted the prohibition on charging interest. As society developed and commerce grew throughout both the first millennium CE and, more dramatically, in late medieval/early Renaissance times, the problems associated with the prohibition became increasingly apparent. All this is well documented by economic historians. In order to make any sort of commercial sense of lending (i.e., capital provision that was needed for growing societies, for building, for ships, for exploration), some form of lending on interest had to be created which at the same time didn't violate the usury prohibitions. Early capital providers needed to lend on interest, without lending on interest.

It is precisely at this point that our legal fictions start to kick in—and in a big way. You see, what began to develop in Talmudic, Roman and through medieval and Renaissance times, were new forms of financial instruments that achieved the same cash-flow effect as interest, but the deals were arranged between lender and borrowers without technically charging interest. These early financial instruments were legal fictions incarnate. They were created precisely to facilitate lending on interest while maintaining the appearance of something quite different—another reality.

There are many examples. Let me take you through a few:

The most straightforward is the repurchase agreement, which is the fiction exemplified in my mini tale of the tall and short man at the beginning of this chapter. If A sells something (say a donkey) to B for $100 on condition that B sells back the donkey to A for say, $110 in one year's time, you have created: a one-year, 10% loan collateralized against a donkey. Yet it appears to be a sale and repurchase agreement. The interest is, as it were, hidden by the legal fiction of the repurchase agreement. So said sale/repurchase agreement is a good example of a financial instrument created as legal fiction to disguise lending on interest by burying it in a mirror structure.

In fact, these types of agreements are still very prevalent in financial markets—they are called "repos" (short for repurchase agreements) and are used for stock lending. Banks and brokers will borrow stock from each other by entering into agreements to buy stock and then resell it back at some slightly higher price; the increase in the price is the interest rate.

Here's another example. Imagine if I were going to lend you some money to allow you to buy a car. Well, I want my interest on my loan—but how am I going to get that if you and I are still supposed to obey the ancient prohibition on usury? Here's what I'll do. I'll buy the car myself and now rent it out to you. You have the car to use, and in the meantime you pay me a rental fee. I set the rent at exactly the same level as the interest I would have charged on the money. Meanwhile, we have agreed that at some fixed point in the future the rental agreement terminates and you return the car to me. We are done. We've now replicated lending-type cash flows/relationships, but this time we've used a lease. You didn't pay me interest; you just made rent payments.

Here then, is one way to understand the financial instrument that's a lease—as another legal fiction that happens to solve the "problem" of usury. Indeed, the lease is still a very commonly-used device to arrange lending under Sharia (Islamic) law, where the prohibition on charging interest remains in place.

Some of the fictions used historically were very transparent indeed. They don't seem like an adequate way at all to create the illusion that they were something other than the forbidden deal. For example, one of the ancient scholars argued that so long as you lend out money in the form of "hiring" out money and taking a rent (akin to hiring out chattels) rather than interest, then that was not usury. Or consider the solution that was worked out by the great Medici banking family in late medieval Venice. The Medicis circumvented the usury prohibition by buying "trade receivables" at a discount. For them, it became a big business. Technically, there was no interest charged. But there was a gap between the discounted purchase price (at which the Medici would buy the receivable) and the face value of the receivable. In other words, if 100 gold ducats were owed pursuant to an IOU, the Medici would buy the IOU for just 90 ducats. Looked at another way, that difference *was* the interest rate. The extra 10 ducats collected on the note was effectively 11% interest (10/90) charged to the seller of the note (assuming the note was redeemed within one year). But no one ever mentioned "interest rate" in a Medici transaction since it was all disguised as the purchase of a receivable.

The usury prohibition even spawned perpetuities or annuity instruments. These were bonds that never redeemed, but just paid a fixed-interest payment in perpetuity. These instruments certainly seemed to charge interest. But since they never redeemed, some institutions successfully managed to argue—against Church doctrine—that they were not therefore loans at all in the conventional sense. Hence the prohibition on lending on interest didn't apply to them either.[4]

Some of these ideas are explored by Professor Michael Knoll, professor at the University of Pennsylvania Law School and Wharton School, in his 2004 article, "The Ancient Roots of Modern Financial Innovation: The Early History of Regulatory Arbitrage."[5] Knoll is principally focused on the theory of Put Call Parity in this article (which we do not need to go into here). But as part of his analysis, Knoll also goes into some detail on historic examples of loans being replicated through other securities. He identifies many of the above legal-type fictions as antique forms of financial instruments that addressed the regulatory challenge created by the prohibition on usury. Business motivation is strong, and when the motive is profit, inventive minds seem always to find a way. In Knoll's view, finding your way around rules turns out to be a key element in the evolution of financial theory. Or, as he sums it up, "The exploitation of regulatory inconsistencies is one of the major impetuses for financial innovation."

E. L. Globus made the same point when he argued that the evasion of the prohibition on interest reflects the conflict between law and life.[6] And indeed, this conflict is addressed with point and counterpoint in the original Talmudic writings on the subject. On the one hand, the restrictions on charging interest were taken very seriously. Indeed, most of the schemes mentioned above were identified and deemed forms of prohibited charging of interest. These indirect forms of interest were referred to as "dust of interest." The dust-of-interest tactics were also prohibited.[7] On the other hand, economic arrangements certainly by early Renaissance times were such that a solution to the restriction had to be found. Hence, scholars also went out of their way to resolve the dilemma.

One particularly interesting solution involved another fine legal fiction or financial product that solved the usury prohibition in a slightly different fashion. This solution emerged in late medieval/early Renaissance times among Islamic and Jewish scholars—called, in Aramaic/Hebrew, the Heter Iska. It essentially said that rather than A (a capital provider) lending on interest to B (a businessman), A and B will be deemed to have entered into a *partnership* agreement. "B" will contribute his business/labor into the partnership, while A will contribute his cash. "A" will effectively be a 50% equity holder in this partnership, but his equity rights will be constituted so as to give him a fixed return on his investment (the fixed return, of course, being interest by another name).[8]

The partnership solution is an especially interesting (albeit difficult) one since it also gives us insights into early notions of equity instruments versus debt instruments. I go into this further in the next chapter, but the key point is that there are fundamental differences of definition between debt and equity. For one thing, the yield on a debt instrument is fixed and is cumulative; for another, the debt instrument has a maturity. The yield on debt is cumulative in the sense that it is (like interest) an obligation which legally, must be paid each year. If it is not, the yield or interest cumulates (or builds up) until it is paid off in full. Contrast this with a dividend on equity (stocks). That dividend is not an obligatory payment that must be made by a company each year. If it has been a bad year, a company may not pay a dividend on its equity, and furthermore the missed dividend will not be owing the following year. And whereas debt is supposed to mature at some point, equity (being an ownership right) is perpetual.

The challenge with the Heter Iska (or other partnership-type solutions) is that the notional lender is being given an equity interest in this partnership. However, to make the legal fiction work, the equity must act like debt. Hence, in many of these Iska arrangements the dividend on the equity (or capital provider's partnership slice) was effectively fixed; and presumably, the capital provider could redeem his partnership interest at a certain point (like the redemption of a loan).

To give a concrete example, imagine I own a shop selling toy models of aardvarks and other obscure animals. My business is expanding as the demand for plastic aardvark miniatures is booming (as you can imagine it might be among the kids of today)! I want to increase my inventory to include the new range of mechanical, computer-controlled aardvark simulacra, but if I'm going to do that, I need a loan. Now, suppose I am bound by the ancient rules on usury. What I'll do is circumvent the rules using a Heter Iska. Effectively, my new capital provider does not extend a loan to me (at least it doesn't look like that). Rather, he takes a share in my business: he becomes my partner. We then fix the return I will pay him under the partnership agreement, and I even allow him a mechanism to redeem his share at some future date. We have achieved the same cash-flow effect as a loan. And this time, we see the *partnership* as a financial concept functioning as a legal fiction to solve the prohibition on interest.

Put like that, this partnership-type solution sounds a bit like something that is hybrid debt and hybrid equity. And that's really interesting since now we see how this little legal fiction has just given birth to another well-known modern financial instrument—namely, preferred stock.

★   ★   ★

Preferred stock is perhaps the prime example of financial instruments acting as the very economic embodiment of a legal fiction. Preferred stock is equity (it ranks junior to debt, albeit senior to common stock), and yet it typically has a fixed dividend. Preferred stock is usually perpetual (like equity) although it can often be "put" by the investor back on the issuer at some point to allow for redemption. So preferred stock is often debt in practice, but hidden in the form of equity.

Sounds very like the legal fiction of the Heter Iska—doesn't it?

Indeed, it is. The concepts are identical.

This way of seeing financial instruments and in particular, preferred stock (i.e., in terms of their functions as legal fictions—debt "hiding" as equity) is still very relevant in today's banking system. In recent history, for instance, legal fictions associated with the Basel Accords had direct impact on the credit crisis. The Basel Accords are a set of treaties outlining the rules which determine how much equity capital banks should keep and in what format. In the banking world, the equity or shareholder capital deemed to be valid for this purpose is usually called "Tier 1 Capital." The point of the Basel rules is (supposedly) to maintain stability in the global banking system by ensuring, among other things, that banks must maintain a minimum amount of shareholder equity relative to all their debts. In other words, if banks are going to be adequately capitalized (in the view of regulators), they must hold a sufficient amount of Tier 1 Capital.

Well, prior to 2007, U.S. banks regularly issued what were then known as Trust Preferred Securities (or TRuPS). TRuPS were preferred stock that paid a fixed dividend and, in spite of being perpetual instruments (and being purportedly equity), could be "put" back on to the issuer (therefore effectively achieving redemption and all the characteristics of debt). Despite this bit of legerdemain, banks treated them as pure equity—which was really a game of "just pretending." Prior to 2007 many banks also managed to get the U.S. regulators to treat their TRuPS as Tier 1 Capital pursuant to the Basel Accords—i.e., getting them to be regarded as if they were pure equity. Even better, while the TRuPS were given equity treatment, the dividends on them were treated as tax deductible (just like interest on debt). The banks were getting the best of both worlds—instruments that were treated by regulators as equity, but in reality behaved exactly like debt (just debt that was subordinate to a given bank's *other* debt liabilities). All this allowed banks to increase the leverage in their balance sheets. The TRuPS were legal fictions themselves.

At the onset of the credit crisis, it rapidly became clear that many banks had much smaller (real) equity cushions than they were purported to have. It was as if the banks had been bluffing all along in an intercontinental card game—essentially pretending to hold a full house when all they had was a pair of twos. The legal fiction (or bluff) of the TRuPS instrument was called by the crisis. Many banks were found to be way short of real perpetual equity capital. This itself exacerbated the consequences of the crisis for numerous smaller and medium-sized banks in the U.S.

Since 2008, the Basel Accords have been tightened to say the preferred stock of a bank will only count as real Tier 1 Capital (real equity) if it is absolutely perpetual; that is, unlike debt, it cannot be redeemed. Furthermore, the preferred stock must be non-cumulative, which is to say the dividend cannot be set at a fixed rate. (So again, in this respect, it is unlike debt.) "The format is that of a true preferred stock, not a debt instrument 'disguising' itself as equity"—to quote from a research paper by Dr Craig Zabala and myself in the *Journal of Risk Finance*.[9] The old trick (smoke and mirrors) of the TRuPS has been consigned to history. But it's a very nice, and extremely modern example of financial instruments fulfilling their role as debt hiding as equity (like the Heter Iska) and being best characterized as . . . legal fictions.

In summary, I would be tempted to agree with Professor Knoll that the solving of regulatory prohibition has been perhaps one of the chief drivers of financial innovation. We might, for example, ask the counter-factual question as to where the world of finance (or the modern economic world entirely) might be today had there never been a prohibition on charging interest. At first blush, you might say that we'd be better off, since it appears as if the usury restrictions slowed down economic advancement. After all, capital provision was a critical element in economic growth, just as it is today. Beyond doubt, the rules on usury created a somewhat artificial barrier that stood in the way of the easy flow of capital.

But I think the very opposite might be more true. Yes, the rules were prohibitive, but they produced benign results. Firstly, the usury rules raised an alarm about exploitative forms of lending—types of lending which are ultimately never healthy for an economy taken as a whole. More importantly, if there had never been a rule that needed to be gamed or worked around, a huge swath of financial innovation would simply not have happened in late Roman, medieval, and early Renaissance times. As we've seen, the whole emergence of financial instruments in the highly creative form of a legal fiction depended on there being this usury rule (one considered important and yet entirely impractical)—i.e. a rule that forced men acting self-consciously in their own business interest to be extremely innovative. In many ways this is the power of capitalism. Very little can stand in the way of the profit motive—rightly or wrongly. We saw exactly the same phenomenon in the case of the *Moorcock* in Chapter 3—men twisting contractual meaning to an extraordinary degree to achieve their business objectives. Likewise, we now see how financial contracts are themselves created as contractual fictions in a multitude of colors and forms for very much the same reason.

I think in fact, much of finance can be characterized by reference to the aggressive use of these fictional tools to achieve certain economic and business ends. The fictional tools are, we might say, only "representative tokens" of the economy, but they are used by financiers for capitalistic objectives. Financiers do not, for example, invest in economic production per se (e.g. machining tools). They are investing, trading, using, and ultimately making money in and from these representational fictions that mirror the economy. This is a fact that I think underlines many themes in this book, but let's come back to that in the Epilogue.

So—can we conclude legal fictions are the be-all and end-all of financial instruments? Solving problems (regulatory or otherwise) is clearly part of what financial instruments do via fictions. But equally, financial instruments must ultimately be understood in broader terms than this. In the most general context, financial instruments are really particular types of contracts, often in the form of increasingly elaborate complexes of rights and obligations. This broader delineation is also what underlies the increasing proliferation of financial instruments over history and in particular, in recent financial times. When financial instruments are seen in those terms, the permutations are endless. In other words, strings of attached economic rights can be created ad infinitum. For example, we might start with a bond—just a right to receive payments in the future. Then we might create a bond call option—i.e., the right to buy in the future, a right to be paid some money in the future. And then you could also have an option over a bond call option: that would be the right to buy in the future, a right to buy in the future a right to be paid some money in the future. And so on and so on. As Michael Knoll also says, "The principle that underlies the rapid pace of financial innovation is that cash flows can be disaggregated and rebundled in almost unlimited combination."

And all this brings us to the question of what cognitive or epistemo-logical process is actually going on as financial instruments are innovated. We have tangentially touched on that question in this chapter. But understanding the nature of that innovation and its implications (including its implications for the recent credit crisis) is another important subject, related to, but separate from, the issues above. And that's really the topic of the next chapter.

WHAT IS FINANCIAL INNOVATION?

Railroads and the Credit Crisis

"As the births of living creatures at first are ill-shapen, so are all innovations . . ."

—Of Innovations, **Francis Bacon** (1561–1626)

The New York and Erie Railroad Company (the NY&E) went through some hard times. Chartered by the New York state legislature on April 24, 1832, it was created as a reaction to the establishment of the Erie Canal. That canal had created a northern trade corridor from Albany to Lake Erie, and the people in the southern parts of New York State had been promised a similar trade route that would go directly from New York City to the nearest of the Great Lakes.

The initial foundation for the railroad was established in 1835. But the Great Fire of New York in that year and the subsequent economic collapse, scuttled the fortunes of most of the NY&E's initial investors. So, from the very beginning, the NY&E's financial standing was extremely fragile. Given these problems, substantive construction of the line did not get under way until 1838, and it was not until 1841 that trains began traveling on part of the line. The whole railway network was not finished until 1851, linking Piermont in Rockland County, New York, with Dunkirk on Lake Erie. But throughout this period, the NY&E was beset with financial troubles.

During the 1850s the company went bust again. This time around, however, it was saved by Cornelius Vanderbilt (among others). The company went into receivership in 1859 and was restructured soon after as the Erie Railway.

The first president of the NY&E was one Eleazar Lord, an extraordinary man who, in addition to his business activities, held the position of Deacon of the first Protestant Dutch Church and was a consummate author and teacher. A resident of Piermont—one terminus of the line—Lord had played a key role in mapping out the route of the original railway and helped steer the NY&E through its many challenging years. While acting as the company's president, he also managed to write and publish five books.

One of Lord's financing initiatives was to prove especially significant.

In 1842, during the extended construction of the railroad, the NY&E was out of money—again. Lord and his board members were contemplating how to raise fresh capital to continue construction. The core problem was that the history of the company had been so perilous (like many other 19th-century railroad endeavors) that it was not easy to find investors who would be comfortable with the risk. It was essential to make the business look as attractive as possible, since the universe of potential investors in North America was relatively small.

Unquestionably, there was an allure, but also disincentives. Eventually, some equity investor in a new railroad would make out like a bandit, but that would probably be the person who came in last when the railroad really started to generate income. In the meantime, various waves of prior equity participants could be wiped out. Perhaps it was better to only be a debt provider to the NY&E; at least you were prioritized to the equity investors and paid a fixed coupon on your loan. Well, not really. Even the debt holders could get stung in a default, and the interest on past loans did not really merit the risk. The cash flows from the NY&E in 1841 were still not sufficient to service a larger coupon, so a straight loan to the company was not necessarily a good investment proposition either.

Given the problems that Lord and his company found themselves facing and the compelling need to draw in new investment, what was to be done?

Well strangely enough, Lord was not the only one contemplating this type of problem at this particular time in North America. And here I do not refer to other railroad executives, but to some of the Native American tribes. Said tribes were still very much a feature of North American life in the mid 19th century. For example, in 1840 (just a year before the NY&E's funding crisis developed) Southeast Texas had been witness to the so-called Comanche "Great Raid," raids that had themselves ended in a peculiar form of economic chaos.

In any event, one of the regular features of Native American life was the harvest festivals. The harvest occurs each year in most states in the U.S. and usually falls within certain predictable parameters. But of course, some years the harvest is very plentiful; whereas other years there may be droughts resulting in the opposite effect. The Native American harvest festivals involved praying to the spirits to assist in managing this particular harvest distribution problem.

Interestingly the risk pattern that concerned the Native Americans was precisely one that could also be harnessed to address the problem with the NY&E. There was virtually always a minimum harvest amount (we might say, the Native American's generally got their "fixed" annual return); but in addition, they also had incremental reward and risk associated with the bonanza harvest years (or, by contrast, the occasional drought years). That base return, but with upside potential, was probably the exact recipe required by rail investors.

And indeed it was—for the NY&E managed to replicate that risk/reward pattern in a new security. And so was born—the convertible bond. The NY&E could not offer bond investors incremental cash yield on its debt (as said, it simply did not have the cash flows to increase the yield above a certain level). What the NY&E *could* offer was exposure to the company's equity, as well as its debt. Under the imaginative leadership of Lord and his board, a bond was created that offered a new opportunity to investors. It paid a fixed coupon (like all bonds), but also after a certain time and at a certain pre-determined price, the bond could be converted into the actual equity of the NY&E, at the option of the bondholder. In that way, the bondholder was given an incremental dollop of yield in the form of a call option over the equity of the NY&E. The investor was allowed to have his cake and to eat it—he got his fixed yield, but also had the chance to participate in the upside (as well as downside) if the railroad enterprise really took off (or not). A bit like betting on the harvest.

As a way to charm new investors and draw them into the fold, the incremental upside offered in the NY&E convertible bond worked beautifully. Sufficient investors were drawn in by 1843, to allow the construction of the railroad to continue. It was a genuine piece of financial innovation, and one that tells us much about the nature of such innovation generally.

As far as I know, the NY&E was the first company on record to issue convertible bonds. It is interesting to see how quickly these convertible instruments were adopted. Before long, they were the favored way to finance railroads in the latter half of the 19th century, particularly railroads that were half built. The instrument could pay some element of coupon serviced by the parts of the line that were already functioning while offering investors a slug of the equity upside as the railroad was further developed. Look, for example, at the sales pitch in this announcement for a $200,000 8% convertible bond to be issued by the Milwaukee and Mississippi Railroad in 1852:

> *Thirty-six and one-half miles are completed and the whole is now under contract to be completed by the first of November next . . . The iron and ties are purchased for the whole distance, and a considerable portion of the grading done . . . The 36½ miles now opened is earning $200 a day, and the receipts for June will be about $5,000. The receipts for August, when the road will be open to Whitewater, are estimated at $12,000.*

In all likelihood, this single financial instrument played a hugely important role in the successful and rapid expansion of railroads throughout North America.

I want to discuss, in the rest of this chapter, what this story teaches us about financial innovation itself. However, before we get there, I will delve a little further into the nature of convertible bonds.

Convertible bonds are very (very!) clever financial instruments. They are best characterized as bonds plus equity call options. In other words, investors in convertible bonds have made a loan to the issuer, but after a certain time and at a fixed conversion ratio, he can call for equity in the issuer (common stock) in lieu of his bonds.

He will do this if the conversion price embedded in the instrument is such that he can call for the equity at a level that is cheap, relative to the price he might have to pay for it in the open market. Being part bond and part derivative (i.e. equity option) the real valuation theory behind these instruments was not fully developed until option theory itself was much more developed—that is, until the Black-Scholes option pricing model had been fully expounded in the 1970s. Suffice to say, today there is a very well-established public convertible bond market, the bonds are actively traded by specialist investors, and many large corporates issue these bonds.

A great deal of serious financial theory has been written about convertible bonds and we won't be repeating it here. But let's just touch on the analogy between convertible bonds and harvests in our story—for while it is not perfect, it helps explain why convertible bonds are useful in various financial situations (not just railroad enterprises!). To see why, all we have

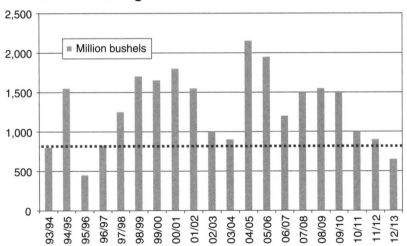

Figure 5.1 Annual U.S. corn ending stocks (million bushels) (1993–2013)
Source: USDA, Economic Research Service calculations based on data from USDA, World Agricultural Outlook Board, WASDE.

to do is take a look at some sample harvest yields over a number of years. For instance, look at the chart of U.S. corn ending stocks since 1993.

The harvest pattern shows certain similar features to the yield possibilities under the convertible bond. Most years the corn stocks end close to or comfortably above a certain base level, typically approximately 800 million bushels per annum. (This is akin to the convertible investor getting the fixed coupon on his investment when it is in the form of debt.) But periodically the harvest provides something more like an equity yield—it can come in with very high volumes (producing an abundance—sometimes over double the 800 million bushels level) or occasionally below the base 800 million level (see the years 95/96 or 12/13). And likewise, the convertible bond gives the investor the possibility of exposure also to the upside of being an equity investor in a company (as well as the downside, if said company fails). Hence the analogy between the convertible bond and a harvest (indeed, the phrase "investment yield" came originally from the notion of a "yield" on crops).

Convertible bonds, in other words, give us a very good insight into the different nature of debt and equity itself. Equity, as basic financial theory explains, provides an investor with real ownership of a company. If things go well, that equity might increase hugely in value. But if things go badly, the equity is the "first loss" and your investment might be written off. As we discussed in the previous chapter, debt is "senior" to the equity and pays a fixed yield (as opposed to a variable dividend). Remember, it also matures at a certain point, as opposed to being perpetual (like equity). The result is, in the usual course of things, a debt holder will get a predictable fixed yield on his investment and does get his principal back. A debt investment won't give the huge upside of a great stock investment, but it should, in theory, be a more stable investment than a pure equity play.

Of course debt holders do sometimes lose their principal also when a company goes bust. But at least their loss only occurs after the equity holders' loss, and their interest and principal payments are prioritized to any distributions to equity holders. The beauty of the convertible bond is that it combines the benefits of debt and equity investment. Hence, why it was the solution to the NY&E's problem. It offered investors a stable, fixed cash yield, but then gave the investors the extra option of participating in the equity upside of the railroad.

Actually, the type of risk/reward profile we see in the convertible bond is one that can be seen all around us, not merely in harvests. The game of Monopoly uses this structure. Every time you go around the board, you are guaranteed to get $200. This is like the fixed yield that keeps a player in the game whether or not his "property" (on the board) is generating income. But the real money is made when you develop real estate (in the form of property developed with houses and hotels) and others start landing on your properties. The hotels come at a cost, but they are the equity upside element in the game. Likewise, they also contain the downside risk typical of equity (you get wiped out if you land too often on another player's hotels).

Another peculiarly philosophical example of the convertible type risk/reward pattern is illustrated in the works of John Rawls, probably the leading 20th-century political philosopher, who I mentioned earlier in this book. His major opus, *A Theory of Justice* (1971), is an admittedly dense piece of work, but there is a fairly simple way to understand one of its central themes. Think of a situation in which people draw straws. From the "drawer's" perspective, all straws appear to be the same length, but of course they're not. So the decision about who ends up with the long straw, and who the short, is random. Well Rawls argued that the only way to understand distributive justice was to imagine we were all in what he called the "initial condition." In this "condition," we assume that none of us has any idea what gifts or limitations we will be born with (intellectually, physically, financially, psychologically, and so on). But we will draw straws to determine these gifts and abilities. The size of the straw you draw will determine the gifts/talents you start out with in life. That's the vision of Rawls.

Now Rawls asked what rules for distributing assets ("distributive justice") would we agree to, *prior* to anyone having drawn his straw?

Well, if you think about it, prior to the draw you just don't know whether you are going to get a long straw, a medium straw, or a short one. So Rawls argued that our determination of distributive rules should reflect this state of ignorance (he called it a "veil of ignorance"). On the one hand I would want to exploit the upside of getting a long straw (i.e., being a hugely talented person with many gifts)—this defined for Rawls the extent of "liberties" that should be allowed in society. Society should, in other words, let us exploit our talents/gifts. Equally, I would want some protection if, perchance, I ended up drawing a short straw. In other words, I want a good element of equalization and redistribution of wealth if it so happens I am born into society with limited talents, into a poor family, etc. Hence, Rawls claimed to deduce a theory to support his liberal economic agenda that favored mixed redistributive economic policies along with the maintenance of certain free human rights.

I don't want to analyze Rawls's ideas in depth, but even on the surface I believe there's a connection between Rawls's theory about justice, and the wondrous workings of the convertible bond. The game of chance that Rawls saw as the game of life lends itself to the type of risk/reward structure provided by the convertible bond. On the one hand, we might want the protection of some element of egalitarian redistribution of wealth (that's like the fixed coupon in the bond). But on the other hand, we also want the liberties (the free rights) to hit the big time if perchance we have unique talents (and that's just like having equity or upside exposure). A strange symmetry indeed between distributive justice, the chance circumstances of birth and the yield mechanics of a convertible bond.

In any event, I say all of the above to give you a taste of how intriguing the convertible bond really is. At the time it was created, it was introduced to solve a very practical problem—getting investors interested in a some-what shaky-looking railroad deal. But as a theoretical construct of a creative financial mind, it proved to be much more universally applicable. What was once an innovation in financial structuring continues to enjoy remarkable success today in numerous investment opportunities. It is an innovation that mirrors an enormous number of risk/reward profiles we continue to face in the real world.

But the real question I want to get at in this chapter is—what was the actual nature of the innovation when the convertible bond was developed by the NY&E? What *type* of discovery was going on when the instrument was developed? And, taking that innovation as exemplary, what is the nature of financial innovation generally?

Answering these questions is not easy and involves a peculiarly philo-sophical puzzle. It also opens up some critical insights into the 2007/8 credit crisis.

The development of the convertible bond was certainly not the only eureka moment in financial history (think of some of the instruments we touched on in the previous chapter). Even the basic idea of common stock itself was a breakthrough at some point. In other words, the idea of splitting the ownership of anything into multiple parts, such that more than one person could own that asset, was itself a moment of financial innovation.

The joint stock company is said to have emerged in mid 19th-century England when the idea of limited liability was formally incorporated into English law. That was the concept that a company could be its own legal personality, that I could own a share of that company, and that I would have no more liability to that company than the purchase price of my share. This is the "corporation" that the fine American satirist Ambrose Bierce defined as, "An ingenious device for obtaining individual profit without individual responsibility."[1]

But the core concept of splitting ownership into pieces predates the advent of common stock by perhaps as much as 2,000 years. There is good evidence that even as far back as Roman times there existed a form of legally recognized organization that had many of the features of the modern corporation. The "*societas publicanorum*" is described by Ulrike Malmendier, Professor of Economics, University of California, as having the "most important elements of the modern corporation." The entity "did not . . . depend on individuals involved, a representative could act 'for the company', ownership was fungible, traded in the form of shares, and separated from the control of the company."[2] Even more surely, split ownership (even if not technically limited liability) was clearly going on in relation to shipping and mining endeavors in the 13th century. Economic historians will tell you that 13th-century Swedish mines were financed using "*stora*" allowing for multiple owners of the mines. Somewhat later, 15th-century mines in various parts of Europe were being financed by shares called "*kuxen*." Again at some point someone had the idea of saying, "Hey, instead of one person funding this endeavor, why don't a bunch of us do it and create one entity, separate from all of us, that backs the venture—that way we'll split the risk and all own a piece of the pie." But what initiated this sort of innovation? How do creative minds work when they come up with something that may revolutionize—or further the evolution of—business enterprise?

Generally, knowledge progresses either deductively or inductively—that is, either by following a path of pure logical reason or through empirical experimentation. Development of mathematical knowledge and theorems is the best example of knowledge progressing deductively, while the natural sciences (physics or chemistry) give us clear examples of knowledge progressing via empirical verification. (This is a huge simplification of a great deal of philosophy on the nature of epistemology and scientific method, but it will do for now.)

Most cutting-edge product development or discovery tends to be driven by developments in empirical science—certainly for products like high-end technology or pharmaceuticals. Products are created when there are new discoveries in science or engineering, and then the product is further tested empirically before being sold in the consumer market (think, for instance, of the trials to which drugs are subjected before being brought to market).

Fine, so what about new financial instruments—or as they are often called, new "financial products?" Well, when someone, somewhere, came up with the idea of joint ownership—or when the NY&E developed the convertible bond—had anyone really discovered something new via empirical testing? I don't think so. There was no way to perform some kind of social or economic experiment to determine which new financial product was going to be safe and effective. Nor in fact, were these new products (such as joint equity ownership or convertible bonds) tested empirically prior to use. Once the convertible bonds had been conceived, the NY&E sold them to investors . . . and the rest is history. There was no trial period for the convertible bond before it was offered to the general investor. Indeed it is hard to imagine what such a trial period could consist of (and I'll come back to this critical point later).

By contrast, the development of financial instruments seems a bit more like (though not identical to) a purely deductive process in mathematics or logic. In the previous chapter, we saw how financial instruments are really just a particular bundle of contractual rights. It seems that when a new instrument is developed, someone has merely extended the logic of these contractual rights and their possible permutations, one step further. That's a pretty good guess about what happened in the case of joint ownership. In all likelihood, someone just said, "Let's split an ownership right into two or more pieces, and then we will 'share' the right."

Think also of our analogy in the previous chapter between financial instruments and legal fictions. We saw how financial instruments were elaborated rights that acted as legal fictions to solve certain transactional or regulatory problems. The elucidation of the instrument (in the form of a legal fiction) is rather like solving a problem in mathematics or logic. Indeed this is surely what Michael Knoll (see previous chapter) meant by saying, "There is a strong incentive to innovate around prohibited or disadvantaged transactions. Such innovations are commonly referred to as regulatory arbitrage."[3]

In the case of the convertible bond, the idea was to combine the rights embedded in a straight bond obligation with the rights embedded in an equity participation. But before that was ever implemented, it was *just* an idea. The convertible bond may not have quite been a legal fiction, but it was a theoretical package of rights dreamed up by Eleazar Lord or his board of directors/bankers, in search of a possible solution to a pressing financial problem (e.g., "How are we going to get this railroad built?")

Actually, as we saw, the convertible bond combines a bond with an equity call option. But then the development of an option is also merely the development of further permutations of contractual rights. As per the previous chapter, an equity call option is merely the right to buy an ownership right in the future. So it seems the innovation here is (again), solely a further elaboration on possible permutations of contractual rights.

The closest analogy may be something like construction—or LEGO. Once the foundation is in place, the builder keeps adding on more blocks. The blocks are all of a similar kind, but the aggregation of improvements results in the creation of a more and more elaborate edifice.

To give you a further example of this elaboration of rights in the area of convertible bonds, let me tell you about one of my own professional experiences. In the 1990s I worked for a while in a small convertible bond group at J. Henry Schroder Wagg. This was a British merchant bank that was sold in 2000 to Salomon Smith Barney (itself by then owned by Citigroup). One of my first published pieces of research was about the way convertible bonds could be used by banks to monetize or liquidate equity stakes they might have in other, non-bank companies. Generally a convertible bond is convertible into the equity of the bond-issuing company itself. But it *could* be convertible into the equity of—another company.

Sometimes banks end up making a loan collateralized against the common stock of the borrower. If the loan goes bad, the bank can end up foreclosing on the equity and effectively owning the borrower (i.e., owning the borrower company). This is particularly common among, for example, German banks where the practice of taking collateral over the equity of a borrower is very prevalent. But of course, banks are not in the business of owning non-bank companies (that is, entities such as auto manufacturers or media companies). One of the ways that banks found they could liquidate their stakes in these non-bank companies was to issue convertible bonds that were convertible into the stock of these other non-bank companies (as opposed to into stock of the bank itself). So long as the terms of the conversion rights were sufficiently attractive, there was every likelihood that investors would at some point convert the bonds and end up taking the non-bank company from the bank. By offering the sweetener of the conversion feature, the bank meanwhile could raise debt at a cheaper rate than it might otherwise do.

This type of convertible bond is itself called an "exchangeable bond." And I tell you this story to show my own real life experience of some of the financial innovations of the 1980s. The "exchangeable bond" just took the rights structure within the convertible bond one step further still—i.e. to allow for the call option embedded within the convertible instrument to be over the equity of another company, and not necessarily the equity of the bond issuer.

So in some respects, the innovation going on here does appear to be the elaboration and further construction of new complexes of rights over some ultimate material asset. Indeed that is why some economic and financial historians have said there is really *no* innovation in finance at all. They would claim that the idea of ownership and of borrowing are as old as society and the rest are just elaborations on these core concepts ("epicycles upon epicycles").

I think, actually, there *is* innovation in finance. There is real new thinking going on here, but as I say, it seems to be akin to extracting a mathematical result from a given equation (i.e. logically elaborating what was already in the original equation, but not immediately apparent).

Still, in another sense, financial innovation does not quite feel like mathematics either. In mathematics, or logic, theorems can be proven definitively. New mathematical truths are not empirically tested, but they are logically proven (think of the phrase: QED). But that doesn't happen with financial innovation. Since this kind of innovation is more like product design, no one can somehow "logically prove" these products any more than I can logically prove, for example, a hammer! We just construct further chains of contractual rights as possible tools to use in our financial dealings, but that's about as far as we can go.

And this is a very fundamental point to arrive at. On the one hand, financial innovation appears to be a bit like pure logical innovation. However, said financial innovation does not generate logically provable theorems. It produces real-life products, used throughout our economies. But *unlike* a hammer or a drug (whose functionality I can empirically test before selling to a customer), financial products are not really testable either (at least prior to being imposed on human beings).

The fact is, we do not have a social laboratory to test an economic theory in the way we do with a theory in physics or chemistry. And that is also highly problematic when we look at government macro-economic policy making. Governments develop their theories and set policies mostly as a way to come up with a "solution" to a given, real-life economic challenge. (The "solution," whatever its nature, is typically based on the theories of economic academics.) Then those policies are directly imposed on society. While policy makers and academics may review economic history and hope that it serves as a guide, no prior testing of a specific economic policy is done, nor could it be. With the trial comes the error.

Many academics will explain this problem is particularly acute given that economic policies and theories try to make predictions about phenomena involving literally millions and millions of people, the equivalent of nearly endless different moving parts. Even in physics (where the basic laws are reasonably well known), no one can predict how a mere 20 marbles will distribute themselves on the floor after having been tipped out of a jar. The mathematical calculations required to do so are so vast that no computer in the world is big enough to handle them. All the more challenging then to anticipate outcomes in economics where you are trying to make predictions involving millions of moving items (people), and you do not even know the base laws of economics to start with. Macro-economic policy making, in this sense, resembles playing chess with a million or more pieces rather than 16. (Indeed, the same point can be applied to most of the predictive claims of your average fund manager—for example, Warren Buffett, "The amount of mental effort the financial community puts into this constant attempt to guess the economic future from a random and probably incomplete series of facts makes one wonder what might have been accomplished if only a fraction of such mental effort had been applied to something with better chance of proving useful.")

These issues are all well acknowledged by economic theorists and were the core of the ideas of the brilliant 20th-century philosopher Karl Popper. Public sector economic policy making is an intrinsically dangerous business for this very reason. It often produces quite unforeseen outcomes (and we'll touch on this again in Chapter 7).

But what we have seen in this chapter is that the consequences of financial innovation in the *private* sector are no more predictable than they are in government policy making. Financial innovation results in new financial products being elaborated and then imposed on society without any testing (or indeed possibility of testing), prior to the product hitting the market. Sometimes the arrival of said product has beneficial economic effects. I think that was broadly the case with the convertible bond that assisted in financing North American railways. And I think joint stock ownership generally had beneficial effects in allowing risk to be spread and therefore facilitating the financing of endeavors which no one person could do alone.

That said, remember how joint stock ownership is ultimately the origin of stock markets. And while stock markets have been hugely beneficial in allowing liquidity into the capital markets and raising funds for hundreds upon hundreds of businesses, they have also had some darker side effects. Stock markets have been the source of some of the worst financial panics and subsequent economic downturns in history. I'm sure that when the first "*stora*" or "*kuxen*" was developed in late medieval Europe, no one envisaged the total benefit of these "products"—nor could any medieval sage have anticipated the damage they would cause, say, during the Wall Street Crash of 1929 or the internet bubble.

And this brings us to the present day and the 2007/8 credit crisis. We will briefly need to step back again and look at some serious financial innovation that occurred prior to that crisis. There were two big financial innovations in the 1990s. One was the credit default swap (CDS) and the other was the collateralized debt obligation (CDO, also referred to as "securitizations"). Again a great deal has already been written about these products, so I don't want to go into significant detail on them, but their story is relevant to our broader thesis concerning the precarious nature of financial innovation.

The CDS was developed by a now-famous team at JP Morgan as, effectively, a form of credit insurance. Prior to the CDS, if a bank lent to a certain borrower, that bank would have to live with the credit (or default) risk associated with the relevant borrower for the life of the loan. The team at JP Morgan realized that you could, however, bifurcate the credit risk from the actual lending. For a premium, you might be able to pay another counter-party (usually a big insurance company) to insure you (the lender) against the risk of your borrower defaulting. So the originating bank would remain the lender, but at the same time it would "hedge" its credit risk. That credit insurance arrangement is a CDS contract.

Meanwhile, the CDO was effectively a debt security that was collateralized against a whole set, or group, of receivables (e.g., mortgages or auto loans or consumer loans). Rather than there being an end borrower, it was the cash flow from the pool of receivables that was to be used to pay interest and amortize down the CDO notes themselves. The products were first developed for use with very homogeneous blocks of receivables, but grew in complexity during the early 2000s. The underlying pools of assets became more and more involved—often being multiple different "cohorts" of mortgages, consumer loans, auto loans, and in some bizarre cases even being pools of other CDOs (so-called "CDO squared"). The CDO notes themselves were also broken into different tranches with different levels of priority as to payment of interest and principal. Technology was undoubtedly a factor in the birth of the CDO product. Banks needed to have huge computer processing power to run the cash flows under what were often hundreds of thousands of underlying mortgages or loans embedded into a CDO. Prior to the 1990s, that sort of computer capability was not commercially available.

Actually both the CDS and the CDO are widely recognized as important and useful financing tools. The CDS does allow banks to hedge their risk against certain credit exposures. The CDO allows asset backed funding (non-recourse to any single borrower) against pools of assets: this can often be a very efficient way to finance receivables books.

But at the same time, clearly a bunch of unexpected consequences resulted from the proliferation of these two products in the early 2000s.

Many insurers that provided CDS coverage hugely underestimated the default risks they were taking on (AIG was just one example). In addition, the product undermined transparency in the credit markets because many banks that had made loans were no longer on the hook for the credit risk. The CDSs were private transactions, so it was very hard for the market as a whole to know who was on risk for what credit exposures.

CDOs, meanwhile, became overly complex with too many tranches and multiple pools of underlying assets. In fact, the receivables pools were so complex that very few people in the market could assess the cash flows generated by these assets. In addition, over time, the quality of the underlying receivables deteriorated (e.g. involving pools of sub-prime mortgages, flakey student loan portfolios, and so on). Exacerbated by a bull market, greedy brokers sold CDO notes wantonly to huge numbers of investors who had no real understanding of the underlying collateral supporting the notes.

The reader can learn much more about these products and the lead up to the 2007 crisis elsewhere. But what is very clear is that new financial innovation (actually quite useful innovation) had been launched onto society with no testing and no awareness of the implications of the widespread use of the products. It is only now, since the crisis, that various mechanisms (central clearing for CDS, improvements in the quality of securitized assets, and so on) have been put in place to moderate the use of these products more effectively.

Was there any way to "test" these products before they were introduced? I think not. And this is where we come back to the nature of financial innovation itself: it simply doesn't lend itself to empirical testing. You can subject a new model car to an endless array of engineering and safety tests before introducing it to the market. But try that with CDSs and CDOs? They could never have really been "trialed," even if anyone really wanted to. (Likewise, the NY&E could not have pre-screened its convertible bond prior to launch).

Hence we are left with the final conclusion of this chapter—again a particularly philosophical one. Certainly one of the causes of the 2007/8 credit crisis was the structure of CDS and CDO products. But it was the nature of financial innovation itself (i.e., the innovation that led to the development of those products) that was also a cause of the crisis. Private market financial innovation, like macro-economic policy, is intrinsically untestable and thus always likely to surprise. It will always produce products that have all manner of unforeseen side effects on an economy.

This is not to say that financial innovation should be avoided. Far from it. But clearly all innovation must come with a caution on the label.

★ 6 ★
WHAT IS OWNERSHIP?

Faust

"Not one is dissatisfied, not one is demented with the mania of owning things."
—commenting on animals, **Walt Whitman** (1819–1892)

Let's start with another brief, thought experiment—one that I suspect will be quite easy for many people. Suppose that you want to become the proud owner of a brand new Ferrari.

To accomplish this, you will of course have to visit a Ferrari showroom. No great hardship. There, displayed in splendor, is a select array of vehicles renowned for their leopard-like ability to spring from zero to 60 in seconds. You will be able to get into a soft Italian-leather seat behind an awe-inspiring control panel, to grip the wheel and imagine yourself flying along winding roads in a vehicle that throbs with power. If you are well-dressed enough and give off all the vibes of prosperity—in other words, if it appears you have the financial wherewithal to purchase the car—you may even be allowed to take it for a test drive, an experience (if you are a true car lover) that is likely to confirm your appetite for ownership.

Now that you are softened up, the salesperson takes you into his quiet office where the walls are festooned with "Salesperson of the Year" plaques. After a cheerful discussion about your lifestyle habits, family, and ambitions, the salesperson finally reveals . . . the price.

Most likely, you then gasp and wonder how you can exit the premises with your dignity intact.

But the sales professional, as it turns out, is quite used to this response. So he begins to discuss the trade-in value of your current vehicle. He suggests some payment plans that you might, just might, be able to afford if you resigned yourself to eating canned soup for the next five years.

So you linger. The salesman can now feel your vulnerability. He's reeling you in, he knows you're close to signing an agreement for this passionately-desired acquisition. And so, he says to you . . .

"Look, I can see we're very close here." (Long pause.) "Here's what I can do for you." (Another long pause.) "I'm going to knock 50% off the price. But . . ." the salesman continues, ". . . on one condition, one little condition . . ."

The salesman now stares hard at you with piercing eyes. He sneers and leaning across the table, whispers, "I want your right to vote . . ."

It is safe to assume that most of us would consider this very strange dealmaking. The first element of strangeness is that this is a car showroom. So why on earth is our salesman willing to deal with our, or anybody else's, right to vote?

But the proposed deal is also strange in a much deeper way. As strongly as you may desire ownership of that car, don't you find it unsettling that you have shifted over from a monetary discussion to a transaction that uses your voting right as a bargaining chip? You may have been casual about exercising that right—for instance, skipping the polls when it comes to voting for county justices and school supervisors. But still. This is your *right to vote* we're talking about. Is that really something you should be trading in, even for a hotly-desired automobile?

And that's the crux of the issue. Transferring rights to ownership over, for example, a car or cash sounds fine; but transferring your rights to vote, now that seems odd. Yet both ownership and voting rights are—"rights." Hence, there must be an important difference between these two types of rights.

In fact, what the Salesman of the Year is proposing, is a bargain that looks downright Faustian.

And therein lies our dilemma. We have to figure out what's going on here if we want to understand the true nature of ownership rights.

That's really what this chapter is about.

The concept of an ownership right is one that has been written about exhaustively since the notion was first addressed by legal, political, and economic thinkers. It was, for example, an issue in Roman law, in the Talmud, and in the medieval Christian Church. After the Renaissance, the issue became even more contested, most notably as addressed in the speeches and writings of John Locke, Thomas Paine, and the French *philosophes.* In the 19th century, the question of ownership was a key part of political and economic discourse as taken up by the likes of John Stuart Mill, Karl Marx, or Max Weber. It is also in the modern political theories of say, John Rawls and Robert Nozick. Not to be overlooked is the fact that ownership rights were a tipping-point issue leading up to the American Revolution, to the degree that quite a number of the Founding Fathers thought such rights were worth fighting and dying for.

Suffice to say, I am not going into the history of thought on ownership rights in any detail right at this moment. Instead, I want to tell a tale in this chapter that has already been suggested (in certain ways) by my car salesman episode above. That is the famous tale of Faust or Dr. Faustus and his pact with the Devil.

At first blush, the Dr. Faustus tale may not appear closely related to the potential trading of voting rights. Yet the deal that was offered both to Faust and by our proficient car salesman will turn out to be very comparable after all. More importantly, the scenarios will turn out to be fairly similar to many of the trades we make in our daily economic and financial lives. And in seeing this, we will get a peculiar insight into the nature of ownership rights themselves—a useful insight indeed, since ownership rights are another of the fundamental building blocks of the financial and business world.

The tale of Faust has been told with many variations by numerous writers. The account of the Faust story by the brilliant German writer Goethe and the account of Dr. Faustus by Christopher Marlowe are just two examples. Other great writers who have adapted the tale include Thomas Mann, whose novel *Doctor Faustus* interpreted the legend in a 20th-century context using as a central figure, the composer Adrian Leverkühn. The tale also inspired films (F. W. Murnau's *"Faust"*), symphonies (by Liszt, Berlioz, and others) and operas. Rather than deal with the great variety of interpretations, I think it far more useful to give the bare-bones outline of the original story highlighting certain common elements that run through most of the derivative interpretations.

There is some evidence that Faust was based on an actual figure who lived in early Renaissance Germany. Certainly the legend or folk tale of Faust was circulating in Germany by the early 1500s. Faust was a man who seemed to spend his life involved in various ascetic, intellectual, and mystical preoccupations. He found himself, however, dissatisfied with the course of his life, unfulfilled by his own seeking of gratification and pursuit of truth. That's probably where facts end and legend begins, for the story tells us that Faust was visited upon by the Devil's messenger Mephistopheles. Mephistopheles offered Faust a pact, a deal (another example of our contracts) whereby Faust would be granted all manner of earthly and material satisfactions, in exchange for his soul.

According to a German source dated 1587 (*Historia von D. Johann Fausten* by Johann Spies), the terms of the contract were written up, with the Devil agreeing to the following terms:

1. To serve Dr. Faustus for as long as he should live,
2. To provide Dr. Faustus with whatever information he might request, and
3. Never to utter an untruth to Dr. Faustus.

On the other side of the contract, Faust was to surrender his body and soul to the Devil. In other words, Faust would be given the worldly satisfaction he desperately sought, but afterwards (after 24 years, according to Goethe and various other sources), his soul would be consigned to eternal damnation in hell. (Twenty-four years apparently signified the 24 hours of the day.)

To Faust's credit, some (if not all) of the satisfactions he sought were quite lofty—intellectual insight, knowledge, the answer to the meaning of life, the design of the universe, and so on. In addition, however, the pursuit of plain old wealth and sexual gratification were also part of the package deal. (Goethe tells us how Faust was the cause of bringing desolation into the life of a lady called Gretchen.) Also, a significant amount of foolishness and mockery of the powerful seemed to have been sought after by Faust, at least in Marlowe's account of his doings.

Both Goethe and Marlowe go into a fair amount of detail about Faust's activities during the years after the signing the pact. In Marlowe's story Dr. Faustus spends his time stealing food, making himself invisible, mocking the Pope, entertaining kings with magic, performing supernatural feats, and playing with or tricking various dukes and knights. In Goethe's story the main emphasis is the seduction of Gretchen. Other versions of the tale regale us with descriptions of Faust enjoying everything from elegant clothing to fine wine and foods, beautiful women, intellectual fame, and other forms of excess and perversion. Some of these activities were done with the support of Mephistopheles. In all cases, however, the fulfillment that Faust really gets from everything the Devil has given him, is limited.

After the 24-year period (or however long it was), the Devil then came to take Faust's soul in accordance with the contract. Both Goethe's and Marlowe's story have key women appearing in the saga at this point. In Goethe's version it is the now-dead spirit of Gretchen interceding for Faust. Marlowe's drama has the compelling image of Helen of Troy being conjured up by Faustus (although conjuring Helen seems to be merely another instance of Faustus showing off). A student or assistant of Faust (Christoph Wagner) tends to make an appearance in some renditions of the story: for example in one account, Faust bequeaths his assets to Wagner near the end.

In any event, some versions (e.g., Goethe's) have Faust being saved at the last minute by the good grace of God. Part of Goethe's interesting logic is that the pact specifically said Faust would go to hell *if* he achieved fulfillment from the gifts of the Devil. Since he never did achieve satisfaction, he is therefore not bound by the pact. Other versions have Faust being taken away to eternal damnation. (I refer the reader to Chapter 3, "What is a Contract?"—every contract is open to interpretation and when Faust was up against it, he certainly did his best to find a favorable interpretation of his pact.) In whatever version it's presented, the story wishes to tell us that Faust had been granted various worldly gratifications, but such rewards came at grave expense—namely, the loss of his moral compass (which itself resulted in longer-term doom). In a sense, Goethe's conclusion goes even further, implying that a man cannot actually realize human satisfaction through worldly pleasures even if he pursues that mission with total abandon.

Much of the historic analysis of the Faust story focuses on it as a morality tale. Indeed it is a moral parable, which is fundamental to its place in the canon of Western literature. In earlier centuries, not surprisingly, there was a great deal of analysis of the tale as it stirred lively debates about Christian doctrine, Satanism, pre-destination, and other religious and moral issues. But whatever the moral or religious freight it carries, the tale is supported within an economic and financial framework—a trade. So my focus in this chapter is to address the trade aspect at face value, disregarding any symbolic ethical lesson. And it is the nature of the "assets" traded that I want to understand. This way of looking at the story somehow speaks to our modern sentiments and again, provides insights into elements of modern finance and financial jurisprudence.[1]

So let's look at the assets in this trade. On the one hand there are material or ordinary world satisfactions being granted to Faust. We may say that what Faust bought were "rights" to certain material and physical gratifications. This seems straightforward.

On the other side of the trade, Faust apparently "sold his soul." Now this other side of the trade is less easy to comprehend since the very idea of selling your soul is itself a metaphor. Few, if any, readers would picture this trade-of-a-soul as a physical occurrence. Instead, what we gather from the story is that somehow, Faust morally compromised himself by going through with the trade. Or, to put it another way, Faust traded away certain fundamental features of humanity that should not really be traded. He sold his basic human dignity or his ethical integrity.

Now, rights to material goods are of course another phrase for "ownership rights," so another way of seeing the tale is as a purchase of ownership rights in exchange for human dignity. And when we look at the Faustian pact in this way, we are immediately given a certain insight—namely, that Faust bought something tradable (rights to material goods) with something that ought not to be traded (his basic human integrity).

From this we quickly see what the Faust story itself tells us about the nature of material rights—rights to physical goods and services—versus certain more fundamental human rights. The fact is that an "ownership right" is precisely the right that allows a human to "alienate" an object. It allows a human to "reify" (or "thing(ify)") the subject of the right. If you have ownership rights over a table, that means the table is subject in all respects to your whims because you are the human to whom the right was granted. Not only is this self-evident, it's also well codified in a wide range of laws. For example, the French Civil Code Article 544 defines ownership as "the right to enjoy and dispose of things in the most absolute way, provided no use is made of them forbidden by law or regulation." Based on such provisions, it can be said that any owner generally has the right to destroy an object, change it, use it for his benefit, or (most critically) to sell or transfer the ownership right: the object is tradable.

In actual fact, in formal jurisprudence the definition above would be considered somewhat oversimplified. Legal theorists will tell you that even ownership rights are usually heavily constrained by all sorts of other legal baggage. For example, ownership rights to real property are these days usually limited by such things as town planning rules, building regulations, or municipal laws. But this is a legal technicality for our purposes. The key for us is that the sorts of things Faust bought in his pact were rights to material things or services and the ability to use those things for his own purposes. And these rights, it makes perfect sense to say, can be sold or transferred.

In today's financial world these alienable rights can become quite fanciful and even hard to comprehend. Increasingly, there are instances of complex rights becoming divorced from immediate underlying hard assets (as we touched on in Chapter 1 regarding Dinosaur Derivatives). Structured bonds or derivatives or collateralized debt obligations or swap contracts are all good examples. In other cases modern finance has disconnected voting rights from the economic benefits of equity ownership (what Henry Hu and Bernard Black have called "equity decoupling" or "hidden (morphable) ownership").[2] Nevertheless, with certain exceptions, these are all contracts representing rights to material cash flows, so it is quite logical for these rights to be "alienable" or sellable. While they may not always be sellable *in practice,* since a liquid market for a given security may not exist, they certainly are *in principle* (morally speaking). That is, they are all appropriate subjects ("things") that are eligible for a sale transaction.

By contrast, when we talk about certain fundamental human rights—like the right to life, the right to certain freedoms, the right to moral dignity, and so on—we are effectively saying we humans are the very opposite of those things that are the subject of ownership rights. We are saying humans are not "things." They (we) cannot be reified or used indiscriminately. We have certain fundamental entitlements that no one should take away. My rights of freedom, in all their manifestations, are not rights that I should sell to another. If I did, I would have compromised those rights themselves. Indeed, that is why these rights (such as those specified in the U.S. Declaration of Independence) are often called "inalienable." This also is the problem with slavery—it turns people into things to be traded rather than upholding the fundamental integrity of all humans. "Every man can contract his services and his time, but he cannot sell himself nor be sold: his person is not an alienable property," says the French Declaration of the Rights of Man and Citizen.[3] And as the greatest German philosopher of all, Immanuel Kant, famously said of all ethics: "So act as to treat humanity . . . in every case as an end, never as a means only."[4]

Actually the gap between inalienable human rights and alienable ownership rights can occasionally get blurred. There are trades in the life policies of the aged (allowing someone to cash in their policies at a discount before their appropriate maturity), in the pawnbroking of wedding rings, and in the trading of litigation settlements (for example, claims under the Bernie Madoff saga can be bought, as of this writing, at about 50% of the face value of the total claim). Some, if not all of these types of transaction, border on the, we might say, distasteful, and raise the question of whether these assets (although having a cash value) should be alienable.

In any event, through the above analysis we see now the basic problem with the Faustian contract. Faust traded ownership rights (which it is fine to trade) for things that we are really not supposed to trade—namely, his human dignity. In this sense, Faust turned his soul into a good to be sold. He alienated himself and thereby compromised his own moral standing as a member of the human race. He treated himself as a means, not an end.

Karl Marx was obsessed with the idea that *every* working man "alienated" himself by essentially consigning his humanity in service to the bourgeoisie. Marx, of course, was exaggerated in his application of this idea, but his words capture some of the Faustian sentiment: "*Alienated* labour degrades man's own free activity to a *means*," Marx wrote (my italics). "It turns the species-life of man into a means for his physical existence."[5]

Now we can also see why our opening story about the car salesman is very similar to the story of Faust. Suppose we took what we consider to be a human right and turned it into a negotiable property? What if we actually substituted the "right to vote" for cash? While it's fine to trade our "ownership" of cash for the ownership of a car, we feel an instinctive aversion to giving up a human right in exchange for property. We should *not* be alienating our basic human right to vote. Doing so bears the hallmark of a Faustian pact.

Funnily enough though, I suspect many people, when really short of funds, would be prepared to cash in their right to vote. The result would, of course, be a slow trend toward despotism (or oligarchy) as certain wealthy individuals buy up everyone's voting rights. Society would indeed have sold its political freedom to whichever buyer or buyers could monopolize the nation's voting rights.

Debt servitude is another case in point. In the early part of the second millennium BCE in Babylon, it was not uncommon for a debtor, who could not repay his debts, to instead become a permanent slave to the creditor. A very Faustian trade indeed with the debtor forgoing his liberty in exchange for debt forbearance. The same point can be made about the old, but now generally illegal practice of debtor's prisons. Even the Babylonians recognized the moral challenges of these practices and debt servitude was periodically subject to annulment by royal decree.

To use another example from the world's oldest profession; consider the ambiguity associated with prostitution. Many of us just do not think rights to sex should be a tradable good since such a sale undermines human dignity. The prostitute and the client are both entering into Faustian pacts (she is selling something that perhaps no one should sell, and he is buying something that perhaps should not be bought).

So the Faust story can certainly be interpreted as a useful economic illustration of the nature of alienable "ownership rights" versus inalienable, more fundamental human rights. In this context we might say, the story suggests a very important lesson in business law or business ethics. At least, it's important for those living in functional, democratic, capitalist-based systems. In fact, these "ownership rights" have been recognized by more than one theorist as the bedrock of the liberal capitalist system, the rule of law and our financial architecture. The social and legal theorist Roberto Unger wrote of the critical role of the "private rights complex" of the advanced Western economies involving "an absolute claim to a divisible portion of social capital."[6] He thought he had an alternative to that complex. (But I am not sure anyone has ever really devised a coherent alternative.)

The Faust story has penetrated the social psyche very deeply, so that a Faustian pact is regularly used as a metaphor in many contexts. If you go into a library or go online and try to dig up articles or books on Faustian pacts, you will find a nearly endless number of accounts of how our society as a whole (or groups within our society) have entered into Faustian pacts. Apparently, industrialization was a Faustian pact that gave humanity much power and wealth, but will eventually lead to the destruction and pollution of the planet. The same has been said about technology and, generally, our modern misuse of the environment. See for example, Wendell Berry in his essay *"Faustian Economics"* where he accuses post-industrial humanity of wanting to consume in a limitless fashion (akin to Faust's demand for unlimited knowledge). Environmental doom is the inevitable Malthusian result, as the earth can only provide limited resources.

In this vast literature of references, the finance and banking industry as a whole is frequently accused by the Left of leading us all into a Faustian pact: this was the industry that offered to create wealth merely by using financial alchemy or to provide mortgages for all, with the consequences being the 2007/8 crisis. By contrast, the Right tells us the U.S. government enters into a Faustian pact whenever it "prints money" to solve deficit problems—with the inevitable consequence, say the doomsayers, of an inflationary spiral that could run out of control.

There may well be important elements of truth in many of these stories. Or they may prove to be misapplied analogies. On a macro level, things tend to turn out in ways we never imagined—sometimes positively and sometimes negatively.

For me, where the Faustian pact is more relevant, is on the prosaic level of our everyday business concerns. We see this particularly when we bear in mind my definition of the pact—as a trade between rights of ownership over something material (i.e. something that can be legitimately traded such as cash, real estate, or stocks) versus elements of inalienable human dignity that (at least ideally) should not be traded at all. In fact, I think part of the reason we find the Faustian pact such a compelling idea is that deep down we know we are consenting to something like it on a fairly regular basis—in our daily business affairs.

What do we all do to earn cash (i.e., to achieve *ownership* over cash)? Well, most of us sell our labor to an employer. We don't have to accept the Marxist creed that this is totally and absolutely corrupt, for there are limits to how much that employer can alienate us, and we cannot be enslaved. But still, my freedom is always somewhat constrained by the choice to take a certain job with a given employer. I have to go to work at certain times, do certain tasks, achieve certain goals, and so on. So it seems every job involves at least a modest Faustian pact: we receive cash by putting some constraints on our essential human freedom. The pact might be regularly repeated during the business day when, say, an employee puts up with the demands of a difficult boss—again, because the employee wishes to stay employed and get the paycheck that comes with it. Here, for the job/cash the employee is trading some of his or her autonomy.

Indeed for some, this pact becomes so unbearable (so Faustian) that they refuse to work for another and become self-employed or become an entrepreneur. But of course at that point the individual has entered into another little Faustian-style pact: to earn money, the individual may, for example, have to dedicate many hours away from his/her family who provide the individual with a core sense of human worth. And there are innumerable other minor human sacrifices that someone often has to make for the sake of a proprietary business.

I don't want to say that on a daily basis, we have to deal with Mephistopheles as did the hapless Dr. Faust. Nevertheless it seems to me that society and economies cannot function at all without us regularly entering into smaller versions of Faustian-style pacts (the trading of alienable rights to material assets in exchange for elements of human autonomy understood in the broadest sense). Clearly it can get out of control; but certainly Western capitalist democracies wouldn't function without this trade. In fact, perhaps Goethe and Marlowe were really telling us that Faustian pacts are all part of what keeps humans going in our typically contradictory fashion.

These Faustian trades are also part and parcel of our ordinary moral dialogue. The fact is, we do not (solely) treat human beings as Kant would have us do—always as ends and never as means. The whole school of utilitarian moral thinking (following Jeremy Bentham and John Stuart Mill) specifically says we must look at the consequences of our actions and see which outcomes generate the most happiness. In certain cases, a utilitarian calculation means we might sacrifice at least part of someone's basic human rights or dignity for a larger social goal or purpose. All sorts of my freedoms are compromised in any organized society so as to generate order, protect society at large, or maintain a basic welfare system. So, utilitarians recognize the social importance of Faustian-style pacts, at least within limits.

And most striking of all, it might be that those small Faustian pacts are precisely the antidote to the larger Faustian scenarios that so many doomsayers see in our broader society. Interestingly, the Faust story is one that seems to have plagued the German mind in the late 19th and early 20th century. Oswald Spengler, prominent among those German thinkers specifically influenced by Goethe, referred to the "Faustian culture" in his great work, *Decline of the West*, which was written after World War I.

In Spengler's view, this culture began as early as the 10th century CE and by the time of his writing, had overcome the West. He believed the West had sold its soul to technology and industrialization in exchange for global power. Ultimately, he asserted, this would spell doom. Germany would be at the forefront of this decline, spelling the final chapter in this disastrous piece of Western history.

Similarly, Thomas Mann's *Doctor Faustus* is also interpreted as the author's thinly-veiled account of German destiny and misadventure. Probably all these German thinkers were themselves in the thrall of an even more famous (or infamous) German philosopher, Nietzsche, who in fact rather sounded like Faust himself. Here was a figure who wanted to be a "superman" and in so wishing, sold his soul (perhaps?) to fascism.

In any event, Spengler also thought that the Western world had effectively turned everything, including humanity, into a commodity. He viewed this world as the ultimate materialist society. And seeing the consumer culture around us, we must have some sympathy with Spengler's view. (We certainly have to recognize that Spengler was grimly prescient in his day, about the near future of Germany.)

But we also have to see where Spengler went quite wrong—i.e. in his predictions of what lay ahead for Western-style culture. Spengler's view about the decline of the West was in fact, spectacularly wrong. The real dominance of North-American style Western culture hadn't even begun. And I think part of the weakness of Spengler's vision is precisely our point above. Namely: while society can, for sure, become materially obsessed, some element of the Faustian trade is required for a society to grow. Within limits, people need to trade elements of their autonomy for material goods to allow for social progress. In other words, Spengler's Faustian vision of Western society was wrong precisely because capitalist democracy flourished in the second half the 20th century; and it flourished through the controlled use of the Faustian pact itself.

Whether that analysis still applies to the West has yet to be seen. Spengler may turn out to be right yet. But whether or not he is, I doubt we have seen the last of Faustian pacts. Such pacts are not some ultimate doomsday scenario for humanity as a whole, but part of the condition of being human itself. We all find ourselves (within certain parameters), trading elements of our dignity we would rather not trade, for material needs.

To survive we must manage our daily internal Faustian conflicts since they drive us on; they are like blood required by our psyche. Many of us expend much energy trying to iron them away entirely—looking for simple solutions in the Right wing or the Left wing, in God or against God, in anarchism or nationalism, or whatever it may be. But the tensions never do go away and instead we are each asked to harness them. For above all, Faustian pacts are part of the very conflicting nature of man as a "zoon politikon" (using Aristotle's phrase)—i.e. as a "social animal." Certainly they are inextricably part of our lives as economic or financial animals.

★7★
WHAT IS MONEY?
Cyber Cash

"Bitcoin may be the most dangerous technological project since the internet itself."
—internet entrepreneur and blogger in Forbes magazine, **Jason Calacanis** (1970–)

I think we all recognize that we live in a world where most money sits in an account on a computer screen. What we call money is a product of so many electronic impulses.

Needless to say, it was not always so. Starting millennia ago, money appeared in its original form as gold coins of real value. Later, money then became bearer notes backed by gold and then mere bearer notes themselves with no intrinsic value. In time, money became legally authorized mechanisms to exchange value, but not convertible into anything else—so called "fiat money" (see John Maynard Keynes, N. Gregory Mankiw et al).[1] Money in fact can take any format so long as trust in its exchangeability is established (and we touched on this in Chapter 1). As Niall Ferguson tells us, ". . . money is a matter of belief, even faith: belief in the person paying us; belief in the person issuing the money he uses or the institution that honors his cheques or transfers. Money is not metal. It is trust inscribed."[2] In fact the "fiat" nature of money was recognized by Chinese society even in medieval days. Nearly 1,000 years ago the Chinese were already regular users of paper money backed by nothing much save the (very flaky) guarantee of various Chinese potentates.[3] And today we have the most insubstantial form of money ever created.

Any brief history of money could include many amusing tales. There is, for example, one relevant story of the venerable Nathan Rothschild. When I went to work for the Rothschild banking group, I was told many stories about its founder. I have no doubt some of them were apocryphal, but be that as it may, one in particular made an impression on me. It was said that in the early 19th century, one banker who was a competitor of Rothschild refused to accept for value, Rothschild's bearer notes—the IOUs, then in circulation, that were considered equivalent in value to one pound of gold. The other banker's objections had nothing to do with the worth of the notes. He declined them purely on a racist basis—namely raising the objection that Rothschild was a Jew. So Rothschild sent a cohort of clerks to present IOUs of the competitor's bank, demanding (as was the bearer's right) that the clerks receive one pound of the actual gold that backed each note. Of course, by then these notes had already become quasi-fiat themselves. The bank had printed more notes than it could actually "back" with pounds of gold. There simply wasn't enough gold to meet Rothschild's demands. The competitor banker rapidly realized he had no choice but to accept the face value of Rothschild's notes after all.

But as we all know, you wouldn't get very far trying to exchange bank notes for gold these days. In fact, you couldn't conceivably pile up any amount of precious metals or valuable goods to exchange for the electronically generated digits that today inhabit large and diffuse systems, representing "money." We also know how these systems are susceptible to invasion, to intrusion by governments, corporations, and undoubtedly by some spies. And perhaps the greatest hacking minds do not work for our governments or institutions at all, but are the clever kids working in their garages, living the internet dream.

So, let us now tell a tale about someone who does indeed break into the systems of a nation's great money-center banks. These are systems that manage the accounts of 90% of the country's population. While these systems are supposedly secure and well protected from software manipulation, I want to describe how they met their match in an IT wacko called Terry.

Quite casual in appearance, usually sporting jeans and a T-shirt, Terry was the kind of guy who, in another era, would have one eye, a peg leg, and a parrot on his shoulder. Using strange and unique algorithms formed from many further and more transcendental logical patterns, Terry stumbled on the codes to break into these systems.

Wishing to make himself rich in a piratical-type manner, he decided that he would like to plant a large wad of cash in his own account. But Terry was a far more moral type than the average pirate, and he really didn't wish, or need, to steal anything at all. He possessed the know-how to plunder individual accounts but decided instead that he would work a grander scheme which would assure that no one would find their bank balances diminished. On the contrary, Terry found a way to fill people's coffers with cash just by increasing the digits in their electronically stored accounts.

Granted, the method was a crude tool, not least because Terry "the hacker" chose to make random adjustments to each person's account. Revealing his plan to no one (with the single exception of his friend Bill from the local Irish bar), Terry chose *not* to exercise any discrimination in choosing the computerized accounts he would fill. Nor did he determine exactly how much he was going to put into those accounts. Profoundly and ethically confused though he was, Terry just didn't want to rob from others and give to himself. Rather, he attempted to enrich his own account without stealing in any direct fashion from others.

So, Terry created the code and tapped the keys to make his bizarre vision come true and in so doing, he pressed what became something of a financial button of doom. For in the twinkle of a cryptographic moment, his program sent the numbers in everyone's bank accounts (let us not even call it money, much less cash) upward. Millions upon millions of digitized accounts were enhanced by Terry's spontaneous donations. In an instant, the numbers increased, spiraling skyward in a great wave, a binary swarm dispersed in totally random fashion.

Some accounts increased by 10%. Others doubled or trebled. And so it went on—with some enhanced fifty or a hundredfold. For sure, our pirate friend made a substantial contribution to his own account. But the beneficence was widespread—a deluge of numbers in so many accounts of individuals, of companies, of LLCs, of non-profits, of municipalities, and so on. The "program"—or rather virus (as those in the know call them)— was aptly labeled the "Midas Touch." An equal-opportunity donation, it even populated the many accounts of government agencies—among them, agencies that were already preoccupied with defending themselves from devious cyberterrorists with far more destructive motives. Though relative to Terry, the terrorists, whilst being mad and bad, were quite amateur in comparison.

To cut a long story short—suddenly, and everywhere, there was an abundance of cash and all were rich—or so it seemed . . .

Now imagine if you will, the astonished look of pleasant surprise on many bank customers' faces when, on the morning of the great hacking, they checked their bank accounts. By 8.01 a.m. (exactly one minute after cash flows hit the accounts), thousands of people who happened to be checking their accounts on ATMs or computers or wireless systems realized that some significant cyber event had occurred. Some now saw huge balances—figures so large they defied any explanation. Not surprisingly, the first assumption was that there had been computer error. Among those with startling balances, some proved themselves honest, immediately calling their banks. Others, less scrupulous, endeavored to use the money rapidly, fearing that the error might be detected before the new funds could be spent.

Of course, there were still others among Terry's beneficiaries who decided that moderate improvements in their accounts could credibly be accounted for. (Perhaps a late payment coming through? A refund of some kind?) These recipients also reacted in a variety of ways. Some embarked on a small flurry of spending. Others did nothing. For every customer who called his or her bank to report the discrepancy, there were hundreds who merely remarked on their good fortune to spouses, friends, or family.

Eventually however, there was general awareness that something was afoot in the monetary system. The "great deluge," as this leviathan of cash dispersion soon came to be known as, had immediate effects. On the morning of the great deluge, the uptick in spending was rapid and consequential. Stocks surged. Fine cars were in great demand. Retail purchasing ran rampant, as a newly-enriched population chased after dresses, shoes, diamonds, paintings, gourmet food, PCs, phones, gaming devices, new furniture, handbags, uncountable bottles of better-than-usual wines, rich seams of pornography, and even, a few new books.

Meanwhile, the monetary authorities were soon on the case, issuing immediate warnings. People were strongly urged not to rely on the figures that appeared in their bank accounts. But relative to the scope of the operation and the suddenness of its onset, the initial government response seemed to be shock and perplexity. Reaction was slow. By midmorning, as the Chairman of the Federal Reserve was making his first appearance on television, already many billions (perhaps trillions—who was counting?) had been spent or else transferred around the system.

First out, from the Federal Reserve, was a dire warning. Let no one make use of the apparent cash that had suddenly materialized. The penalties for using the "cash" would be "grave indeed." The chairman made dour pronouncements about reckless spending suggesting that transactions would be reversed as matters were set right. Let spenders beware! They were to be held accountable for using money that was demonstrably not theirs.

Scarcely an hour after the chairman's first appearance, it became clear however that his words of warning were blown away by the inexorable winds of human craving. The extent of purchasing, investing, and trans-ferring activities included such a wide swath of the economy that everyone quickly realized the viral damage was not going to be easily reversed. And this was not necessarily a good thing, at all. While financial markets surged in the early morning, by midday traders were starting to feel distinctly unnerved by the likely chaos caused by the deluge. Ebbing away from giddy joy, enthusiasm faded as all considered the likely consequences. As for the Fed chairman's early comments, they had done nothing more than spook the markets. His threats regarding the reversal of transactions had been unhelpful at the very least. Already television pundits were on the case, aghast at how such a technical breach could have occurred and saying how the authorities must be to blame. Whatever their particular views, these commentators expressed what seemed to be a consensus, that the situation has been made materially worse by the Fed chairman's comments. In the blogosphere, among those most irate about the situation, the culprit taking most of the blame had been newly designated "Chairman of the Federal Hors d'Oeuvre."

What was to be done? First, there were thoughts of closing down the whole banking system—an alternative neither possible nor practical. Electronic transactions were so crucial to the daily life of businesses and individuals. So little cash circulates today in physical form that the concept of somehow reverting to that more primitive form of payment was quite unfeasible.

Still, something had to be done!

Some weeks after the deluge had begun, inflationary pressures started to kick in. Individuals, apparently grossly enriched by the newfound sums in their accounts, were now spending aggressively—or rather foolishly, like kids in a candy store. The very thought that these funds might subsequently be taken back via a Federal Reserve order made many people less prudent about their spending rather than more so. More new fancy bags, more new cars, more new furniture—the appetite of the public seemed insatiable. There were pointless upgrades to electronic gizmos and soaring demand for liposuction treatments. High-priced dresses, shoes, watches, and other items fled the shelves as never before, coming to rest in the closets, cupboards, and drawers of unrestrained consumers. The consumption was more than conspicuous, it was intense. No one seemed to question the vacuity of it all. An age of bounty seemed to have been visited upon society, falling like rain to nurture a new harvest that was abundant and wholly poisonous.

Alas, this harvest season was short. Just as in Joseph's dream (Chapter 2), the thin cows began to consume the fat cows and yet remained scrawny and limp. In other words, as demand for goods dramatically rose across the economy, prices rose still more rapidly. And then it was only a matter of months (for the cancer of inflation spreads fast) until salaries, pay and wages also had to rise to match these price hikes. Measured against most other major foreign currencies, the national currency began falling, at first modestly, and then with alarming speed. Slowly the world was becoming aware of the howling of this inflationary wind.

And the wind became a great storm, building in intensity as the spiral soared out of control, leaving behind a pungent inflationary stench. The vicious circle swirled ever more swiftly, as if a plug had been removed from the base of a massive tub, draining everything out of the economy. Each consumer awoke to the realization that the economy really had not grown at all. What had occurred instead was, perhaps, the biggest and most egregious exercise of money printing (albeit in electronic format) in human history.

In addition, the unfolding tragedy was made materially worse by the nature of the complex IT virus that had launched the "deluge." The critical part was the way the virus had multiplied account balances in a purely random fashion, bestowing different multiples on each account. The huge inequities that resulted—one account being doubled in value while another might be increased tenfold—was at first hardly acknowledged. It took a few weeks for society at large to appreciate the horrible implications of this particular feature of the deluge. One interesting analysis of the resulting disparities came from a TV pundit, delighted by his quite sudden fame, who described what he called "the mess" in the following way:

"Say there were only two people in our economy—me and my greedy friend Midas. My net worth was just $1,000 held in an account before the deluge, and say Midas had $2,000 in his account, which also represented Midas's entire net worth. So, the day before the deluge, Midas was twice as rich as me. But here's the thing . . . imagine if the deluge had increased my account eightfold (leaving me with $8,000) but only increased Midas's account twofold (leaving him with $4,000). Well, both Midas and I appear richer, but I am now twice as rich as Midas. It looks as if our little economic pecking order has been reversed. But since the economy will be inflating (or the currency depreciating) at the same rate for all of us, with no real new economic production having been created, it must be that my increase in relative wealth has come at the expense of Midas. Generally, disproportionate increases in my account balances must come at the expense of those people whose accounts have been increased at lower multiples than mine."

"What is this, then?" the pundit went on, raising his dark eyebrows dramatically (an expression of wonder that showed up well on camera). "The only possible result must be a huge and quite arbitrary redistribution of real wealth across the economy. Part of Midas's wealth has simply been taken from his account and given to me. Through the deluge, some got plain richer (in real terms) but only at the expense of others . . ."

(What the camera did not catch was his internal reflection at that moment—namely, the thought, "What a clever (and now famous) little economist I am.")

It took many people a while to grasp the huge ramifications of this issue. For most, understanding did not arise from contemplating the theory but rather because they could observe in reality the hellish imbalances in "post-deluge" purchasing power. It was simply and fundamentally the case that the deluge had not only triggered rapidly accelerating inflation but had taken wealth in absolute terms from some people and given it to others.

The central bankers of course understood this ghastly problem sooner than most. This random wealth redistribution meant the one crisis solution that had initially looked viable, was no longer available as a course of action. An obvious initial solution to the spiraling inflation would have been a sudden, one-time rebasing of the currency. For instance, $100 would be rebased to $10 with the hope of resetting the currency's worth. On the face of it, resetting the currency should have cut off the inflationary pattern. But this trick—sometimes used in inflationary crises—would inevitably be effected evenly across the whole economy. And what in turn did that mean? Well, it was most coherently explained by the acutely bright, but equally weak chairman of the Federal Hors d'Oeuvre. Delivered in his all-too-familiar high-pitched, nervous squeak, his explanation to his Monetary Committee went thus:

"If we rebase, it may indeed stem inflation. It's been done before in various economies. It doesn't always work if there are deeper structural causes for inflation. Given the highly artificial causes of this particular currency crisis, it may well work for us. But, my economist friends, to rebase will of course crystalize the gross and random redistributions of wealth that this horrid deluge has caused. The man whose account was doubled in value will face the same rebasing multiple as the man whose account was quadrupled by the deluge. We may end inflation but we will forever entrench a gross redistribution of wealth—pure theft. In fact, daylight robbery! Those in society who experienced account increases at lower multiples than the average will be incensed." (Here, the chairman paused in his ruminations. Clearly, he was thinking of the sword that would fall on his own head if certain powerful forces came in to play—not least of which were the members of Congress who once upon a time had meaningfully large account balances.) "In other cases," the chairman stumbled on, "it may be many poor, minor depositors who will have lost out and be even more aggrieved by their still further withered purchasing power. Oh dear, oh dear," the Chairman squeaked in conclusion.

Against this thin dyke of words crashed a wave of rumors. It was said that imminent currency depreciation by the Fed would be implemented to try to quell the inflation. And the realization that this policy would lock in random and grossly unfair "real" wealth redistribution began to take root in the public consciousness. As usual, the potential behavior of the Federal Reserve had as much effect as its actual actions.

Our proud little TV economic pundit was a shadow of his former self when, in a later appearance, he came to realize that his own bank accounts had grown, via the deluge, by a much lower multiple than the national average. Further interviews turned into rants, with the anchor of the show looking on smugly (he knew his own accounts had, by chance, been inflated sixtyfold).

Now lobby groups were forming across the nation. Some comprised the rich (or the once rich) who were terrified a currency rebasing would crystallize huge losses. Other groups were the poor who also feared the worst. A strange alliance in fact, formed between those both rich and poor whose accounts had only been grown by low multiples in the deluge. Though appearing to be economically incompatible, the two groups were now bound together by the implicit transfer of wealth triggered by the historic hacking.

Against them were those who now realized they had somehow won a curious national lottery, those who had seen their account balances multiplied many times, far above the national average. Plenty in this group were the former poor, now desperate to hold on to their windfalls (among them, small account holders who had seen their accounts increase in value by fifty times or more). But some of the big beneficiaries were also those who had started out rich and were now, well, ridiculously so. Having already been wealthy prior to the deluge, they kept quiet about their pumped-up fortunes, clearly satisfied that they were the most well endowed by the crisis. In any event, the winners from the deluge were deeply in favor of the Fed rebasing the currency with its prospect both to end inflation and to lock in their newfound wealth in real terms.

Of course, there were some who seemed not to care about the whole deluge at all. About 30% of the population didn't have any type of bank account in the first place—the "unbanked." These people, so poor already, saw the affair in glorious anarchistic terms: to them this was the final (and so well-deserved) punishment that had fallen on a corrupt banking system marred by its exclusivity. Accustomed as they were to scrimping and saving, they felt a certain *Schadenfreude* in seeing the great electronic mountain of money come tumbling down around them. Still, the ultra-poor increasingly found that what little hard cash they had in their possession rapidly became even more worthless.

Meanwhile there was the usual array of crazed preachers who saw the failure in religious terms. "'Tis the end of days, when the Lord cometh and smasheth the tables of the money changers!" rose the cry from many pulpits.

As the system was fracturing around them, some even laughed, looking quite wild, even deranged.

Paralyzed by the unfolding economic chaos, the Treasury and Federal Reserve continued to dither. They could no longer adjust each individual account, ratcheting back to the original balances. Even had they wanted to, it was technically impossible. Since the day of the hacking, vast numbers of purchases and transactions had flowed through the system. Inflationary pressures which had first crept along, then walked the shadowed streets at night, finally broke into a full gallop. The disputes among the lobbying factions became steadily worse, periodically becoming violent as some took to the streets. The national mood turned bleak. Bank runs became the norm. Outside the closed doors, lines of the forlorn and desperate snaked around for several blocks. Soon it became apparent that patience was futile. Why wait for cash that lost value even as depositors shivered in the damp cold blast of a new economic depression?

Then some of those whose accounts had been accelerated two or three hundredfold (or even one thousand hundredfold) by the deluge, became known to the public. Once exposed, those individuals became a new form of social pariahs—a new breed of distorted "fat cats." The press, filled with bile, exposed them in the strongest terms. Some received death threats. Kidnappings were reported.

Terrified now by mass social unrest, the government forbade the Fed to rebase the currency. Losing what looked like the only option, there was nothing left but to let unabated inflationary pressures play out the ghastly endgame. A climax, a tipping point, arrived when inflation hit 20% per month. After that, it turned exponential. At the dark climax, prices were doubling daily. The economy exploded (or was it imploded?) into a deep hyperinflationary storm.

The inflationary vortex became a huge, life-sucking beast, denuding all value from money. Now even those who had benefitted disproportionately from the deluge saw the value of their cash deflate and vaporize. If it was $100,000 for a meal one week, it was $100,000 for a packet of chips the very next week. Of course, there were no barrels of cash to wheel around since physical cash was altogether obsolete. People needed electronic accounts filled with an ever-increasing number of digits to cover their monthly costs. One million dollars in a pointless digital bank account would be just enough to pay for a new pair of pants.

The government was paralyzed. The president resigned. The Fed chairman was indeed, finally offered up for hors d'oeuvres. People who had lost jobs were starving, rioting, or just dying. Hospitals closed. The fabric of the legal system came undone.

And why? Well, all because one hacker didn't want to steal. True, he wished to get rich, but he had hoped, with a utopian type of naivety, that all those around him could become rich as well. What he had envisioned was a unique gift to society. It was the new age of digital money that had, for the first time in history, given one man the power to implement this type of plan. But like so much economic intervention, the consequences were quite different from those initially envisaged. His electronic gift had morphed into one of the most hideous economic atom bombs of all time.

End of another peculiar story. But this time the story seems not merely to be about finance, but also about technology. Actually it is about the collision of technology with finance that has itself created a new creature in the financial zoo—electronic money (or more precisely, electronic assets). There are various strands to our hacker story, and each of them tells us something different about our modern monetary system.

The first element in the story can be summed up in a question: "What is the physical nature of money today?" There is, of course, a certain amount of physical cash—notes and coins—in circulation in our system. But in modern times, certainly in the Western world, the vast bulk of what economists think of as money is represented by the numbers that appear in electronically stored account information. More striking though, it is not merely pure cash money that is mere computer data, it is money (and even securities) in a much broader sense.

Central bankers and economists have various measures of money— sometimes called M1, M2, and so on. M1 is what we might call pure, entirely liquid money—the money in cash and checking (or current) accounts. M2 is a slightly broader concept of money including not just checking accounts, but also, for example, money market mutual funds, time deposits, and savings accounts—highly-liquid assets that are some-times referred to as "near money."

Our story could undoubtedly apply at the very least to M2 since most forms of M2 listed above are today manifest solely by numbers appearing in electronically stored files. However, we can also go much further.

Many securities today (including fairly illiquid long-term investments) are really no more than numbers appearing in special securities accounts. If you invest in a bond issue, you may never receive a bond certificate (indeed, such certificates may never be produced). Rather an electronic register will show how many bonds any one individual or institution owns. You will simply view your account statement showing the number of bonds you own. These are called "registered bonds," and the title to the bonds is determined by the details on that electronic register. When such bonds are bought or sold, the electronic register is simply updated accordingly.

Most bizarre of all, however is when your ownership of a "bearer bond" also becomes solely a blip on a screen. A bearer bond is one that is supposed to be owned by whoever holds it physically—i.e., whoever "bears" the bond certificate. In this respect it's similar to paper currency. The Euro bond market (originally a huge London-based market for internationally issued bonds) was, and still is, premised on the idea that the bonds issued in that market were "bearer" in legal format. The market was constituted that way for tax reasons, the idea being that individual bearers of the bonds would be liable for paying the tax on the interest received on the bonds rather than the tax being "withheld" by the issuer as it typically is with a registered bond. (This, it should be said, generally favored private investors simply not paying the tax at all—but that's another story).

You would have thought that bearer bonds (like dollar bills) must, at a minimum, be produced in physical format precisely because they are, bearer instruments. Well, not at all. For at least the past 20-plus years, the physical evidence has not been required. It became cumbersome and dangerous (among other things, due to potential theft) to have huge numbers of bearer bonds floating around Europe. So in time, the bonds were all kept in a vault. Legal title to a bond was still *theoretically* based on who the "bearer" of the bond was. But, in practice, the notional bearer was determined by the number of bonds against a given name on an electronic register.

In due course, there really was no point in printing individual Euro bond certificates at all. Instead, just one "global" bond certificate would be produced representing an entire Euro bond offering. (I worked on documenting some of those bond offerings in the early days of my own career in the UK.) Again, in reality the amount of bonds you owned could only be determined by the number against your name on the electronic register. However, through an incredible sleight of hand in English law (and in order to preserve the fact that interest on the bonds pays gross of withholding tax), the bonds were, and still are, deemed to be "bearer" securities. Technically, title to the bonds continued to depend on who was holding them, notwithstanding that there was actually nothing to hold at all.

On its current Eurobond web page, HSBC, the British-based global bank, states this peculiar state of affairs very succinctly: "When sold the bonds are made to the bearer, however, physical delivery to the buyer in reality is not possible." A bizarre situation indeed, since to *bear* a bond means to hold the bond *physically*. Perhaps this is a strange form of what we might call "particle finance" (analogous to "particle physics"): what investors hold in their hands are nothing more than electronic pulses.

Clearly this is another one of our little financial paradoxes, but no great surprise since (as we saw in Chapter 4), many securities are really "legal fictions" of some kind or another.

So, many more assets besides checking account money are in pure electronic format. This all works (sort of), because as we discussed in Chapter 1, there are established (and legally enforced) practices that allow the "exchange" (or rather transmission) of electronic pulses to represent the exchange of economic value.

And here we might also think of Bitcoin. Yet another medium for exchange of value that was (and still is in some places) not just incorporeal, but even divorced from government or institutional backing at all. So long as Bitcoin participants have/had faith in the exchangeability for value, of the particular Bitcoin electronic pulses, Bitcoin too could act as a functional currency. Of course, lacking legal validity it was (is) intrinsically vulnerable. It has therefore been susceptible to rampant inflation and devaluation. So long as that trust is there Bitcoin works. But when, in a moment of group angst, the trust goes, well then, it doesn't work at all.

All this in turn leads us on to the next questions related to our money story. How is this electronic money actually produced?

People still talk of "printing money," and for sure our physical bills and coins need to be produced through a manufacturing process. Technically, it is only the Treasury—not the Federal Reserve—that can exercise the option to print actual money. But in reality the vast bulk of our money is created purely with a few taps on a computer keyboard. As a consequence of monetary policy since the credit crisis, the U.S. Federal Reserve has been "printing" a fair amount of money and using it to buy bonds in the market. (I'll return to that so-called policy of "quantitative easing" shortly, as it has direct bearing on our story.) But let's look at what exactly happens at the Federal Reserve when it "prints money."

In a nutshell, if the Fed decides to buy, say, $1 billion of Treasury bonds with new money, there is effectively a system allowing the Fed to input a new $1 billion of what is called "credit" in one or more of its relevant accounts. The newly-minted electronic credit is then used by the Federal Reserve's trading desks to buy, for example, Treasury bonds in the market, and in this way this new $1 billion gets disseminated into the wider financial system. Those who have sold the bonds (whether it's the Treasury selling a new issue or institutional investors selling bonds in the secondary market) take the new electronic cash and reinvest it for their own purposes. So the new cash might end up in infrastructure projects, or in other assets, or it might be lent out to other institutions or individuals. In this way the new $1 billion is slowly showered like a widespread rainfall falling into a wider, thirsty economy. (The reality of the process is somewhat more complex, but this is the core concept.)

We might imagine some lucky people at the Federal Reserve who have the job of "creating" the "credit" just by imputing into the relevant account systems the $1,000,000,000 figure. Truly a sweet job—and a uniquely easy way of (apparently) "creating" economic value. This process at the Fed, and indeed at all major central banks, is therefore very similar to the process used by our hacker in the story to inject new money into the system. Our hacker too had the capability of simply increasing the volumes of money in people's accounts just by use of his computer program or virus.

It becomes clear from all this that never in history has it been so (mechanically) easy to create money. Back to Peter Bernstein's *Power of Gold* where he continues regarding modern money that ". . . all of which is costlessly produced at the touch of a computer's keyboard."[4] The production, sorting, and transfer of money has therefore never before been so efficient and yet also so vulnerable. When money was represented by real gold coins, the only way to mint was by obtaining and molding real gold— never an easy process. Even when our money was largely in paper format, printing durable counterfeit-proof currency required a highly-sophisticated production process. Bills had to be produced with all the exactly required features of legal tender—the correct chemical constituents in the paper, precisely-etched designs free of all imperfections, not to mention watermarks, hidden strips within the paper, and so on.

Comparing that to the current-day production of most of the "cash" in circulation, it must be acknowledged that it is still not easy for the average IT maniac to introduce or withdraw new electronic currency. The big money center, and central, banks have incredibly sophisticated, well-protected systems designed to prevent hackers from having a field day. These systems ensure that it is only through very unique portals (such as those at central banks) that new currency can be electronically created.

That said, if a hacker could really break into those systems, he would probably have the ability to put in, take out, or transfer more volumes of money than ever before in history. You do not have to be an alarmist to envision that happening. Let me hasten to add that I am not aware of anyone breaking into the big money center bank systems. Yet it is certainly possible. Credit card accounts have been hacked and raided on a scale that has required massive effort to undo the damage and restore confidence—for example, the large-scale theft of the credit and debit card data of some 40 million Target store customers between November 27 and December 15, 2013.[5] In these and other instances, hackers have gained access to the very meta-database of the credit/debit card accounting system itself. Indeed, the public may never been informed about some instances of large-scale money center hacking, for precisely the reasons illustrated in our story—the danger of setting off economic panic. The breaching of a security system may be known to just a few—and partially or completely concealed.

In the lengthy discussions I have had with specialists in banking IT systems, all concur that it would be theoretically possible for hackers to break into even the most secure Federal Reserve or money center bank account systems. The ability, certainly in principle, exists for a program or virus to break into those systems and decrease, increase, or transfer the numbers (i.e. the money) in endless accounts. The general response from IT professionals is that, if this happened, it would be rapidly spotted by the system and could then just as easily be reversed.

But let's not forget Terry and his rollicking good time with universal handouts. Reversing transactions may be possible so long as the hacking is on a limited scale, where a certain cohort of accounts or transfers can be ring-fenced, identified, and hence reversed. Indeed, errors do occur in money center systems and transfers can be and are regularly reversed. But I'm not sure this would be the case if the hacking was on such a wide scale as contemplated in our story.

Remember in our story the change in account balances was so ubiquitous and sudden that it resulted in multiple real-world transactions being rapidly executed? As the minutes turned to hours, countless physical items were bought, sold, and consumed. To reverse all of that would have required not just the re-jigging of all the relevant electronic money accounts but presumably all the physical purchases as well: goods would need to be returned to stores. This, as our story says, would not in reality be practical both because of the sheer volume of executed purchases and also because many goods are rapidly perishable or consumed. As for services, well, it's obviously impossible to refund services like haircuts, car washes, or medical treatments. In a Western economy where perhaps 70% of transactions are the provision of services, the concept of reversing such transactions is unfeasible.

Remember also, as I mentioned, that many securities accounts are constituted as electronic account entries. While our story only went as far as contemplating a hacking of something like M2, if the narrative progressed in real life, soon the runaway digital frenzy could be extended to include all those security accounts. We would rapidly be contemplating the dislocation of many, many trillions of dollars of assets. This is a scale much, much greater than even the hugest government interventions at the height of the last credit crisis (e.g. the $700 billion Troubled Asset Relief Program). It defies reason that any central authority, however efficient, could reverse changes of this financial scale across a nearly endless number of accounts.

So again our story appears *not* to be mere fiction. What we're contemplating is a real possibility, albeit not one yet realized. There are certainly many, many terrorists and enemies of, say, the U.S. who would show no hesitation in triggering the type of virus contemplated in our tale.

In the story we see therefore how the electronic architecture of modern money allows, effectively, for ease of industrial-scale money printing. That itself brings us to the next key feature of the speculative narrative—the huge increase in the money supply triggered by our hacker Terry. What the story indicates here is not news but is consistent with modern macro-economic theory. Material increases in the money supply initially provided a fillip to demand in our tale, but ultimately created uncontrollable inflation. That is why the creation of new money by Terry turned out to be just as damaging as if he had stolen it all.

You might call that the Monetarist feature of the story, although I will say rapid inflation is only one possible result of Terry's virus.

And here we arrive at what is probably the central debate of macro-economics. I really don't want to get bogged down in this, but let's briefly touch on Monetarism. The Monetarists, led by the now-deceased brilliant economist Milton Friedman, generally hold to the belief that government intervention in our economies rarely has any beneficial effect and more often results in a negative impact. Increasing the volume of money in the system does not create sustained long-term increases in demand, the Monetarists observe. It just creates inflation. Or, in Friedman's own words: "Inflation is always and everywhere a monetary phenomenon."[6]

Friedman was, of course, reacting to the Keynesian economic school which held that the best way to get an economy out of recession was for government to spend heavily on infrastructure and projects. Any devoted Keynesian would claim that this is the best way to spur employment; hence, demand could be "artificially" created, which would theoretically restart an economy's engine. (This has sometimes been referred to as the so-called multiplier effect—where each dollar spent by government was supposed to produce more than one dollar of incremental demand).

The opposing views of Monetarists and Keynesians have been debated exhaustively by many academics. I won't step into the quicksand of that debate here. Suffice to say the reaction of the Ben Bernanke's Fed to the 2007/8 crisis has been a sort of hybrid between Monetarism and Keynesianism. I call it such because there is a distinct difference between mere monetary intervention (increasing the volume of money in the system and keeping rates low) and fiscal intervention (involving government actively spending on new jobs programs and infrastructure programs). While we've seen little fiscal intervention in the last five years, there has been plenty of monetary intervention through the provision of liquidity and new capital to the banking system, maintenance of very low interest rates, and subsequent Fed bond buying programs ("quantitative easing" or money printing).

In other words, Fed policies since the credit crisis have been no different from Terry's hacking, which resulted in the expansion of the money supply by providing everyone with cheap (free) money.

As I write, many economic pundits are expressing the belief that Bernanke's policies will eventually lead to creeping inflation and hence the need to carefully "taper off" his quantitative easing program. But it is hard to get an economy, like a person, off drugs. Having seen Bernanke's policies go into effect and observed the consequences, we saw that inflation (and related interest rate rises) did not immediately occur. Did that mean Bernanke's policies made sense, at least for the term in which they were applied? Maybe the patient really needed drugs—at least for a while. The deflationary and recessionary forces triggered in the Great Recession were very strong. Without liberally sprinkling free money onto our society and keeping corporate borrowing costs very low, the economic downturn might have been considerably worse. Indeed, to the extent that Milton Friedman believed the only tool available to government was control of the money supply, even he may have favored some of Bernanke's monetary interventions. Equally Friedman may have just noted that the inflation is now with us after all, it has just manifest itself in new ways—namely in a fairly irrational run-up in the value of equities since 2008.

Either way, voluminous increases in money supply can, but do not necessarily, translate into inflation—just proving, as usual, that nothing in economics or finance is black and white. In our story the increased demand from the deluge is short-lived, and inflation rapidly sets in. But that's because (in Terry's day) there was, pre the "deluge," no established counter-vailing recessionary force to check the inflation. Terry created increased money supply when no such increase was needed in any way. In those very artificial circumstances—circumstances themselves created by the flexibility of electronic money—rapid inflation would surely be the result sooner or later. Whether it would become the hyperinflation seen at the end of the story is another matter; for there to be a real hyperinflationary explosion, various fairly specific economic conditions need to pertain.

In any event, electronic-style money printing is clearly central to our story, and that in turn brings us to the next theme. What are the distributive effects of money printing?

Well, the fact is, money printing in whatever form tends to create some redistribution of wealth. Imagine if Big Bank, Inc., goes bust and the government decides to bail out its creditors for fear of a systemic knock-on effect in the economy. By providing money to make the bank's creditors whole, or at least partly whole, the government is effectively using some of the money supply to fill that gap. So the losses of a few (the creditors of the particular bank) have now been socialized across the whole economy. The slight devaluation of the currency that should follow (all other things being equal) reflects the loss that the currency has absorbed by this bail-out.

But let's not go too far into the rather dull politics of all this. It is, of course, one of the facts that so infuriated many on the Left (and even the Right) during the credit crisis. It seemed that the debts of a few Wall Street investment banks and high-flying insurers were being socialized and carried by the whole economy. They were—but of course, these views by the Occupy Wall Street crowd are also gross simplifications. Many of the government's bank re-capitalization plans were really filling temporary liquidity gaps in the system, and the money has now been recouped by the government (e.g. the Troubled Asset Relief Program). In some cases recovery was not there (e.g., AIG), although again, had the government not intervened in AIG, the consequences could well have been yet more horrendous.

I'm not really interested in whose is correct in this debate—in reality life is nuanced and both the Left and Right seem blinded to this by their pre-conceived agendas. The point is, we need to recognize the curious fact that money printing very often creates some form of wealth redistribution. This was certainly true in our little tale, although as conceived, the wealth distributive effect was quite random. In the Big Bank case, the debts of a smaller group get foisted onto the whole society. In our story everyone's balances increased, but by different multiples. In the absence of any new economic growth, the end result was that those whose accounts were increased by above-average multiples were effectively being subsidized by the rest of the economy (just like Big Bank creditors in the case above). Conceivably, a one-time uniform increase in everyone's cash holdings, if done proportionately, would not create this redistributive effect. But usually, increasing the money supply is done to solve some specific purpose, and it affects one set of groups more than another.

"Inflation is taxation without legislation," wrote Friedman. But on this point Niall Ferguson himself quotes Friedman's nemesis Keynes saying more or less the same thing, "By a continuing process of inflation, governments can confiscate, secretly and unobserved, an important part of the wealth of their citizens. By this method, they not only confiscate, but they confiscate *arbitrarily*; and while the process impoverishes many, it actually enriches some."[7]

Notice also the situation of the so-called "under-banked" referenced in the story—that is, the people who have none of their money in bank accounts. Based on 2011 statistics, about 28% of the U.S. population really does fit into that category.[8] For these under-banked (in our story), money printing created no benefit whatsoever, since they could not be recipients of electronic money. But nevertheless it did devalue their physical cash. Again they were affected in a particularly negative way relative to the rest of the population, making the deluge look like a regressive wealth redistribution.

In summary, increasing the money supply is really a form of taxation. Terry's virus created a taxation applied quite inequitably across the economy.

That brings us then, to the final theme of the story. Let's go back to the question of what Terry was really trying to achieve. His motives seemed to have a utopian element to them. He wanted to increase his own wealth, but without stealing, which led to his plan of showering largesse on all. But as so often occurs with economic and financial policies, Terry's bold move resulted in unforeseen effects.

The market often reacts to anticipate economic policy and in a circular fashion, market dynamics have often already changed even prior to, but in anticipation of, a given economic policy. The hideous side-effects of the utopian vision of Marxist economics are easy to see, but some unintended consequences are usually the result of any economic policy. We mentioned the 20th-century philosopher Karl Popper in this context in Chapter 5. He even went as far as to say that the main task of the social sciences was, "to trace the unintended social repercussions of intentional human actions."[9]

Utopianism is always dangerous. Certainly Terry's ill-conceived plans had hugely destructive effects. Terry himself became an unintended dabbler in monetary easing and everyone in the story suffered as a consequence.

And so . . . well, that's it really—a story of many different, yet strangely interrelated financial facets—one that I think resonates with much of the current economic zeitgeist. A story of quantitative easing gone mad, as well as a story showing the potential side effects of any act of economic intervention—whether by governments, or by a Terry. We also see how any account of modern electronic money is incomplete if it focuses solely on the efficiency of such a system. And a system in which "money" has never been so easily replicable, is by its very nature, always vulnerable.

WHAT IS TAXATION?

Better than Theft

"And it came to pass in those days, that there went out a decree from Caesar Augustus, that all the world should be taxed."

Luke, Chapter 2, Verse 1

"Money is like manure. You have to spread it around or it smells."

J. Paul Getty (1892–1976)

Plenty of archeologists have researched the lost city of Atlantis. Its location is not known—if it ever existed at all. What we do know about it, through hearsay, comes from various sources. The first mention might have been in Plato—or, as some believe, in Homer's account of Scheria or Ogygia.[1]

From these accounts we can surmise that Atlantis was certainly a prosperous place. Plato says of Atlantis that it contained "all that nature had to offer," and Homer described Scheria in similar terms. The island is said to have had a king named Atlas and a constitutional framework that became the source of discussion among Plato and his fellow philosophers. But I believe (and based on absolutely no evidence whatsoever), that we can take things a step further and deduce a great deal about Atlantis' politico-economic system—and in particular its taxation system. In taking this imaginative leap, I want to describe in speculative terms, how a system of taxation might have evolved in that society. So, here goes . . .

Let us assume the population of Atlantis was very small, certainly by modern standards, bearing in mind that the world population in Platonic or Homeric times was a mere fraction of what it is today. We shall take the total population of Atlantis to be, at maximum, 20,000 people, and I'm including children as well as adults. While Atlas was supposedly the king, we shall assume he was just a figurehead (a constitutional monarch) and that the island was really administered by an alternative set of philosopher kings or princes. (This was Plato's concept of an ideal constitutional framework in which an oligarchy of supposedly wise men would run the affairs of state in a benevolent fashion for the greater population.) Still, these were also the days of Greek democracy, so I'm going to assume the system had, in addition, a serious overlay of democratic values. In fact, given the small population on the island, there was probably a form of direct democracy where any matter of importance was put to the population as a whole to decide by referendum. It seems conceivable that all, or many adults of voting age, could meet every week on the so-called Elysian field (to confuse our Greek myths) and vote on that week's political agenda. (The Althing, the Icelandic parliament founded in 930 CE, originally met in Þingvellir or the "assembly fields.") The philosopher kings or princes of Atlantis were, therefore, really just administrative executives who would implement the pure will of the people.

Now let's muse that for many generations, the affairs of Atlantis were run very poorly. There were economic booms and busts on the island. Some people became filthy rich while others remained dirt poor. Many of the philosopher kings ended up richer than most of the others on the island (strange really . . .), although some of them were wise and benevolent nonetheless. Meanwhile, the government always struggled to manage its budget. Most state funds were used to finance the huge fleet that Plato tells us the island possessed, leaving little else for other important social necessities. Indeed, prior to our modern welfare systems, it is true that most state budgets throughout history, were largely spent on a nation's military.

We will surmise that matters progressed in this fashion until one particularly brilliant philosopher king arose. He was known always to talk in a puzzling fashion. His real message was often hidden, or only touched on obliquely with a side comment at the end of a sentence. His name was Parentheses II of Atlantis (otherwise referred to as Parentheses).

Parentheses had many brilliant and sparkling ideas. However he was not much of a communicator, and Atlantis was, as we said, a popular democracy. By public vote, a number of policies could be enacted that might prove to be disastrous, simply because the people were wowed by demagogues and popular media figures. So, early on, Parentheses partnered up with another philosopher king—a man, in fact, who possessed very little thinking or knowledge at all. This partner really didn't merit the title of philosopher king, although he was a consummate salesman—and that's what Parentheses needed. His name was Mediacretes and typically sold the ideas of Parentheses through circus spectacles at the Greek amphitheaters.

Now Parentheses' big idea, the so called "Parenthetical Revolution," was related to taxation and wealth distribution (also known as the great Philosophy of Meritocracy). Under this philosophy, Parentheses wished to end gross inequalities, injustices and inefficiencies in the Atlantian economy by ensuring that wealth was allocated according to—*merit*. It was a just, noble and (broadly) economically-sound idea.

So, naturally, the first step was a basic form of taxation. Those who were earning excessive income or capital gains on transactions, amounts that really were quite disproportionate to said individual's merit or contribution to society, would be taxed on a portion of their income and gains. This was considered just because it ensured wealth accumulation was more closely aligned with merit, while also reducing income inequalities. And taxation had a secondary benefit as well. With the collection of taxes, much-needed funds were collected to manage more effectively the Atlantian state deficit.

This idea was not hard for Mediacretes to sell to the public. After all, the heaviest burden of the tax would land on a small, wealthy minority of the population. We do not know from the ancient records the percentage levels of these taxes (particularly since I made them up). But for the sake of argument, let's assume they were fair, generally popular, and sensible.

Of course, Parentheses was always well ahead of current affairs. Even as his basic tax regime was implemented, he was already thinking more deeply about "merit." In short order, he realized that huge inheritances were also gross contradictions to the Philosophy of Meritocracy. Many of the new generation inheriting large farms and land holdings in Atlantis were lazy and vain. Since the inheritors did not have to work at all for their inheritance, it could hardly be said they "merited" such gifts. Next, therefore, was the introduction of an inheritance tax. Here was another tax that seemed to make sense, both from the perspective of justice and economics. It also gave further funds to the government—enough now, to create a surplus over the monies required to service the military. This allowed the Atlantian state to begin providing much-needed welfare support to the poorest and weakest in society, such as shelter for the homeless and unemployment benefits for those out of work.

Atlantian society undoubtedly started to flourish under the Parenthetical system. The taxes were not so onerous that they undermined economic growth. And the system enfranchised much of the population who felt they had a fairer share of the total island's abundance. These were good times. (No doubt, the "island of riches" that Plato mentions is a reference to this period in Atlantian history.)

Still, the tinkering genius of Parentheses was unstoppable. He thought passionately, profoundly, and long on the concept of "merit." Soon it became clear to him that many people were born with various types of gifts (not just monetary gifts, such as inheritances), but also gifts from nature. Some were more beautiful than the majority, others more intelligent, or stronger, or taller. There were some who seemed to be "natural entrepreneurs," others who lacked this gift. And so forth. It dawned on Parentheses that these natural gifts were not "merited" either—they were also the product of mere happenstances of birth. So if Parentheses was truly to implement his Philosophy of Meritocracy, he would have to take the next logical step.

This of course meant that taxations would be applied reflecting also the *natural gifts* each Atlantian was already born with. What mattered was the "effort" or active fulfillment of your natural born gifts—this was "merit," and for this (in the Parenthetical view) an Atlantian should be rewarded. But to be rewarded merely because, for example, you happened to be born bright or strong, surely, mused Parentheses, that was no more "just" than being rewarded solely because your father was rich.

So a natural-born salesman, who was making money in business, should only be rewarded to the extent that he had truly made an effort to use that sales gift in a positive way for society. If he sold worthless kitsch to the most gullible members of society, this was not meritorious. Likewise, a man who made his income through his brute strength needed to exhibit a real commitment to using that strength in a positive fashion. He had perhaps to work the field, not just win arm-wrestling contests in the local beer halls. And what about the gift of a great intellect? Surely, someone with such a gift should only be rewarded if he used his mind to produce important works and ideas that enhanced society, not merely because he could come up with clever witticisms at fancy dinner parties.

So a committee of the philosopher kings was formed to determine the extent to which each person exercised their natural-born gifts to the fullest. It was up to the committee to decide who was really making an "effort"— that is, making meaningful use of their talents to contribute to society. "Real effort" would keep your taxes down, whereas the lack of it would mean higher taxation of your income and capital gains. This of course meant the state had to keep more and more information on the Atlantian population, but the country was small enough for this to be manageable (even in a non-digital age). Members of the public could also appeal against the determinations of the committee if, for instance, they felt the philosopher kings were underestimating the "effort" a given person was making in their life. This appeals process appeared to add a further element of fairness to the system.

Now, adapting the tax system to reflect the above meant both the richest, or most elevated in society, as well as the poorest, could be impacted by this tax. A rich businessman typically had high taxes, reflecting the fact that he might be idly receiving income from established investments ("clipping coupons"), or because he was merely sitting on real estate assets and selling them for huge gains. In other words, he was not really tapping the full potential of his energy as a businessman. But, equally, the welfare system abusers could be caught in the net. Since the Parenthetical Revolution had begun, there were now plenty of jobless who rather exploited their unemployed status. They would pick up their weekly drawings from the state, displaying little effort to find work, while still expecting some form of housing to be provided by the Atlantian government. The philosopher kings came down hard on them too, reducing their drawings, or taxing said drawings, unless the individual could show real "effort" in rejoining the workforce.

For the above reasons it became increasingly difficult for Mediacretes to sell to the Atlantian electorate this latest piece of the Parenthetical regime. After all, it meant many were facing higher tax bills, and everyone was being whipped by the state to show their hard work. Atlas, as monarch, could have interfered with the passing of the new tax laws, but like all constitutional monarchs, he was too daft to do anything but wave at passing crowds. Still, it was clear that the largest burden would fall again on the rich. Plenty of the latter were indeed "crony"-style capitalists, rent seekers, merely enjoying the benefits of the assets they were sitting on, with little incremental "effort" involved. Given this, the average Atlantian in the street still favored the new policy.

So the new "effort-based" tax rules did get passed, but they also created some friction in society. Many businessmen were now facing daunting taxation levels on income and capital gains. Inheritance taxes were also very high. And, as often happens in high tax regimes, the incentive for new business activity started to be affected. Supposedly new business initiatives should have been seen as real "effort"/real application of skills (and therefore really "merited") and not taxed. But often that was not how the philosopher committee saw it (these were subjective judgments). The less well-to-do also resented being constantly told their benefits would be taken from them unless they showed renewed "efforts" in all they did. Many felt they had natural entitlements to minimum wages and government housing, effort or no effort. And meanwhile, the Atlantian state always wished to increase the reserves in its coffers, so the government authorities generally favored higher taxation.

Still, day-to-day life continued and the economy somehow functioned.

But then an extraordinary moment came. Parentheses had a final epiphany, a "Eureka!" moment as profound, in its own way, as that of his buddy Archimedes. What Parentheses realized was that "effort" itself ultimately was a gift from birth. Some people were just born more energetic or more willing than others. So even the "effort" or "energy" you might expend in applying your God-given gifts was itself not really a consequence of merit either. It, too, was an undeserved gift.

This extraordinary thought led Parentheses, in a typically puritanical Greek form of logic, to a final conclusion—namely, that no material achievement was really a product of "merit" as such. Every achievement, he concluded, was a product of a roll of the dice. The happenstance of birth determined all. Being born with wealth was luck; being born with gifts (like intelligence or physical strength) was luck; even being born with a proactive mindset to exploit those gifts usefully was a fortunate gift of birth. It must follow, therefore, that any economic inequalities (any whatsoever) were contrary to his Principle of Meritocrary—that is, contrary to the idea that each should receive only according to his merit.

Hence Parentheses concluded that all must be taxed so that each person had income and wealth exactly equal to that of the next person. It was a great insight for Parentheses and he decided at that point to change the name of his philosophy. He now called it . . . communism.

It would perhaps have been hard for Mediacretes to impose this final piece of the Parenthetical Revolution on the Atlantians, but by now Mediacretes had taken to fixing election results anyway. So that is what he planned to do now. After all, wasn't it the state, Parentheses, and the philosopher kings who knew what was best for the people?

But natural events intervened on the very day when the (apparent) referendum on the final stage of the Parenthetical Revolution was to be implemented. That day, a strange phenomenon was observed. The water at the shore receded until vast expanses of beach were exposed. It was, as we now realize, the precursor to a huge tsunami. And indeed a great tsunami did come. It covered the whole island; buried it deep under many feet of water—every single part of the island, including even the lofty ivory tower of Parentheses II. And so that's how it was. That's how Atlantis was lost to the sea forever.

This totally apocryphal little tale brings out various ideas (beyond merely taxation), but we will comment on only a few aspects relevant to the main financial themes of this book. It goes without saying that vast libraries could be filled with books written on taxation policy and redistributive justice. It's a topic on many people's minds today, particularly following the credit crisis, and is certainly germane to some of the profits made in the finance business.

In speculating about the system used in Atlantis, I focused on the curious value of "merit" as it plays out in this debate. It is certainly an important philosophical ingredient in the analysis of distributive justice, but by no means the only relevant concept. "To each according to his merit" is not, *prima facie*, purely an egalitarian concept. Yet the notion of "merit" can itself be confusing. And we see that in its limiting case it may, strangely, collapse into total egalitarianism.

In any event, the only point I really want to extract from our ancient tale is how little original thought seems to be expressed on the subject of redistributive justice today, either by the Left or the Right. That's true certainly in popular debate, the debate that drives elections. We continually seem to be coming back to the same old ideological positions, ideas that have been tried and tested over and over again—and all found wanting. Let's understand that a little further.

It is true that in the business of financial arbitrage, huge gains are sometimes made that are totally (profoundly) disproportionate to any sort of merit associated with said transactions. There are confluences of events when certain key investors make bets (buying or shorting an asset) often for quite a limited period, and they make enormous profits on those trades. In fact, it is fair to say some of the greatest financial fortunes were made in one big trade. Nathan Rothschild made much of his fortune taking a huge long position in British consols (UK government securities) from 1815 to 1817, making about £600 million (or approximately $1 billion in today's money and exchange rates).[2] George Soros also made about $1 billion by short selling a notional $10 billion sterling position during the 1992 Black Wednesday U.K. currency crisis. John Paulson was reported to have made approximately $4 billion by using credit default swaps to bet against U.S. sub-prime mortgage pools in 2007.

Being gains from an arbitrage, these extraordinary profits did not come without cost to others. Generally, it was at the expense of other people that the gains were made. In such arbitrage, the losses are usually spread among multiple (sometimes thousands or hundreds of thousands) of investors: the one "lone wolf" investor is typically betting against the market herd, and the wolf gets it right. It's actually not dissimilar to winning the lottery. The cost paid by millions of people buying lottery tickets is aggregated and given to the one winner who makes millions (or billions).

Now we may well believe in the freedom to contract and the freedom of the markets. And it is these freedoms that allow for these occasional massive arbitrage opportunities, as well as the more modest profits (and losses) many people make in the markets. We can also see that the gamble of the arbitrageur, to his credit, might show unique market insight and large amount of guts (plus a good slice of luck). Still, I don't think anyone can really believe the enormous profits made in these historic, once-in-a-lifetime trades can really be justified merely from the perspective of "merit." And hence why the idea of some reasonable level of taxation on these types of large capital gains seems (at least to most of us) quite right and fair.

It is also true that the nature of economics does result in very large income and wealth inequalities. And this observation seems to apply to most economies in general; the inequalities appear in controlled economies like China just as in Western capitalist systems. These wealth accumulations are, of course, what Thomas Piketty has focused on in his recent book *Capital in the Twenty-First Century*.[3] And while there is some debate about the correctness of all Piketty's data, he is generally credited with having put together a huge inventory of wealth inequality which in its broad message is no doubt correct. He notes, for example, that the top decile share of U.S. national income dropped from 45–50% in the 1910s–1920s to less than 35% in the 1950s (a fall also documented by the Nobel Prize-winning economist Simon Kuznets); but it then rose from less than 35% in the 1970s to 45–50% in the 2000s–2010s. In the wake of the credit crisis, and for those observing the excesses of Wall Street in the 2000s, Piketty's analysis is, understandably, attractive to many readers.

Anecdotally, I myself work periodically with wealth management groups managing the money of extremely wealthy families. Doing this type of work, you cannot help being struck by the very large agglomerations of wealth that are in the hands of a limited number of people in most global economies. Such levels of wealth inequality can create a great deal of animosity in a society where very imbalanced distribution is considered unjust. It can also certainly create a type of "cronyism," the behavior of the "rentier," which can be very counter to economic innovation. Once one group owns large vested assets, it is not in their interest to have new innovative businesses arise to compete with them—for instance, by bringing in new industrial methods that potentially impinge on the incumbent's monopolistic position.

Still, even if all the above is quite true, we also know that excessive taxation can be very debilitating to economic growth. Again this insight has been analyzed at different times. It was basic to the ideas of Adam Smith, the Scottish philosopher, and often cited as being the heart of the neo-conservative revolution of the 1980s. Excessive taxation was clearly targeted by the policies of Reagan and Thatcher, both of whom identified debilitating taxation as crimping growth in the 1970s. These politicians were themselves backed by thinkers such as Milton Friedman, *et al*, who we have already touched on in this book. They were supported also by the self-evident failure of the centralized wealth distribution system of the Russian Communist experiment.

We seem today, in other words, to swing between redistributive philosophies (Roosevelt), to low taxation philosophies (Reagan), and back again (Obama). In other words we've sort of seen it all before. We've seen the failures of radical socialism and we've also seen the excesses of unbridled capitalism. As our tale of Atlantis shows, a system with *no* redistributive taxation plainly doesn't work (morally or economically), but then a system with excess redistribution doesn't work very well either.

The real problem with the work of Thomas Piketty is that for all his fine analysis and data, his conclusions and prescriptions are just too unoriginal. He concludes merely that the only solution to wealth inequality is higher taxation. In particular, he wants at least a 50–60% taxation on inheritance. He argues for this in a 2013 paper[4] dense with formulae which can potentially mask somewhat subjective moral judgments. Again, many (most?) of us already recognize that enormous inheritances are somewhat unjust, and we all know that markets can create unfair wealth distributions. But we also know people are atavistic and (quite rightly) want to protect their family and seed. So to take away entirely the motivation for providing wealth and protection to a businessperson's future generations will inevitably be debilitating to the business motive and to growth. Excess taxation is yet another tired old solution. Piketty might look at the U.K. "Super Tax" of the 1970s that generated a "super" income tax of over 90% applied to very high earners. The tax was of course unworkable, since anyone earning levels that made them eligible to pay this tax either left the country or just plainly lost their incentive to continue in business.

So whatever your political leanings, one thing is for sure. Both hard redistributive philosophies on the one hand and very light-touch taxation on the other are just not very original ideas. Nor do either of them seem to contain the whole truth when it comes to distributive justice. That, too, is plain from our tale of Atlantis.

I personally think what may be going on here relates to the rapid transformation of society into its current industrial and post-industrial format, proceeding at a rate that has outrun the more normal pace of our social evolution. This is not a developed theory on my part; still, if you look at early hunter gatherer tribal societies various things are clear. Firstly you had to look after yourself; you had to succeed in the hunt and survive in the wild. But secondly, you had a whole wealth of social interrelationships to fall back on. In your tribe were people who would assist each other with a degree of reciprocity that ensured mutual survival. So tribal people were self-reliant. And in that sense they were capitalistic. But in addition they had the natural safety net provided by the family and tribe. (So perhaps they were not very capitalistic after all!) Still it was not really a "safety net" as we might understand it today. It was not provided by a state that imposed rigid taxation and redistributive laws. What sustained the safety net were informal kinship relationships (so it doesn't sound much like socialism either).

But of course the atomization of modern society means we have lost much of that tribal reciprocity. Virtually all of the classic 20th-century studies of then extant tribal lifestyles (Malinowksi or Llewellyn or Hogbin) will tell you about the much greater level of kinship relationships that sustained these tribal societies—relationships that were much more powerful than in our modern cultures. In other words, it may be that our debate over state intervention and redistributive taxation is so stale today simply because we are no longer in social environments that are very natural to us. We are, you might say, imprisoned in our societies and no manner of social engineering (or lack thereof) will create the more natural safety net that existed when there were only tribal arrangements. The Parentheses' of the world, even through the instrument of democracy, can provide welfare via taxation, but it's really not the same as the familial bonds of the tribe. (This is also a theme we'll pick up again in later chapters when we discuss the curious state of financial services regulation.)

I think this is what the extraordinary 18th-century Swiss-born French philosopher Jean-Jacques Rousseau meant when he famously said at the beginning of *The Social Contract* that, "Man is born free but everywhere he is in chains."[5] For after this enigmatic comment Rousseau rapidly speaks of what he calls "The First Societies." Of those he says man's "first law is to provide for his own preservation, his first cares are those which he owes to himself." But Rousseau then immediately continues by observing that the first social unit is the family. And the problem we seem to face in modern large-scale, urbanized society is the natural love that parents have for their children in a familial/tribal unit simply cannot be replaced. As Rousseau puts it, "The whole difference is that, in the family, the love of the father for the children repays him for the care he takes of them, while, in the State, the pleasure of commanding takes the place of love which the chief cannot have for the peoples under him."[6]

So we were born to be balanced, self-interested beings functioning naturally in a group where support for each other was built into the social fabric ("free" in that sense). But now we are "in chains" in modern commercialized society. Even in the early days of the Neolithic revolution, in the Fertile Crescent, men had to farm for themselves, but there was also the warm embrace of natural and familial charity (think of the Biblical tithe). But, no longer.

Hence it is a caricature to see early tribal hunter gatherers as lone fighters who survived by exercising their instincts for self-interest. But that said, state-imposed wealth redistribution does a poor job of replacing natural tribal support systems. Taxation is better than theft (theft by individuals of the wealth of other individuals or theft by the state), but it can hardly replace the love of a tribe or of family.

As we said in the story of Joseph, the concepts of socialism and capitalism had very little meaning before the Industrial Revolution. They're simply not ideas grounded in our primordial social past. The dichotomy of the "Left wing *versus* the Right wing" is, itself, a recent invention of the 18th-century revolutionary French Estates General, merely designating which physical wing of the assembly certain members were sitting on. So at least when it comes to taxing wealth and trying to legislate distributive justice, perhaps all these concepts had a limited shelf life, and their moment has now passed.

Isn't it time we looked at the whole issue of distributive justice in a new way, through some kind of new telescope? This is not to say, therefore, that the solution lies in some "middle political ground" either. Don't we need an entirely new angle on it all, perhaps based on a deeper understanding of how our natural self-interest meshed with tribal fealty in prehistoric days? It's possible, of course, that the questions of just taxation and distributive justice will remain intractable. Still, new perspectives cannot be beyond human wit, for it does seem time to try a new road, some road "less well traveled." And the economist who really can find that new perspective may turn out to be the next economic equivalent of Einstein.

★ 9 ★
WHAT IS FRAUD?

When We Meet the Bad

"Because sentence against an evil work is not executed speedily, therefore the heart of the sons of men is set in them to do evil."

Ecclesiastes, Chapter 8, Verse 11

R on met Frank in the former's office in Chicago about six years ago. It was hard to tell whether Frank was wearing a toupee or not. The bulk of his hair appeared to levitate, ever so slightly, above his skull, but it was quite natural-looking hair, so it may have been the real thing. To this day Ron does not know if the hair is real or not.

Frank had the usual permatan, with a small mark on the left-hand side of his chin—probably the beginning of a melanoma from too much sun (or sunbed) exposure.

You would instinctively mark Frank down as a typical lizard that you see on a regular basis in the money business. Nothing very special in that, and his plastic look was mere noise. He represented himself as, and had all the air of, a long-term Wall Street veteran. Ron, whilst having been a successful wealth manager in his own right, was on the other hand, a more sensitive guy. He too had a large shock of hair, but it was certainly the real thing. Ron was an old friend of mine, actually a man I have a great deal of time for. It is he who told me the tale around the core events I am now recounting.

Knowing Ron, I understood that he was driven by what I would consider a perfectly healthy desire to make money. And he was upbeat and optimistic by nature—perhaps, as events would prove, too optimistic.

Frank and Ron bonded. Both were in their late fifties. To Ron, Frank seemed like someone at a similar stage in life who also shared parallel ambitions. Over a few months they had drinks together, joked about the old times on Wall Street, and strategized on the latest developments and opportunities in the financial services sector. Taken by Frank's apparent financial experience, his dashing and forceful manner, Ron was soon inviting Frank to be his partner.

Ron already had a going concern, a specialist financing business called De Metro Ber & Co. What he offered Frank was the position of senior partner. In return, Frank agreed to inject about $500,000 into De Metro Ber to buy a stake in the business. That in itself was enough to make Ron a wealthy guy, albeit, by Wall Street-type standards, no more than a medium-level player. The legal documents were put together and Ron assumed this cash injection was as good as done and dusted. All that remained was the usual transactional treacle for the lawyers to wade through to close the deal.

Now an active partner in the business, Frank advised Ron that De Metro Ber needed to upgrade its CFO and Frank had just the man. Derrick was his name. He was a long-term business friend of Frank's, and in no time Derrick was given the role of supporting both Frank and Ron. As described to me, there was a sense of real momentum around De Metro Ber at that time. Ron and Frank, now in tandem, would be proactively driving the firm forward with a series of what they described as "transformatory" transactions—either acquisitions or developments of new product offerings. Both men had the feel of experienced dealer makers.

Very soon Frank was pushing for new capital to be brought into the business. In this he had Ron's full agreement. Only that way could the firm be turbo-charged to achieve its full potential. Cash was needed for staff, working capital, and acquisitions. De Metro Ber was *going places*; bringing clever new angles, novel services and products into the whole financial services arena.

So Frank and Ron rapidly orchestrated the production of marketing material in anticipation of attracting new investors into the De Metro Ber story. In quick succession, would-be investors were approached, meetings were held, and interest was solicited.

So far, the relationship between Frank and Ron had gone swimmingly. However, in occasional conversations with Ron, I learned that there were some early signs of strain. Even at this initial capital-raising stage, Ron said, the dynamics between Frank and him were being tested. The same applied to some of the other key executives involved in De Metro Ber. Ron thought these challenges were noticeable even in the management presentations to prospective investors. Frank, in particular, appeared on the one hand dominant and off-hand with many of the other senior executives, including Ron. And yet Frank didn't seem to have the sure-footed knowledge of the whole business that was shared by the other executives. But so far, Ron took this in stride. Some stresses and strains in a new partnership are inevitable, and Ron could write this off as an adjustment period. Humans are humans, each with flaws and virtues, and once you put said humans into a business context—where money is at stake and egos can clash—short-sighted and boorish behavior is often the norm, not the exception.

Some months passed, and De Metro Ber's capital-raising efforts continued. But it soon became clear the capital exercise was not going quite as well as the company would have liked. This was in part because of the difficult economic environment which made all such deals demanding. But it was also partly because De Metro Ber was still a relatively young business, and the total management team had not been fully tested, nor did it seem to have quite "jelled" as a single unit. Once again, not an unusual situation. On the face of it, nothing appeared out of order at the business.

Still, I continued to get the impression from Ron that Frank was something of a lightning rod around these issues. Ron told me how, to some investors, Frank came over as very much the experienced financier— a player, a man of the world, a man of financial substance and acumen.

But other investors picked up an impression that in Frank's attitude there was something not quite right—a certain insouciance, or was it nonchalance. He seemed just a bit too relaxed for comfort.

Yet, in the end some new investors were found, and this must have been a big step forward for the company. I did note, however, that De Metro Ber had not been able to attract the usual crowd of professional/institutional investors who typically come in to these types of deals. Those investors had passed on the opportunity. Instead, interest came from a select group of very high-net-worth individuals. Interestingly, these were mainly contacts that were initiated by Ron himself. These were guys for whom dropping a million dollars here or there was like dropping a dime for most of us. It might be inferred that their investment decisions were totally random, but these were not investors who had more money than sense. Many of these individuals had made sound business decisions in prior investments. Still, they were rich enough to have become slightly careless with parts of their capital. Mayer A. Rothschild was known to have said, "It takes a great deal of boldness, mixed with a vast deal of caution, to acquire a great fortune; but then it takes ten times as much wit to keep it . . ." Some of these very affluent individual investors were indeed less than diligent when it came to holding on to the great fortunes they had acquired.

In any event, the news got around that these investors had subscribed for new stock in De Metro Ber and the company continued on its merry rise. As so often happens, there were immediate ideas for further expansion. Ron was certainly the imaginative thinker here, but his generally sound ideas could be sidelined by Frank's overbearing character.

But then, in a case of very unfortunate timing, Ron was hit by something quite out of the blue. He was taken seriously ill. Stuff happens—nothing really to do with the core plot line of our lives, but these events create detours and new effects. In this instance Ron was hospitalized for an extended period. For a few months, he effectively had to drop active involvement in the business.

Dealing with his own health issues, as one could imagine, was a consuming preoccupation for Ron. Nonetheless, from a financial perspective, Ron felt reasonably secure. As far as he then knew, all was going as planned with De Metro Ber, even in his absence. When I spoke to Ron, as I did occasionally during his hospitalization, he expressed no concerns about the state of his business life or De Metro Ber. He felt that De Metro Ber was safe in the hands of his partner, Frank, and both enjoyed full confidence in Derrick, the CFO. All would be well.

One thing that Ron did notice however during his hospitalization, was that he began to receive fewer and fewer calls about the business. To some extent, that was to be expected, given that Ron was unwell. But nonetheless, he sensed something increasingly odd about the extended silence between calls. After all, this was effectively a partnership between Ron and Frank, so Ron was surely needed for various decision-making processes and issues. On the other hand, Ron was genuinely preoccupied with his health, and it made sense that he would be less involved until he returned to day-to-day activities. In any event, he continued to assume the business was in good hands under Frank's stewardship.

Ron's recovery was slow but steady (he fortunately recovered—at least healthwise). Nearing the end of Ron's time in hospital he received a call from one of the senior executives in the business. At first, it seemed just a friendly catch-up call, both to see how Ron was doing and to discuss latest events at De Metro Ber. But as the conversation continued, the executive began to say more than he had perhaps planned to say. He seemed to find it cathartic to be chatting to Ron, and as he mused about the company, Ron began to pick up some intimations of concern. In the still calm of his hospital room, Ron found himself growing increasingly alert as he heard the executive indicate that while all appeared to be running fine at De Metro Ber, appearances could be deceptive. What concerned this executive was a range of somewhat irregular money transfers. In particular, one person seemed to be orchestrating these transfers—Frank.

Initially, Ron's response was calming. He assumed the executive simply didn't know what he was talking about. Ron shrugged off the matter. The executive was worrying too much. Frank had matters entirely under control. It even occurred to Ron that this executive was holding some grudge against Frank. Still, after the conversation ended, Ron found himself with a lingering sense of concern.

Finally, curiosity got the better of him. Ron started following up with other sources within De Metro Ber.

I estimate it was about three weeks after this when I had my next conversation with Ron. By then he was out of hospital and no longer physically sick; however he was now mentally sick and increasingly, financially sick too.

Ron began to tell me what had transpired during the interval when he received that call from the executive and our present conversation. What emerged was an extraordinary tale of activity at the company, sagas and machinations—some of which were so outrageous they seemed almost impossible to believe. It was all fairly incoherent and Ron certainly left me confused. However, there would be further calls during the coming weeks. Ron was often rambling, increasingly frantic, wild, or anxious. But over time, as I listened, I began to understand the facts of the case. It was as if a mist gradually lifted to reveal, in all its horrifying details, the full outline of . . . fraud.

What emerged was a clear portrait of Frank as a man who could only be described as a psychopath. I don't mean he physically attacked people. But he was a professional, full-on, conman. And here we are not talking some cheap street conman, but a highly experienced executive who had plundered and stripped various companies over time. His pattern of behavior was not like that of more ordinary human beings. People do make mistakes. And yes, there are people who sometimes do bad stuff. But Frank was something else, the kind of individual I have rarely crossed paths with— that is to say, a highly-established executive who is a proactive and brazen fraudster.

For starters, remember the capital raised from those wealthy individuals? On the day it came to closing that raise—on the very day when these investors were to wire in their monies to the company—Frank had called each one to give new wiring instructions. Since for many of these individuals, this was a minor expenditure given minimal attention, they unquestioningly followed the new instructions. As I indicated, a bunch of these wealthy guys were just too wealthy for their own good. They had no problem trusting Frank and happily wired cash to the new account numbers that had been given to them. What none of them realized, of course, or even bothered to investigate, was the nature of these accounts. Needless to say, all were personal accounts of Frank himself. In addition, Frank had multiple personal accounts in multiple legal entities. Even if an investor had shown some curiosity about the account destinations, it would have involved laborious investigation to find out where the money went. Yes, the capital raise had actually occurred. But by the time it closed, most of the money had gone directly to Frank, never even reaching the accounts of De Metro Ber.

It is hard to see how Frank thought he was going to get away with this scam, although we will see at the end of this tale that there was a twisted method in his madness. In any event, psychopaths rarely think about the rational consequences of their actions.

You might have thought Ron would have got wind of these misdirected wire transfers, but it escaped his notice for one main reason. Frank's handpicked CFO, Derrick, turned out to be more than just your average CFO. In fact Derrick was an old-time accomplice of Frank. Men like Frank always need technician types around them, the guys who cover the details in terms of fixing and cooking the books. Well, that was Derrick—as Frank had said, "just the man to be the new CFO." And it was Derrick who had concealed where the monies had really been wired to.

Then Frank got plain lucky. Ron's illness was like a gift from God (or rather, from the Devil), for now Frank, with Derrick's help, effectively monopolized the accounts and finances of De Metro Ber. During Ron's hospitalization, Frank had begun all manner of wire transfers to personal accounts, not only financing his own expensive lifestyle but also initiating changes in the corporate ownership of various entities within the De Metro Ber group. It also transpired that the original $500,000 Frank was supposed to have put in the business for his stake (see the beginning of our story), had never been sent in either. Derrick covered that one over, too. So the multiple frauds were egregious and deliberate.

To top off the story, while Ron was hospitalized, Frank went out of his way to tell all concerned that he was now effectively managing the business. He had informed everyone that Ron was no longer well enough to be involved. (Indeed, he strongly implied that Ron was so gravely ill it was unlikely he would recover.) Both investors and company employees were told that they should speak only to Frank when it came to company affairs. With Ron's illness Frank had been granted an extraordinary window of opportunity, and he exploited his now-exclusive authority to the fullest degree possible.

By the time Ron was out of hospital, Frank and Derrick were already heading for the hills. Anticipating his imminent confrontation with Ron— and before all his company authorities were taken from him—Frank was wiring out as much money as he could from De Metro Ber to his own empire of accounts and personally-owned entities. Ultimately some $40 million plus was stolen from the company or investors. Even on the very day that Ron confronted Frank and secured his departure from the company, Frank spent the morning wiring himself cash. This was certainly not Bernie Madoff level of fraud in terms of quantum, but it was incredibly calculated, brazen, and proactive fraud.

Of course, it was apparent to anyone following this tragic string of events that Ron had been suckered by Frank. Clearly, the temptation for Ron was to make money himself, so he had a strong incentive to believe in Frank in the first place. In fact, until the very end, when the total scale of fraud was revealed, Ron had never suspected Frank. But then neither had the rest of the team, with the exception—of course—of Frank's collaborator Derrick.

After it all broke, Ron began to dig further, uncovering that Frank had been involved in a bunch of these scams before. Other companies, Ron learned, had been similarly cheated by Frank. Which left one question that to Ron seemed totally mystifying: why had these other companies not sued Frank or reported him to Federal prosecutors?

Well, Frank had been reported for his previous malfeasances, but here was a further twist in the whole grim tale. For Frank was not just brazen in theft, he was also brazen in playing the financial services regulatory game. Unlike the Ponzi schemer, Bernie Madoff, who pleaded guilty once exposed, Frank would do no such thing. He took from each of these companies he defrauded, an arsenal of cash which he then used to hire expensive lawyers. Mounting a phalanx of legal defense, he denied everything, and he had the resources to bleed dry financially anyone who came after him with any type of action. His maneuvers and transfers were brazen, but they were also so complex that he knew there was no straightforward proof of his guilt or liability, either in criminal or civil courts. A sophisticated player at this game, Frank knew that the U.S. financial regulatory environment was dense with complex, overlapping rules and different regulators that could be played to his advantage. He could hide in the tangled forest that is the U.S. financial service compliance landscape. Within the heart of the system itself, with a deep reserve of funds, Frank made himself impervious to the system's own rules. This was the hand he had played in defrauding previous companies and it was how he handled Ron's ensuing five-year legal battle. And during the legal wrangling that followed, Ron would learn how Frank had played this game again, and again, and again.

We'll discuss the U.S. regulatory environment further in the next chapter. But for now we need only know that, on the one hand, Frank had run a coach-and-horses through endless regulatory and legal prohibitions; on the other hand, the mess he left behind was essentially obscured by the sheer morass of the U.S. regulatory regime.

Five years later, Ron was financially ruined. His reputation with many investors was in tatters. Yet he had still not succeeded in bringing even a civil action against Frank. Nor had Federal or State prosecutors been able to marshal a coherent enough case to bring criminal charges against Frank.

Ron has given me periodic updates on the whole extraordinary affair over the months and years since the case broke. Ron still has his hair, but little else. Frank, meanwhile, continues to live the good life, no doubt with his toupee (or hairdo?) still in prime condition. In my career, Frank represents the one and only quintessential, bare-faced white-collar psychopath that I have at least witnessed in action. Frank is precisely the type of man which our financial system should surely protect us against. And yet he's also the one type of operator who all our rules, regulations, and laws seem quite unsuited to bring to ultimate justice.

That's the story for this chapter. For obvious reasons, I have changed all the names of the individuals and the companies involved, even altering many factual details and the nature of the company's exact business activities. But the circumstances are very broadly true, and Frank is still a free man and, as far as I know, an active player (in whatever game he happens to be playing now). Certainly the story is relevant in obtaining an understanding of the nature of fraud. And that understanding, after all, is the focus of this chapter.

The extent of Frank's fraud should be clear to the reader, including (in summary):

- Creating a fraudulent "history" of himself and his prior dealings. (On this the reader should know Frank would regularly spend significant money on IT experts having his internet details heavily doctored; itself an interesting insight into the importance of our modern online images and representations);
- Making false representations ("fraudulent misrepresentation") to his partner (Ron) about how much money he (Frank) was investing, where he was putting that money, and how it would be used ("breaches of contract" among other things);
- Making fraudulent claims about how investor money was being "invested" and, of course, fraudulently siphoning off the money to his own accounts ("unjust enrichment" or else plain "theft");
- Gross mismanagement and misconduct associated with the daily running and affairs of De Metro Ber, including misuse of investor money ("breaches of fiduciary duties");
- And in the end, instead of owning up and making amends for his actions, he used the legal system to deter justice; to obfuscate and intimidate any potential prosecutors.

Much has been written about the criminal mind and the punishment or rehabilitation of perpetrators. But let's simply touch on the role of fraud in the world of finance. And there are a few core conclusions that I want to make based on this story, that are germane to the finance themes of this book.

First, I believe that the finance world—necessary and important as it is—inherently tests the moral integrity of all men and women. Secondly, among the many who are tested, there are a few who just stand out from the crowd—those whom I have labeled "white-collar psychopaths." And it is when the real bad guys, those psychopaths, meet and test the already morally challenged but otherwise "normal" guys, that there can occur a moment of what we might call "criminal financial fusion." So far, this may seem obvious. But then there's a further, final twist—namely, that our over-regulated financial system may actually be making life easier, not harder, for the Franks of the world.

Let's go into this in some more detail.

So, first and foremost, fraud is an intrinsic side effect of the financial world. It can never be dissociated from that world. The valuation fluctuations, the ability to make gains, the risk of losses, and the fundamental uncertainty of the finance field (per our discussions in previous chapters) means there is an inevitable appeal to greed and fear in the game. These emotions test anyone who plays at the table, just like gambling on a horse or in a casino. However, the greed and fear in finance goes deeper than in typical casino games. In those games the outcome for a given player is largely determined by external events (the turn of the cards in punto banco, the spin of the wheel in roulette, the role of the dice in craps). But the finance game involves more complex forms of risk phenomena: multiple types of "uncertainties" (to use our term from Chapter 2) are interwoven. For finance is associated not only with external factors (the future performance of an economy, or interest rates, or the performance of a business); risk in finance is also self-fulfilling, embedded in the group psychology of the players (for instance, the collective panics of the market). In that sense of course, finance is much closer to group gambling games like poker: that game mirrors thought patterns associated with contractual negotiations (such as bluffing and psychological interplay) conjoined with the hard facts of the cards dealt.

In addition, finance, unlike gambling, is more than a pastime chosen by those who wish to indulge. Providing finance is a service that is genuinely and universally needed for growth in any economy and for many people's well-being. So in finance, we are also dealing in something that ultimately has a real-life impact on many people whose lives and welfare depend on the outcomes of financial transactions. Among those affected are many innocents. So while finance might at times appear to be a game, it's actually something much more important. This itself, I believe, adds a certain *frisson* to the emotional and moral impact of finance. Yes, it's just money, but you are not just playing with casino chips. There is, to exaggerate a bit, an element of Russian roulette. People really can get hurt.

So finance will always test the integrity of every man or woman (that's also what the Faustian pact is getting at). And actually, when tested, most people are found wanting. We don't have to look very far to see an abundance of moral failings. These occur even when people are (as they should be) just trying to earn a decent living in life and make some legitimate money in the finance industry. There's moral vulnerability, even among those who seem quite comfortable with the financial machine.

Now all this means that in finance, there is an added challenge in spotting the white- collar psychopath (like Frank) whose moral turpitude is a whole level different from the rest. It is, in other words, very hard initially to differentiate between just a typically ethically-flawed person and the actively bad guys. It's hard, because when it comes to money, most of us are sometimes . . . real "jerks." Let's, for example, touch on some of the hypocrisies found among those in the finance world—even among fairly normal, relatively balanced people:

- First, there's the politically-correct type who claims various socialistic and liberal moral principles, but is in fact just as envious of money as any other group (and sometimes more so). Often Democrat voters, this type (also called the "armchair socialist") can be really quite puzzled in his hypocrisy. The PC finance guy knows that his position is incoherent, but he struggles with the lack of moral integrity of his position;
- Then, on the other political extreme, are those who really believe in the money credo. They actually think they can or should judge their and other people's self-worth by their financial status. These are typically Republican voters and sometimes people who really think that free market economics do (somehow?) match conservative (or even religious) values. Deep down (in fact not that very deep) we all know that our human worth cannot possibly be based on our financial status. Hence you can usually see the fear in this individual's eyes (after all whatever monetary worth a person now has could well be lost tomorrow);
- Then there's the type who are proud that they made it (or sort of made it) having come from a modest background. Sometimes entrepreneurial types, they tell endless stories of how tough it was for them as a kid being brought up on the mean streets—proud at having pulled themselves up

by their own boot straps. Often they find that while they have talent enough to achieve a certain level of money status, it is actually much more difficult to achieve still higher levels of financial success;

- That group again contrasts with the good little boys or girls who have managed to do just fine by always being protected in well-established institutions. Often lawyers or bankers, they progress smoothly from private schools to established firms that they never leave. They too, know in their hearts that without the protection of these institutions (or their family money), they would struggle in the tough old world. They are the private sector equivalent of the government bureaucrat protected by his job;

- And then finally, there are those who are not really finance or business people at all, but have somehow come into the money world through popular media success. They have ended up having a public-speaking platform, but are often neither really intelligent nor wise enough to be public thought leaders (and again, they know this in their hearts). In this category I include: many media pundits/celebrities; some, albeit not all, religious leaders (be they priests, rabbis or imams); many politicians; and (all?) pop stars.

Perhaps many of my readers will recognize themselves somewhere in the above taxonomy, or in more than one of the above categories. I certainly do. And the above list only touches on those who have actually gained something vaguely positive out of the money world. Many have lost the game, been rejected or humiliated by it. This might perhaps have moderated their arrogance or sense of self-aggrandizement; still, their own material challenges could just as easily (in fact probably more easily) lead these individuals to all sorts of financially-related ethical improprieties.

Of course, men and women can be incredibly generous and kind and sensitive. And very few of us are psychopaths. But the intrinsic fear and greed of the money world ultimately undermines many people's moral and psychological compass. In other words, with such a panoply of the weak-willed in the business sphere (indeed in life in general), the real crook, the real financial sociopath, can often go unnoticed for a very long time. The human vulnerabilities of ordinary men and women act as a sort of camouflage for the real baddies. Thus has it always been throughout history.

And you see that over and over again in the deep psychology of say, Shakespeare's writing (look at the machinations of Iago or Richard III[1]) or, more entertainingly, in the manipulations of the stylized Gordon Gekko caricature (the bad) over the broker Bud Fox in the movie *Wall Street.*[2]

In fact initially, the ordinary guy often finds the psychopath or narcissist alluring, attractive. He has a certain compelling drive and passion—just the kind of allure that Ron, no doubt, saw initially in Frank. And that attraction is maximized precisely when we face the supposed temptations of something like—money. The most egregious psychopaths, of course, are the ones who become tyrants and dictators, as has happened in many centuries. But it's commonly observed they are empowered by believers, or followers, and those who simply fail to stop them. It is ordinary people who allow the monsters to rise largely through our own (typically human) ethical indifference, fear of standing out from the crowd, and lack of moral courage.

But let's now turn back to Frank, a rather small player on the big stage of psychopathic behavior—but a danger nonetheless. In our original story, we can see the specific impact that such men have on others. His plastic looks and rather unappealing outward demeanor were noticeable, but not enough to make anyone believe he was much worse than your average wheeler-dealer looking for his next trade. He hid, furtively, among the rest of us morally-compromised humanity. And yet he did ultimately turn out to be quite different from most of us.

I realize that calling Frank a "psychopath" is harsh, but I think it's essential to make a distinction between him and someone who, out of need or desperation, simply breaks the law. Certainly the (average) ethically-challenged money man can find himself in trouble with the law. Perhaps a good example of this is, say, the lawyer or fund manager (call him Joe) who is holding client money on trust in a separate client account. One year things go badly for Joe's business, and his money management firm is short of working capital. In desperation Joe dips into a client account to cover some debt. He's sure things will be better very soon and he'll rapidly return the "borrowed" money to the client's account.

Unfortunately, things do not improve in Joe's business. He just no longer has (or can generate) the cash to return the money. In fact Joe has to borrow some further cash from other clients' accounts also. The situation starts spiraling out of control and clients are curious about their balances. This type of fraud is actually very common in the real money management world and one of the reasons why the regulatory rules relating to the handling of client money are so stringent. You are *never* allowed to dip into a client's account to sort out the working capital requirements of your own money management firm or brokerage or law firm. It's just theft. Client money must always be ring-fenced from use other than on behalf of the client. It must also be ring-fenced from bankruptcy of the relevant money manager or broker. It is solely the money of the client, no one else's. These issues are of course at the center of the derivatives broker, MF Global's collapse and scandal in 2011.

But here's the critical point: the average finance guy like Joe usually gives up the scam after a fairly short while if ever he finds himself in the above predicament. He did dip into client funds at some desperate moment of weakness and now cannot pay back the money. But Joe, while indeed having done things really wrong, is at least by disposition within the "normal" ethical spectrum. For example, guilt at his actions gets to him. He cannot sleep at night. What should he tell his wife? He starts to feel the anxiety and the horrible pressure of potential public exposure. Joe thinks of having let down his family, friends, and employees. In fact he recognizes that he has let himself down.

Normally in these cases, the relevant individual sooner or later confesses to his fraud and takes the consequences. Perhaps Joe loses his professional license and does a couple of years in prison. It's awful for sure, but he just didn't have a sufficiently twisted moral fabric to go on with the client money abuse for that long.

Now let's contrast that with the real white-collar psychopath. Frank was one. So was Bernie Madoff. Before we focus on Frank, I want to touch very briefly on the Madoff story simply because Madoff really did start just like the Joe described above. Others have written about Madoff extensively,[3] so I'll keep it brief. Essentially Madoff was a fund manager who one day dipped into client funds. However, when one or two years later it became clear he was not going to be able to pay off those funds, he didn't stop there. He didn't throw in the towel like the average Joe. No, Madoff institutionalized his use of client funds for his own benefits. He simply covered shortfalls in one client's account by taking from other clients' accounts. Hence he slowly and deliberately built his notorious and mammoth Ponzi scheme. He industrialized the fraud and then systematically managed it for some 20 or so years.

Madoff would never have thrown in the towel, but for the fact that the 2007/8 credit crisis triggered very high levels of redemptions by clients of their money. He simply didn't have enough new money coming in to cover the redemptions of existing clients. So the structure exploded and Madoff caused enormous damage to thousands of people's savings and lives, not to mention schools, universities, charitable institutions. And of course, he destroyed his family. (One of his sons tragically committed suicide.)

So coming back to Frank—he was very similar to Madoff in this sense. Frank just did stuff that most of us would never do. He certainly matched with some of the technical psychiatric definitions of "psychopathy." Dr. Christopher Patrick, a specialist in the study of psychopathy at the Florida State University, defines psychopathy as involving: boldness, disinhibition and total lack of empathy.[4] These were all traits recognizable in Frank. He perpetrated egregious and intentional theft, continually and brazenly. And he would specifically target fairly well-to-do guys who Frank thought he could exploit (like Ron). Like other psychopaths, Frank had a sense that he was special. He plainly "deserved" to be an extremely rich guy (or so he thought); he could not define himself in any other way. There is a great sense of material entitlement in our modern societies, but the Franks of the world are the extreme embodiment of that sense. He had to get money in any fashion he could to support his self-image. In Frank's twisted morality, he had the "right" to take from whatever "sucker" he could find out there.

This type of moral pathology can be deeply entwined with the financial game, but it's really quite unique to come across individuals who perpetuate fraud with such a consistent sense of entitlement and lack of what normal human beings refer to as conscience. Those operating at the Frank or Madoff level are very special types, and of course I don't mean that in a good way. Like most human traits, moral sensitivity is generally *normally* distributed. While none of us is completely virtuous, most of us are somewhere near what we would define as the norm. But those like Frank are outside that range (they are in what is called the very "thin tail" of the normal distribution curve). When it comes to the way they operate in the financial world, they behave like a different type of human being entirely. Their moral sense—or rather total lack of morality—makes them fundamentally different. They become quite another, no longer a "zoon politikon" at all.

It's the same really with the true genius or perhaps the autistic savant. We can recognize some of their traits in all of us, but they've become (through the extremity of their gift or condition) something quite different from the rest of us. I would recommend the reader perhaps see the play/film *Amadeus*,[5] which shows the entirely incomparable nature of Mozart's musical genius. Of course I'm not comparing genius to psychopathy (far, far from it). I'm merely saying that once you get so far from the human norm in any feature (particularly psychological and cognitive features) you seem to end up with quite alternative types of humanity entirely. Perhaps even our greatest saints and moral leaders are themselves identifiable just because they too are off the normal human scale in their uniquely beneficent ethical temperament and behavior. Frank was certainly unique too—in a bad, bad way.

I don't really know too much about the persona of Madoff. That said, I do, personally, know one of the men who ran a feeder fund into Madoff— he'll certainly also remain nameless. But I do not believe said feeder guy was especially twisted (although he certainly ended up doing great damage). He was just another prime example of a moderately (just averagely) greedy individual suckered by the Madoff psychopathy. And this is the distinction I want to make: while the "white-collar psychopath" is an entity unto himself, he is likely to find many who are susceptible to his allure.

This was what characterized the dynamic between Frank and Ron, although I believe what happened to Ron could absolutely happen to any of us. Ron was actually not that greedy at all. Still, he was looking to make money, quite legitimately, in partnership with Frank. So the money temptation immediately made Ron vulnerable to Frank. And in fact Frank was perhaps, in personality, even worse than Madoff. For while Madoff confessed his guilt once exposed (perhaps to protect family members), that was the very last thing Frank was going to do. In fact, as we saw in the story, Frank proactively used the U.S. financial regulatory system to his own sick ends. He was a master at playing the counter-claim game in litigation, using his ill-gotten gains to hire expensive lawyers to twist the meaning of regulatory prescriptions and contractual terms.

And this brings us to the final piece in all this—namely that we really do need protection from the Franks of the world. That is, we do need some regulatory protection, and protection that works. All of us need it, not just the financially vulnerable or the less well-to-do. We need it to establish the boundaries of justice, but also because the whole economy suffers when unprotected by the rule of law.

We also need (for sure) protection from those normal moral failings that occur when the "average Joe" commits acts of financial folly in moments of misguided desperation. But we can understand it is not always easy to figure out how we should be treating the Joes of the world. They're not the bad guys— they just have human limitations that are put to test when confronted with Faustian financial challenges. (Joes do need to be regulated against, punished, or, more precisely rehabilitated—certainly a complex area for discussion.) But Joe is not Frank. Frank was a sicko, who broke every moral and legal rule in the book. And if we're going to have an effective regulatory system, it seems to me absolutely necessary that it's at least able to get the Franks.

And yet again as we saw in our story, in today's financial world there's a real struggle pinning down a Frank. And that's not for lack of rules. In fact I want to argue (see Chapter 9) that it might even be because in our current regulatory system, we have *too many* rules. For it seems the sheer complexity of the U.S. financial services regulatory system makes it harder, not easier, to get the likes of Frank. I go into the gargantuan mess of the U.S. regulatory system in the next chapter. But suffice to say here, some financial psychopaths like Frank really do exploit this mess. They can duck and dive within the system like a scavenging fox hiding in the alleys and empty houses in a run-down, over-populated, dilapidated inner-city slum. Nor are the authorities (including the FBI and the SEC) sufficiently competent to penetrate the dense thickets of legal defenses that someone like Frank can throw up as barriers to prosecution.

For an experienced player like Frank, the sheer complexity of the system can act as cover in so many ways. And here are just a few possible tricks:

- Expensive lawyers will both defend and then counter-claim on every action. Each claim and counter-claim takes exhaustive diligence and review by the courts. It's expensive. And one side (like Ron) can simply run out of money. Then a Frank can throw in claims that are totally irrelevant to the core issues just to obscure the situation. (In Frank's case, he quite falsely made allegations against Ron amounting to defamation);
- Meanwhile attorneys will reinterpret and twist the meaning of contracts between the parties. As with the *Moorcock* story, the Franks of the world know instinctively that a contract, or any rule, is open to endless interpretation and hence manipulation, and this is a key part of their psychopathic arsenal;
- Then of course, the evidence of money transfers is very confusing to trace, utilizing the latent complexity of U.S. corporate law. The money goes to account X, then account Y, then Z, all under different names, exploiting a plethora of allowable legal entities. Frank used so many corporate entities that you needed serious forensic accountants to see where the money really went (it's called "layering"). It's a ploy commonly used also by guys active in the money laundering business;
- Even if you can "follow the money," new legal games are then available. Having (illegitimately) changed the tortuous constitutional and partnership documents of De Metro Ber, Frank would claim the above transfers were not "*ultra vires*" (to use the legal phrase: i.e. he was acting within his authority). He was merely paying himself legitimate dividends;

- Meanwhile, there are today, so many regulatory bodies, supposedly protecting the practices of the financial services industry, that good attorneys can play them off each other. Who has actual authority over a given situation or breach? Is it FINRA, or the SEC, or the FDIC or the OCC or the CFTC or the CFPB or the Fed, etc? (And those are just to name some of the Federal authorities: never mind all the State authorities.) A good financial services attorney can continually frustrate the actions of any given body by arguing they are stepping outside of their jurisdiction or authority. On top of it, the regulatory code of each authority is dense with rules, all of which an attorney can try to reinterpret (more rules make for more interpretative possibilities, not fewer);
- Finally, of course, criminal actions anyway need to be proven "beyond reasonable doubt." That's a high bar to reach, particularly when there's someone like Frank obscuring the facts. Authorities just won't bring a case unless they feel fairly confident they will get their conviction. A con artist like Frank can wear down the authorities in criminal cases just as ruthlessly as he wore down Ron in his civil actions.

And these phenomena have been recognized in other industries too. There's evidence, for example, that Medicare fraud is exacerbated by the complexity of the rules of the system. "If the rules were simpler, defrauding Medicare would be harder," wrote the *Economist* in May 2014.[6] Medicare alone apparently has a backlog of half a million appeals.

Procrastination and inaction by the authorities, also characterize many cases like Frank's. Bernie Madoff, of course, was a prime example. He remained active in his egregious breaches of the financial regulatory environment for years and was not generally spotted, inspite of all the rules. As the reader may know, the few Madoff whistleblowers were ignored by the SEC. "This is a debacle for the SEC. The commission has a lot to answer for," said Joel Seligman of the Madoff case, an SEC historian and president of the University of Rochester in New York. [7] Even today it is still not clear why the SEC missed Madoff for so long, but no doubt it was in part because they were (and are) just too over-burdened with all manner of possible breaches of rules. Madoff was also certainly helped by some other insiders who sorted the technical details (just like Frank's CFO Derrick).

So here's perhaps a curious, yet perfectly logical way to think about this: if you did choose to breach various SEC or other financial services rules on a fairly regular and professional basis, you may still be more likely to be run over crossing the road than caught for said dealings. I am certainly not advocating breaches of the law. But if you are a morally bankrupt money man regularly breaching legal prescriptions, then perhaps you do not need to be too scared of going to prison after all. With some clever regulatory gaming and some good attorneys to help you exploit the rules, it's quite unlikely the authorities will be able to get you. Breaching financial regulations may be highly unethical, but it may also be a crime that pays. (Ask Frank!)

I have even had this discussion with serious compliance officers of major financial institutions. As said, most of us are somewhere close(ish) to the mean on the moral spectrum, which means we don't systematically break the law just because we don't think it's very ethical to break the law. But there's a huge imbalance between the compliance costs incurred by many financial institutions and the actual results that we get—in terms of fraud prevention—by paying these costs.

As I will point out in the next chapter, about 12% of the operating cost of the U.S. banking system today is taken up in compliance—that is, the cost required to manage the sheer volume of regulation in the U.S. system today. By contrast the chance of banks paying 12% of their operating costs out in fines for periodic breaches of the law is really quite remote (for the reasons explained above). The regulators might (conceivably) put a financial institution out of business entirely for consistent abuses, but even that's unlikely given how hard it is to implement the rules effectively.

In other words, perhaps some twisted firms might determine it is economically rational to allow a certain level of lawbreaking in their firm and just to pick up the consequent fines. They will allow it as it inevitably generates a lower cost than putting in place a full and immensely complex compliance infrastructure. Awful though it may sound, this is not an impossible position for say, some smaller less well-established finance firms to take. Particularly since keeping to the law for some shadowy firms may not really be a moral issue—it may just be a cost-benefit analysis. Some element of legal liability is an inevitable part of their business, and why not take that risk if the costs of complying (to avoid the liabilities) are so onerous? Why, in other words, shouldn't some small, shady, off-the-radar finance company actually institutionalize the Frank method of making money?

There are serious studies on financial regulation that bring this issue out. Here's what Oxera (a U.K. consultancy) wrote in a 2006 research paper on regulatory effectiveness: ". . . detailed rules—instead of high-level principles—may give room for regulatory arbitrage or otherwise distort incentives of firms and thereby increase risk. Regulatory failure occurs where the costs exceed the benefits of regulation."[8]

Actually, some of the smaller, less scrupulous hedge funds in the business of say, buying Non-Performing Loans (NPLs) do (effectively) make this trade. They will be sued or face fines in collecting on certain assets, but it's worth carrying that burden rather than be fully compliant and clog up their business with large costs. These funds may even have a certain utility in our system. For when mainstream banks are in trouble with excessive NPLs (as we saw in the last credit crisis), the best way to rehabilitate said banks is to sell these NPLs at a discount to a third party, such as the hedge funds above. The selling bank takes a big one-off loss for sure, but at least it has then stopped the hemorrhaging of cash.

This is quite a shocking and paradoxical conclusion to arrive at. The Frank story is telling us the regulatory mess in the U.S. means that certain of our more opaque, and less ethically robust, finance firms might conclude they are (economically) better off actively breaking the laws than keeping them. It's a huge issue, for the rule of law is a critical moral and economic imperative in any functioning society. But the seeming excess of the rules may result in the opposite of what the rules are of course supposed to achieve—i.e., bring law and order, morality and fairness to the financial markets.

Understanding this regulatory mess, what financial regulation really means, and how we ever got to where we are today is the subject of the next chapter. But the story of Frank is a salutary one. The financial game intrinsically makes us all vulnerable to improprieties (the Devil can so easily get the better of us). And even more so, the money world is a veritable feast for the Franks of the world. But is our currently dysfunctional regulatory regime merely adding more alluring delicacies for the gluttony of Frank to feast upon?

★ 10 ★

WHAT IS REGULATION?

Antique Maps

"Rules and models destroy genius and art."
On Taste, **William Hazlitt** (1778–1830)

The history of antique map dealing over the last 40 or so years is a fine story, filled with beautiful objects, important historical artifacts, colorful brokers, great trades, rapacious dealing and theft, but also the emergence of a unique asset class.

Let me give you a brief, entirely true account of that story.

Maps hardly existed prior to the Renaissance and the beginning of printing. There may have been medieval or ancient maps but very, very few still exist. More likely, before the advent of printing, people found their way across large distances by going from town to town, picking up local guides on the way. The maps that emerge with printing in the 15th century tended to be elaborate affairs—part geography, part art, part history (since the maps were full of historical/cultural details) and part fiction (since large elements of the world were still unknown to men). Mapmaking continued as a high art form, perhaps reaching its zenith with the Dutch map makers of the 16th and 17th centuries, the era that produced the greatest of them including Mercator, Ortelius, Adrichom or Blaeu. But their era of glory was not to last. By the late 19th century, maps were becoming machine printed in vast quantities and no longer had significant artistic merit. Suffice to say, original maps dating from about 1450 to 1850 are an antique art form. In the current market of map dealers, some of the unique pieces—including full atlases—are worth millions of dollars.

But as recently as the 1970s, there was not much of a trade in antique maps. Instead, the vast majority of the most precious maps or atlases were housed in museums or major libraries or universities. Very few people knew about the asset class. In fact, very few people ever saw the actual maps. Most were hoarded by obscure librarians and curators, treasures that had yet to be offered to a wider public.

Beginning in about the 1980s, however, a few entrepreneurial art dealers emerged who began to make antique maps a more recognized collector class. One of these is a man I know personally from my own map collecting—a brilliant maverick character called Graham Arader. Today, Arader has a suite of galleries across the U.S. and figures as one of the most important dealers in antique maps in the world. Arader, along with a small group of like-minded dealers, worked (globally) over the last few decades to commercialize antique maps, buying and selling them privately and in auctions. They also accumulated huge marketing material on the maps to educate the buying public. Their inventory is now classified in various ways, depending on the countries, ages, and origins of the maps, the provenance of the map makers, and the quality of the maps themselves. The most striking and unique maps have been included in beautiful displays that have succeeded in capturing the public imagination. This accounts, in part, for the many antique maps you are likely to see hanging on the walls of home libraries, living rooms, or dining rooms. Most of these home maps are not old enough to have real historic value or are copies, but that does not matter. The point is, antique maps have now "arrived" to be regarded as part of our cultural heritage. Their artistry has now been impressed on the public psyche.

But here's the thing about the antique map market: there are no rules. Outside of the bare bones of the usual laws of contract, map dealing is free of any regulations. In this respect, map dealing resembles most fine art markets. From its inception until the present day, no one is watching over the trades and auctions to make sure that the work is genuine or that dealers are licensed to carry out their practices. So it is fair to say the dealers in this market have gotten up to some "funny" stuff over the years.

One of the common practices was plain destruction—that is, destruction of antique atlases for profit. The market for intact stand-alone 16th or 17th-century atlases is limited. Dealers found that whatever you might be able to get for a whole atlas was materially less than what you might fetch for the sum-of-the-parts—that is, if you carefully disassembled the atlas and sold each map separately. So, many map dealers would wantonly cut up the atlases, separately frame each map, and sell it as a unique item. This practice still goes on, but was even more prevalent 30 years ago.

In addition, some maps were not very colorful: some were just black ink, sometimes faded, printed on blank paper. Even though they might have historic significance, their allure would be strengthened if a little color were added. So certain dealers also started painting the maps to give them some of the more vivid hues of the great maps of, say, the more famed mapmakers Blaeu or Adrichom. As they say in the business, this was a bit like painting a moustache on the Mona Lisa, but the practice caught on for the simple reason that it sold maps. Buyers who are essentially "tourists" in the map market still buy the over-painted products. Serious buyers, however, make a clear distinction. They recognize that newly painted maps are not more attractive at all, they are just damaged goods.

As for dealing practices, these were ever more aggressive (or clever, depending on how you see it). Arader himself was known to sell maps "short." In other words he would sell a map that he didn't even own, based on the assumption that he was pretty sure he knew where to get one, at short notice, that would be materially cheaper than the one he had just sold. He was also known for dominating entire auctions. He put syndicates together that would buy the complete inventory of an auction on the day it was due to begin and before anything was offered to the general public. The auction house would announce to the gathered public that the auction would not take place after all, as the entire inventory had already been sold in one block. This was a brilliant method to corner a given market, and since the market was unregulated, there was nothing illegal about this practice at all.

Prices for certain maps tended to skyrocket, and there was very little transparency in this market. One dealer could buy a piece in the morning for, say, $100,000, promising that he had a long-term holder/collector who he was representing. By afternoon, the dealer might sell the same piece for double the price to some unsuspecting rich guy with plenty of money and zero experience in map dealing.

The more unscrupulous dealers made a practice of misrepresenting their offerings. They would pretend something was an original Blaeu, say, when it was not. Dates were misstated. Some claimed the paint on a particular map was original when in fact it had been daubed on the day before. It was not uncommon to make numerous false claims about the rarity of a given map. As for paying taxes on gains on a map trade—don't be silly . . .

And then there were some dealers, like the fraudster I described in the last chapter, who just went way too far. I would call them "map-dealing psychopaths." Such was a gentleman by the name of E. Forbes Smiley III who stole maps from the Yale collection and would then on-sell them. (Arader himself was instrumental in catching and exposing the practice.) In his heyday, Smiley would go to the Yale library, find an old atlas, and when no one was looking brazenly tear out one of the maps. He would roll it up, put it in his sleeve and then leave. This was the cheap source of Smiley's extensive inventory, which netted him a small fortune in his retail trade before he was caught. Fortunately, at least basic laws of theft *do* apply to the map market. Smiley eventually went to prison.

So it was a wild ride. Some people made out like bandits, others lost the shirt off their backs. Some behaved more decently than others, while quite a number went to jail. But one thing is for sure, antique maps arose as a fine-art asset class. They came to the attention of the general public. As the market flourished, their beauty, and their historic and geographic significance, was revealed to us all.

As a collector I can tell you that antique maps are very special and can have particular meaning to different people depending on where they live or what culture/country they belong to. They are also great educational tools for adults and kids alike. They can also have enormous aesthetic merit, with unique cartographic styles that reach the level of high art.

Of course, as is evident, the map-dealing business is still filled with tricksters and sharp practice. Most of the shenanigans go unpunished. And antique maps remain an unregulated asset because fine art is generally considered a private asset class usually bought by relatively sophisticated investors. Art is not widely offered to the general public like stocks, bonds, life insurance policies, or mortgages, and so investors in the art market are not thought to need the protection associated with more ubiquitous financial products. We might say art, therefore, remains the one unregulated asset class left in the Western world. And the antique map market is a particularly interesting case because, unlike some other classes of art, the market itself hardly existed even up to a few decades ago. So it serves as a recent laboratory case study of the emergence of an asset in an unregulated environment.

And here's the thing—if you do not know the provenance of certain maps and map makers, if you cannot spot authenticity, determine the oxidization of ink, assess the correct patina on a map, and so on—well, for sure you will be taken to the cleaners. This is just part of the "sport," and no one is going to protect you from your own folly in dabbling in this market. Perhaps then the game really should have been regulated—to stop the double-dealing, the cheap misrepresentations, the insider trades, the flipping and short selling. It would surely have made the game much fairer and some people would not have lost their shirts.

Or perhaps not. Perhaps such regulation would just have meant that antique maps remained an obscure item held in dusty rooms by big institutions. In other words, without a lively market, there's a chance that maps would never have emerged from the bowels of university libraries in the first place to earn the appreciation of a wider public.

It is this conflict—the conflict between fairness on the one hand and economic growth on the other—that the whole issue of regulation in financial markets is concerned with. This is the core subject of this chapter.

The very first thing to note here is that this is not supposed to be a politically or ideologically-laden chapter. The ideological debate is one you can see on TV every day as one candidate from the Right and one from the Left talk "at" (not "to") each other. I also do not want to look at these issues from the perspective of a lot of rather technical academic writing on the subject—which itself is both (strangely) highly politically charged and can often miss the forest for the trees. My view is based on my own practical and professional experience in the financial services industry—and that view from practice does, I think, allow us to identify certain aspects of the debate as self-evident.

So, my position in a nutshell, which our map story tried to illustrate, is something as follows: on the one hand a financial services industry, open to the general public, without regulation is virtually doomed to organizational and moral chaos due to certain inevitably dysfunctional patterns of human behavior. On the other hand, excessive financial regulation is the death knell of any market or form of economic growth. And that seems to be the case in the U.S. banking system. In other words, the problem we face today in finance is *not* in the concept of rules and regulation per se (which are, give or take, an important feature of any mature market) but in the excessively pedantic nature of said rules. We need, in other words, to relearn what "regulation" is really for and what it means.

What seems to have happened, at least in the U.S. financial services industry for over more than a century, is something as follows. We started many decades ago (in fact in the 19th century) with a financial services industry that could appropriately be labeled the "Wild West." It looked something like today's antique map market. It grew exponentially in line with the whole growth of the U.S. economy, which ultimately benefitted many. (I personally believe there is a real positive "trickle-down" effect from capitalism, but it works over many decades, even centuries, not years).

But it also came with continual patterns of dysfunctional behavior— with systematic cheating, moral deviance, egregious inequality, and other highly distortive ethics that resulted in a regulatory backlash. In addition, there was instability that is a hallmark of capitalism, most dramatically illustrated by the 1929 Wall Street crash, the 2007/8 credit crisis, and similar market collapses. As each twisted mode of human failing man-ifested itself, a new rule was created in an attempt to prevent that form of behavior from repeating itself. (I will give some concrete examples of this later.) Each rule in itself made abundant sense, but over time a type of "Leviathan" (to use Thomas Hobbes' phrase[1]) emerged. That Leviathan today, is potentially stifling longer-term growth in the financial services industry and in the broader U.S. economy. And that's rather like regulating the charming antique map business to such a point that it would have never taken off in the first place.

This is not something that happened *suddenly* in financial services because, for example, a Democrat government came to power a few years ago. This has been a century-long trend. Nor was it true that the financial

Figure 10.1 U.S. financial service regulation—more and more . . . and more

services industry was unregulated prior to the 2007/8 credit crisis. It was highly regulated, although—as often happens with regulatory micro-management—the business practices of bankers had just out-innovated many of the rules. (In other words, there were plenty of rules, it's just that many of them were no longer relevant.)

Take a look at the Figure 10.1—it gives you the brief (but exhaustive) history of U.S. financial services regulation.

To also give you some data here, let's first start with regulation across the whole U.S. economy. According to the Office of Management and Budget, Americans spend 10 billion hours a year wading through federal paperwork;

in March of 2014 alone, regulators added a further 6.7 million hours of paperwork.[2] Meanwhile, since 1997 an average of 12,000 new restrictions per year have been created in the U.S.[3]

In an article in *The Journal of Economic Growth* [4] Dawson and Seater note that the number of pages of federal regulation increased almost sevenfold from 19,335 pages in 1949 to 134,261 by 2005. They estimate federal regulation has shaved off 2% from U.S. GDP growth for every year since 1949–2005. (This I suspect is exaggerated since it does not capture the benefits which that regulation would have also brought, but you can see the point.)

More interestingly for our purposes, look at these statistics: the law that created the U.S. banking system in 1864 ran to 29 pages; the Federal Reserve Act of 1913 went to 32 pages; the Glass-Steagall Act, that transformed banking regulation after the Wall Street crash and acted as an outstanding template for U.S. financial services regulation for about 70 years, took up 35 pages; but, the Wall Street Reform and Consumer Protection Act of July 2010 (the notorious "Dodd-Frank Act") runs for 848 pages. And, as Niall Ferguson and others have pointed out, it still requires a further 243 sub-rules to be created, 67 further studies, and 22 periodic reports. Meanwhile, compliance costs—which include new hires, technology and training— now account for 12% of the total operating costs of the U.S. banking system (see previous chapter).[5]

You can more or less see this trend in some of FINRA's examinations, particularly the Series 24 exam. FINRA is the chief (although not exclusive) body that regulates the U.S. stockbroking business, and the Series 24 is the FINRA exam required to be passed by all those who wish to manage a brokerage firm. As you go through the maze of myriad requirements in that examination you find yourself traveling through the history of stock market abuses, which is then followed by a rule to cover each abuse. Since the U.S. market is mature, every possible trick in the trade has been tried at one time or another (or so it seems), and so every possible gate has been shut after every possible horse has bolted.

For example, once upon a time someone tried "front running" stocks, so there's a rule on that. Then someone tried "splitting orders," so that's blocked, theoretically by another rule. Another ploy was "painting the tape" (another rule), then some tried "interpositioning" (prompting another prohibition), then "insider dealing" (resulting in a big, big prohibition). And so on. It does not matter what all these practices mean, but the exam itself is, unintentionally, a potted history of the century-long trend I have summarized above. Since regulators were dealing with an environment that started in the Wild West where, one by one, dysfunctional patterns of behavior were spotted and prohibited, each rule in itself made good sense. But the end result, one hundred years later, is a genuinely unwieldy and amorphous system of rules. What we now have in other words, can perhaps be seen as a bureaucratic zeitgeist. We might call it: the American mind manifest as the history of form filling.

Of course, in reality, there will always be some new mode of tricky behavior—perhaps a product of the financial innovation discussed in this book—which has not yet occurred. So we will continually come across uncouth practices that have not yet been regulated. When that new scam is perpetrated, the cry goes out again that the financial services world is under regulated and a new rule (or usually cohort of rules) is added to the beast.

I think we all recognize a similar trend has happened with the legalese in contract drafting, partly facilitated by the invention of the word processor, which allowed lawyers endless scope in amending and augmenting contracts. As an anecdote, I have on my wall a handwritten English bond from 1773 between a "merchant" (a businessman who presumably needed the money) and a "gentleman" (an aristocrat who presumably had the money). It is a bond for £6,000, which in those days was a sizeable amount of money, equivalent to a major corporate bank facility today. The bond takes up one page of drafting (one page—and in beautiful calligraphy). Today, bank facilities usually close with a board room table that's piled high with documentation (and it's all dull type!)

From my experience, this problem is particularly acute in the U.S., although also present in other parts of the Western world. Italy, for example, is also catastrophically wrapped up in red tape; in 2012 there was, reportedly, a backlog of some 9.7 million legal cases stuck in the Italian legal system. The U.K. financial services system is increasingly bogged down with the detailed rulings of the U.K. Self Regulatory Organizations. That said, the U.K. Takeover Code—the rules governing U.K. public takeovers—is in many ways still considered a model of a regulatory framework. The Code is short, and it is based solely on general principles that are opined upon by a Takeover Panel when required. As a code, it is very effective.

So getting the regulatory balance in society right is important, certainly in financial services. Without it, rules cannot really function at all, they cannot achieve what they are supposed to achieve. We end up with a system that tends toward confusion and delay, with highly arbitrary outcomes. And it is a problem that periodically rears its head in modern economies. "Rule density is a familiar feature of modern industrial societies. It often leads to complaints that there is 'too much law,'" wrote Professor

William Twining as far back as 1976.[6] Think of our story in Chapter 9, "What is Fraud?" There we saw a man who was running roughshod over endless rules, a man who society really needed to be protected against. Yet the sheer regulatory miasma meant that he could exploit the system to avoid being brought to justice. That to me, is where we are today, at least in the U.S. financial services industry and at least as it impacts on practitioners in that industry. We are in a state of regulatory excess resulting in a troubling level of disorganization and dysfunction.

I experienced this very directly and recently in relation to work I was tangentially involved in for certain clients in response to one of the myriad provisions of the new Dodd-Frank Act. One such provision covers the requirements for large and potentially systemic banks (banks with assets of greater than $50 billion) to write so-called "living wills" (see Title II of Dodd-Frank). These are supposed to be bank resolution (restructuring) plans in the event of a given bank going into financial distress. Specifically they are intended to be contingency plans (ahead of a potential crisis) that do not involve huge dependence on government support. The concept, in theory, is an interesting idea since the regulator wants to try and reduce the burden on the tax payer in bailing out, or propping up large banks—as happened in 2008—in the event of a future financial crisis.

But of course, all that was actually required by the rule was the production of a resolution plan (a "living will") by each qualifying bank, even if it could not really be connected with what might actually happen in the event of another financial crisis. For example, in the "living wills" of many banks, certain financial assets are earmarked for potential sale in the event of distress. That's fine, except the plans do not—because they could not—analyze the chaos you would have, and do have, in real financial crises. Many of the assets highlighted in the plans as potential assets for sale would simply not be sellable in the middle of a crisis since what partly characterizes a financial crisis is that all buyers disappear from the market simultaneously. Every bank runs for cover. And even if said assets were sellable, they would probably go for a material discount to the value contemplated in the resolution plan.

You see, financial crises are complex and unpredictable, and all their twists and turns simply cannot be regulated for or micro-managed upfront. Hence, while the idea of rules demanding that specific resolution plans be written by large banks may sound like a good one, it is not very meaningful in practice. Instead, the relevant banks just produced their entirely hypothetical plans, spent large amounts of money doing so, and burnt-up significant human resources. Still, at least they conformed with the Dodd-Frank requirement . . .

The really curious heart of the "living wills" regime is that it was created as part of Dodd-Frank by a relatively liberal set of legislators—the 'moral' logic being that the Government should not have to bail out a bunch of wealthy Wall Street/big banks or insurers next time. But of course it is ultimately an attempt to hark back to a world pre the Federal Reserve Act of 1913 (a world involving a decidedly free, even Wild West type, bank market regime). After all that 1913 Act was developed precisely to protect the 'people' from the devastating effect of bank collapses by creating a Government central bank that could provide liquidity to banks (i.e. prop up those banks) in times of crisis. So it really is legislation coming full circle—an attempt (apparently) to protect the consumer by telling big banks the Government no longer wants to prop up said banks, or therefore protect the consumer, when big banks collapse!

Actually, even the regulators recognize the shortcomings of these "living wills," although they currently blame the banks for not producing robust enough plans. On May 7, 2014, FDIC Vice Chairman Thomas Hoenig, speaking of the "living wills" regime, said in a *Reuters* article that, "What's different today than in 2008? . . . We still have major exposures from a systemic consequence point of view, and if I were to say otherwise I wouldn't be doing my duty." Subsequently, on August 5, 2014, the Federal Reserve and the FDIC began asking several banks in the U.S. to re-do their "living wills" (or at least try again?) precisely because the regulators don't think they achieve what they are supposed to.

In addition, the "living wills" rule applies to any $50 billion asset institution that has a U.S. banking license, even if most of the assets are outside of the U.S. Hence it captures all manner of fundamentally non-U.S. banking businesses that have a minor presence in the U.S. and just want to do some business in North America. Faced with such a burdensome (and ultimately meaningless) regulatory requirement—well, many foreign banks might just decide to stop bothering doing business in the U.S.

So what might the solutions be to all this, if there are any? Well, certainly *not* no regulation. Nor should we entertain the naive belief that the market always looks after itself or our society as a whole. We need, I think, simpler, shorter and more effective regulation. We need to revert to laws that outline principles like the UK Takeover Code of old, rather than laws that try to act as micro-managers. We need the precise meaning of laws to be determined by judges when a conflict and need arises, but not before. We need zero tolerance for vexatious litigation. We need, in general, a reduction in all forms of litigation in the U.S. economy—since it is itself a key cause of much of the disclaimers, form filling, and legalese that is so clogging the system. We need regulation that reflects the fact that more elaborate rules do not mean more determinate outcomes. (On the contrary, they just create more interpretative noise.) Think again of the *Moorcock* story and the interpretative possibilities embedded within rules.

In practice, we can fairly easily distinguish regulations that are workable and meaningful from those that are not. Let's go back to the laboratory of the antique map market. Had it been determined that the market should be regulated, here are some general principles that might make sense:

- Atlases over a certain value ($x) and pre (say) 1850 should not be cut-up;
- For maps over a certain value ($x), statements as to their provenance and originality should be supported by certificates from qualified third party appraisers;
- Maps cannot be painted over without the specific permission of the buyer of said map, and over-painted maps must always be disclosed as such;
- If a dealer buys a map for $x, and wishes to sell the map to another buyer for more than (perhaps) 200% of $x in a short period of time (say within one or two weeks), the dealer must at least disclose to the buyer the price at which he acquired the map in the first place;
- Each dealer should keep a record of the price at which he sold the very highest value maps (i.e., maps with a value of over say $x0,000)

Now the above rules would create something of a burden on map dealers, although it may also bring some incremental transparency—and ultimately further liquidity—to the map market. That would be positive for the dealers too. The rules are just principles in many cases that would probably need to be settled in court proceedings when a dispute as to conformity arose (e.g., what really counts as a qualified appraiser, etc). Of course the private nature of the art market means these rules would never be implemented in practice, and in any event, they are overly simplified. But the sense of the above principles is clear when we contrast them to the following types of legal pedantry:

- Every map displayed in an art dealer's window must have pasted on it (across the front of the glass frame): full details of the map's chemical condition; a full listing of all prices it has been previously sold at; and the name, address and telephone number of all previous owners;

- Every map must be sold with a large disclaimer notice on the bottom left-hand corner stating that the value of the map may go up or down, the map might be torn, the map may not after all be original, the map could be considered ugly and worthless by some people, there may never be another buyer for the map, and the map will for sure disintegrate (eventually);
- No map can be over-painted under any circumstances, and that includes small pencil marks anywhere on the map or restorative work by an art restoration professional. Maps should be inspected for these marks on a daily basis;
- The maximum price a map can be offered for sale is no more than 20% above the weighted average (inflation adjusted) price that the map was sold for in the last 50 years.

I am reminded of something akin to the above pastiche whenever I watch any type of pharmaceutical advertisement for a drug on TV. These are not advertisements for financial services products, but then the pharmaceutical business is plagued by the same regulatory excesses. Typically a man in late middle age appears on the screen. He is fit and handsome for his age and he is with his late middle-aged wife. They prance merrily across a sandy beach. We are told briefly, by a warm smooth voice, the name of the drug—call it "Happidom." But then before we can be told anything else about Happidom, a man with a gasping, rapid-fire voice comes on and reads to us a bunch of disclaimers. The disclaimers are however long and extensive and *must* all be read. We are told at breakneck speed that no one over the age of 70 should take this drug, nor however, should anyone under the age of, say, 69; nor anyone who has not yet consulted his doctor, nor even with medical consultation. We are told that this is certainly not for pregnant women, although best if you avoid taking it even if you are not pregnant. But the prattle will not stop, for we are also told the drug may give you cancer, a stroke, liver problems, arthritis, psychological problems, and could (most likely will) result in death. This fiasco rumbles on even as our couple on the screen continues frolicking on the beach. Finally, after all the disclaimers have been rattled off, there is simply no time left for the advert at all. The smooth voice returns at the very end merely to tell us, "Happidom—for a joyful life" . . .

Now there are financial services advertisements that are somewhat like the above also with long disclaimers about investment risk. And while the above is, I think, amusing, we instinctively know something has gone wrong with many of our pharmaceutical adverts. We know no one is really listening to all the disclaimers, we know they are being read out just to comply with some rule. And most importantly, the regulator couldn't possibly believe he is doing his duty to protect the public just by having a long list of life's contingencies pelted out during an advert. So these ads are very good examples of the public *not* being protected by the rules precisely because the rules are not being used in the right way.

Niall Ferguson has said the U.S. economy has gone from the "rule of law" to the "rule of lawyers."[7] Philip K. Howard, the American legal campaigner for better governance, called it in his recent book, *The Rule of Nobody* . . . .[8] I would call it more the rule of . . . procrastination. Still, in Ferguson's sense we must disenfranchise a bureaucratic pattern of thought, and hence more meaningfully *return* to the rule of law. And for those really interested in this subject, other serious academic works have been undertaken on how to reduce the U.S. regulatory burden—for example, by Patrick A. McLaughlin and Richard Williams of George Mason University,[9] some of whose data I relied on above. Their analysis highlights some historically successful clean-up attempts—e.g., the 1988 Base Realignment and Closure Commission or the Administrative Burden Reduction Programme in the Netherlands. Still, to effect change is easier said than done. It may take literally a revolution over many decades for there to be a shift in approach, if indeed it ever comes.

You see, in addressing today the regulatory problem in financial services—and I daresay in the wider economy as a whole—we need to see it as conceptual confusion. It goes to a collective misunderstanding of the concept of a "rule" or of "regulation" itself. (Philip Howard, referenced above, sees the issues also in terms of philosophical mistake). As we saw in the chapter "What is a Contract?" and in this chapter again, to conceive of human prescriptive "rules" in the economic sphere as deterministic tools like a mathematical equation is just to misunderstand the very function and nature of regulation entirely. In a board game or a chess game, you can have precise and specific rules precisely because such games are limited, they are bounded. But economic and social reality is much richer than that and highly unpredictable—too nuanced for micro-managing rules. So our regulatory prescriptions need to be malleable enough to reflect that immense complexity.

I think in fact this is obvious to most of us, just as it is obvious that something is wrong with my little pharmaceutical ad above. So that begs the question of why we have lost sight of the nature of social rules. Rules are important social instruments after all. How then have we come to the point where we could be misusing regulation so proactively?

This is another curious question, but it is perhaps linked again to the atomization of modern society that I mentioned in Chapter 8. One of the features of modern society, particularly urbanized Western society, is this breakdown of the natural human bonds between people. It is commonly observed that though we live in huge conurbations, nevertheless we live highly individualist lives with limited emotional connection to those around us. The result is a loss of trust between people, which perhaps means we feel a constant need to control other people's future behavior. If you are close to someone and function in a symbiotic fashion with that person, you just don't need to regulate in any detail that relationship. There's trust and confidence that the other party will behave in a decent way towards you. But it seems, in the absence of that social trust, we will inevitably tend toward regulating in detail every social interaction—hence the genesis of over-prescriptive government regulation and contractual arrangements that try to legislate for all contingencies. This is only a theory, but if true it indicates our regulatory problem today is ultimately symptomatic of a larger malaise in our societies generally.

In summary, I would venture to say that anyone who really wants to understand the regulatory chaos in the U.S. financial services industry today would best be advised to read yet another story quite unrelated to finance— namely *The Trial*, by Franz Kafka,[10] surely one of the great works of 20th-century European literature. In the book a curious figure, Josef K., is accused of a crime without ever being told what it is. He goes through years of excruciating dealings with the law trying to wade through the system and find some rational system of justice. But all to no avail: eventually K. is executed by some government officials in a dark field without knowing anything about his case or having managed to penetrate even the surface of the legal system.

No doubt, U.S. financial services regulation is not quite such a grotesquely unjust nightmare. Still, the parallel with the haunting story is striking. For the horrific demise of Josef K. was not necessarily because of some single, all-powerful force acting malevolently behind the scenes. For sure it didn't take much paranoia by K. to create the suspicion that a hidden demonic authority was at work. But actually that authority is not apparent from the face of the text. There is no single powerful government body or figure that Kafka wished to define ostensibly or explicitly point to. Rather, what destroyed K.'s life was just the sheer weight of the system, the inability to make rational sense of the rules, the time wasted on those regulations, and the endless shut doors—each one only leading to another shut door.

We have then in financial services, a regulatory preoccupation that favors no one really. It does little to assist or enfranchise the man in the street. On the other hand, it limits the prospects for broader economic or entrepreneurial growth and prevents banks from providing much needed credit to the system. If anyone, it may favor established capitalistic oligopolies ("rent seekers") who can exploit the existing system, although in the longer term it eats away at their profitability also. For sure, human misconduct and unfairness in business matters is not something that we can deny, but neither will it disappear solely by imprisoning us all in a Kafkesque hell. There must be a better solution. We just don't need to live with either raw, uncontrolled capitalism nor tolerate death by a million rules.

WHAT IS A
BANKRUPT?

A Financial Institution

"How did you go bankrupt?" "Two ways. Gradually, then suddenly."
The Sun Also Rises, **Ernest Hemingway** (1899–1961)

I n this final chapter let me tell you just a little bit more detail of my own career. Most of it, as indicated elsewhere, has been spent providing a range of financial services to *other* financial services companies. In the industry parlance I have been a "Financial Institutions" (sector specialized) banker, investor, or adviser where my clients have always been other banks or non-bank finance companies of all sorts—as opposed to companies, say, in the telecom, healthcare, or manufacturing sectors. The services, products, and investment solutions that I have been involved in with this client base is very wide, but one activity has been a regular feature of my career—dealing with bankrupt banks and finance companies.

These bankruptcy-related dealings have themselves been various, including investments into busted banks and finance companies; providing or arranging for bankrupt finance companies access to new sources of capital; or advising these bankrupt entities on their options and best route to recovery. It's actually a fascinating business because these bank failures raise so many interrelated financial issues and problems. That is, it's fascinating so long as you are not left holding the bag—i.e., holding a bad investment in one of these entities or sitting on deposits in a busted bank or being a board member who's held liable for the collapse—in which case (needless to say) it is not so fun after all.

Still, in one sense, these situations have in recent years become much *too* "fascinating." By which I mean, some of the financial institutions' related restructurings have become so complex, so involved, and so interconnected that the whole game has changed. In some instances, restructuring situations have entered the financial twilight zone where the core logic of financial and restructuring theory starts to hemorrhage. As you can imagine, it is one of these situations that I want to focus on in this chapter—a situation filled with absurd complexity, vicious circularity and ultimately financial irrationality. It is a situation that, through all this, teaches us a great deal about financial institutions themselves and their intrinsic vulnerability; about debt; and, above all, about the concept of bankruptcy.

This story is in fact the compilation of three complex (broadly true) situations, although I have brought them together for illustrative purposes. There was a great deal of very involved financial theory, accounting issues, as well as tax and legal considerations in this web. But I will endeavor to keep to the core of the issues and make it digestible as a tale.

Actually it is hard to know where to start, but the best place is probably with—aircraft. To give some background, many aircraft are not owned by the airlines that use them. Commercial aircraft are very expensive, ranging in price from a few million to over $50 million each. Often, airlines do not want, or do not have the cash flow, to buy these aircraft outright. Instead they borrow them—or, more correctly, lease them—from aircraft lessors. (Remember how we saw in our chapter "What is a Financial Instrument?" that a lease is just a form of borrowing under another guise?) Aircraft lessors are special types of finance companies that provide aircraft to airlines on lease.

Now, leases can take various forms. The lease type most commonly used by aircraft lessors is the "operating lease." Under an operating lease an aircraft is leased out to an airline for a fixed period (say five years) during which the airline pays rentals. At the end of the five year period, the aircraft is returned to the lessor who continues to own the aircraft. At this point the lessor may sell the aircraft or merely re-lease the aircraft. You will notice that the operating lease has one particular feature that's very important in this transaction: the lessor receives not just rental income, but also gets the aircraft back at the end of the lease. (This contrasts, for example, with say a "hire purchase" arrangement under which the lessee of an asset pays rent for a certain period at the end of which the lessee is then the full owner of the asset.)

I tell you these rather dry details because the nature of an operating lease has specific implications on the risks taken by aircraft lessors/aircraft finance companies. Since the lessor takes back the aircraft at the end of the lease period, the lessor is taking not just credit risk on the lessee (i.e., risk that the lessee will keep paying rent akin to a lender taking risk on interest payments) but also risk on the value of the underlying asset (the aircraft themselves). If, during the period of a lease, aircraft values go up, lessors tend to make out like bandits since the value of the assets they are ultimately holding/owning has gone up. Of course, if aircraft prices go down, the lessor may be getting his rentals, but at the end of a lease the lessor can find himself holding an asset which has heavily depreciated (i.e., depreciated way more than its natural depreciation from wear and tear).

The upshot of all this is that when you look at aircraft lessors over a long period, they turn out to be less in the rental game and more in the business of gambling on aircraft prices. They can make very good profits for a number of years, but then during a downturn, when aircraft prices collapse, often five or even 10 years of accrued earnings could be wiped out. I would venture to say that even if aircraft lessors can be very profitable in certain years, for many of them the long-term (average) return on equity (or profitability) is probably negative, for the reasons explained above.

And indeed, aircraft lessors are very vulnerable to downturns since aircraft usage is closely tied to the macro economy. During bad times, people simply fly less (there are fewer "bums on seats"), so the airlines need fewer aircraft. Hence, aircraft rentals fall and hence also, aircraft values fall (often plummeting). As aircraft come off lease, the lessor finds he is sitting on an asset he can hardly sell. In fact, he may not even be able to find any other airline that needs it for rental. You may have seen pictures of an endless line-up of aircraft stranded in some U.S. desert: this is a portrait of unused (off-lease) aircraft during a recessionary period.

While all the above is well known to aircraft leasing executives, this situation alone creates some absurdities. One of which is that just about every executive in this industry ends up having to lie—or at least be selective with the truth—when it comes to their business projections. They typically provide projections that assume gradual increases in aircraft prices and a healthy rental environment, implicitly going on ad infinitum. But a truly honest executive in the industry would produce projections that perhaps showed nice profitability for a few years, after which the whole business would just fall off a cliff—reflecting a downturn in aircraft usage and values. (Of course, said executive would not keep his job for too long, so they are rare to find).

Funnily enough, there are numerous businesses that behave in similar ways. In other words, they go through periodic cycles that regularly wipe out many, many years of historic retained earnings when the value of some asset collapses. Investment banks are, obviously, among these businesses.

But to return to my situation, here's how things stood. A busted aircraft lessor had been wiped out by a collapse in aircraft values and rentals. It was, in other words, an aircraft lessor in distress. In the interest of anonymity I will call it Lessor A.

Lessor A was close to bankruptcy. You can see Lessor A in the diagram below. I haven't yet explained this diagram, but showing it now, I think, will help you follow the rest of my exposition. Here is a chart of relationships among financial entities at the beginning of this bankruptcy case.

The diagram gives you a view of the way that Lessor A was financed. Generally, aircraft lessors have a layer of equity capital (you might call it their own cash from shareholders/the owners), but the rest of the money comes from borrowings. Lessors, being finance companies, are themselves highly-levered entities with often five to ten times as much debt as equity. All the rentals they receive go largely to pay the interest on the lessor's debt, with the hoped-for increases in aircraft values driving much of the profits. So someone (or some entity) has to fund both the equity and the debt of the lessors themselves.

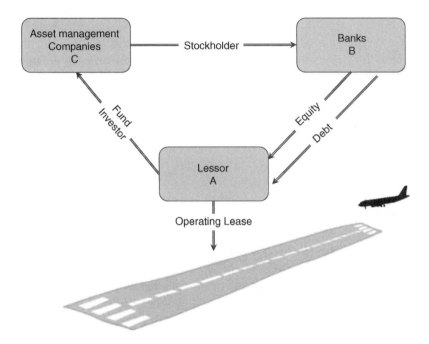

Figure 11.1 A vicious financial circle

In this case, that entity mattered a great deal. That's because the asset losses of the lessor, due to the collapse in aircraft values, were enough not only to wipe out all the value of the equity in the business, but also significantly impair the debt. The equity funder of Lessor A was therefore itself facing a large loss—and so, also, were the debt providers.

Who were those equity and debt providers? Well, the debt is usually from banks (that is, depositary institutions where you and I put our money). They are you might say, the real lenders behind an aircraft lessor. Using all our deposits, they provide large bank facilities to supply the financing the lessors need to purchase the aircraft. Usually the owners of the lessor (the equity provider) would be separate from the debt providers. The owners might, for example, be specialist asset managers. But, surprise, surprise—not in this case! In this case the equity holders and the debt holders were the same banks. The banks (actually, a syndicate of banks) were "shareholder lenders"—they both owned Lessor A and lent to it. Let's call them Banks B. Again, take a look at the diagram above.

Well, this itself made for a unique challenge. Usually in a restructuring, there's a sort of "fight" between the debt holders of a busted company and the equity holders. Debts are prioritized over equity ownership rights in a bankruptcy; so normally, debt holders get all or part of their money first before anything goes to the equity holders. In other words, the debt holders—by virtue of their lower risk/lower return investment—get prioritized at the expense of the shareholders.

But in our story, the tug-of-war between the debt holders and the equity holders was entirely muddled. Here we had an instance where the shareholders *were* the debt holders: they were one and the same. So to the extent that the debt holders were going to be kept whole, it would be at the expense of themselves (or, more precisely, at the expense of just another department in the same bank). As you can imagine, it becomes difficult to manage a situation where a bank gets paid out on a debt at the expense of screwing itself.

But even as we tried to work out that problem, we realized we were far from the bottom of a virtual mountain of curious financial relationships. You see, the collapse in aircraft values was such that, for sure, Banks B were *themselves* going to have to take big write-offs. Whether it was from the equity they held in the lessor or in writing off loans to the lessor, the Banks B's own capital was being impaired by all the losses. In fact it was clear that the extent of the losses was such that Banks B themselves now urgently needed new shareholder capital.

Remember how we referenced Tier 1 Capital in our chapter "What is a Financial Instrument"? Well, Banks B were now themselves all short of Tier 1 Capital. In other words, they were short of the core shareholder or equity capital that they were required to hold to be adequately capitalized under the Basel Accords. That meant the Banks B were going bust too, and they needed fresh equity—i.e., a fresh cash infusion.

Of course, then comes the next question. Where was that new infusion going to come from? And to answer that one, you needed to ask a second question. Who owned Banks B?

Well the actual owners of Banks B—the potential source of that new infusion of capital—turned out to be various investment companies or asset management companies. These are another typical creature of the financial services business. Such companies earn fees by investing other people's money (or other entities' money) in stocks and bonds. They operate a bit like mutual companies or the investment arm of insurance companies. There was, in other words, a select group of asset management companies that liked investing in bank stocks; and they were the owners of large chunks of Banks B. These are the ones I've labeled Asset Management Companies C in the chart.

But were Asset Management Companies C really going to refinance Banks B? That remained to be seen. And that's because Asset Management

Companies C were themselves now facing big losses from this situation—namely, losses on their investments in Banks B. The impairment to the equity of Banks B was effectively a write-off of the investments made by Asset Management Companies C. And yet these were the very asset managers who were now being asked to put in *more* equity to make up the losses sustained by Banks B—that is, replenish Banks B equity or Tier 1 Capital. And, and as we know, Banks B had sustained these capital write-offs because they were owners and lenders to Lessor A. And it was Lessor A that had lost all the money in the first place since it had bet on aircraft prices (via aircraft leases) that had collapsed.

Of course, that was still not the end of the chain. And now we come to the *pièce de résistance.* In addition to being shareholders in Banks B, Asset Management Companies C were also, as I mentioned, in the business of managing money of certain third parties. Well, who was one of those third parties? None other than our good friend Lessor A.

You see, Lessor A also needed significant cash balances to maintain liquidity and manage its working capital. This cash itself was invested in liquid stocks. And, lo and behold, some of the asset managers of this liquidity were Asset Management Companies C—yes, the same asset managers who were, in turn, busy losing this money on their investments in Banks B.

So to summarize (now in reverse)—Lessor A had a bunch of liquid investments that were losing money, being investments in stocks managed by Asset Management Companies C. The positions were loss-making since Asset Management Companies C had unfortunately bet this money on the equity of Banks B. This was a bad bet since Banks B were starting to go bust and were sustaining big investment write-offs. They were sustaining those write-offs because they owned equity and had simultaneously lent money back around to . . . Lessor A. And Lessor A was triggering these write-offs because Lessor A was itself losing money on aircraft that it had invested in and leased out.

There it was—a veritable merry-go-round (or domino effect) of financial assets linked to financial assets that were, in turn, linked to other financial assets; and different types of finance companies linked to other types of finance companies—lessors to banks to asset managers. There was, in addition, the circularity within Banks B that was the result of their being both shareholders and lenders. But, more extraordinary, there was also a much larger vicious circularity in the total financial chain. If you asked who ultimately owned those aircraft, the answer was, in effect, no one. They were owned by Lessor A, but Lessor A was owned by Banks B, but then

Banks B were owned (at least in part) by Asset Management Companies C, but then the stocks held by Asset Management Companies C were themselves (again, in part) held on behalf of Lessor A. It was a bit like those chains you can see images of on the internet where one person A is sitting on another person B's lap, B is sitting on C's lap, C is sitting on D's, D is sitting on E's lap and E him or herself is sitting back on the lap of A. Nobody is sitting on anyone since everyone is sitting on everyone. Or to put it another way, perhaps Lessor A did own the aircraft, but then that seems only to be the case because the owner of Lessor A was . . . Lessor A itself!

As you can imagine, sorting out this mess was not straightforward. New capital was required to stabilize both Lessor A and Banks B, but where on earth was it going to come from, and in what format? Given the linked relationships, this question was puzzling in the extreme. And there were other issues that seemed hopelessly intertwined. How were the losses going to be shared out among the various parties? How could new investors be made comfortable unless they had complete confidence that losses had been capped? Who was liable for what? How could Banks B avoid panic among depositors who had learned of the whole situation? What was required to be reported to the public markets? And what were the tax, accounting, and legal implications of all this?

I will not even go into the solutions such as they were. Instead here's where this particular story ends, and where I want to draw a much larger picture of bankruptcy and its implications.

I think the complex nature of this bankruptcy is perhaps best understood by looking at some of its components—in particular, those that created and transmitted what was effectively a debt problem. Yes, the aircraft leasing business is a speculative one for the reasons I explained: you are betting on fluctuating aircraft prices. But that alone could not generate the kind of chaos that ensued when these prices plummeted. What allowed the spread of the cancer had more to do with the nature of financial institutions and of lending.

You see, there's something intrinsically unstable about any chain of debt, notwithstanding that debt is a very necessary and fundamental part of modern finance. While there have been, and continue to be, many attempts to soften that instability, I think that all we can ever do is move the instability around the system.

Let's start with banks themselves. They are by their very nature, accidents waiting to happen. They are fundamentally vulnerable entities by virtue of their make-up and purpose. I think most of us already know this. Banks (that is, real banks—i.e., depositary institutions like Banks B) make money by borrowing money at a low rate and then lending that money out at a higher rate. The spread between these two rates is the banks' "net interest margin" and comprises the basis of its revenues. The banks borrow from you and me: we are lending the banks money when we give them deposits. Of course, banks do not pay very much on our personal deposits, so we're giving the banks pretty cheap funding. By contrast, when the bank aggregates all its deposits and lends out to companies such as Lessor A, it charges those borrowers much higher rates than it is paying on its deposits. And banks can do this because the term structure of (incoming) deposits is so different from (outgoing) loans. Deposits can be withdrawn at any time since they are effectively overnight loans to the bank, so the interest offered is very low. But when a bank lends out to an entity like Lessor A, it can legitimately charge a much higher rate because the bank is locked in for a significant period of time, often a number of years. This is what is captured by "yield curves"—they show how typically, as maturities on debt get longer, the interest rate on that debt increases.

All this of course, means banks are vulnerable to the famous demon of *bank runs*. If depositors to a bank become nervous that the loans the bank has made are unsound, they may start pulling their money out. But the bank no longer has the liquidity to repay all these withdrawing depositors (since, after all, it has lent out their money on longer-term loans). Hence "deposit flight," better known as bank runs, are sometimes caused merely by panic. But whatever the cause, once deposit flight begins, it turns into a self-fulfilling prophecy. (A bank can go bankrupt just due to a liquidity shortfall even if it turns out the bank's loans were sound after all.) Cash liquidity is, after all, the lifeblood of any bank. And this self-fulfilling feature of bank failure can turn a situation from one that is merely problematic into one that erupts into chaos—note the Hemingway quote at the beginning of this chapter.

Most of us know all this: the vulnerability of banks is part of our communal lore and history. We have all seen epochal photographs of people lined up outside banks in distress (or believed to be in distress). It is, of course, also the reason why the government created the Federal Deposit Insurance Corporation (FDIC) following the 1929 stock market crash. In one sense the insurance provided by the FDIC was one of the first attempts to take a large element of debt-related risk out of the financial system. And while I don't believe it really does achieve that, such insurance does nevertheless, assure most depositors that they will not lose all their bank savings in the event of a bank collapse. With that element removed from the equation, depositors no longer feel they have to rush in to rescue their savings. That in turn staves off the very type of panic that used to precipitate bank collapses.

Deposit insurance has been incredibly successful. Deposit runs rarely happen anymore, at least in societies where depositors have confidence in the solvency of their governments. But on a more holistic level, deposit insurance ultimately just moved the risk of debt mismatches elsewhere. Deposit insurance means that, in effect, banks are subsidized (guaranteed) by our government through the insurance the government is providing the depositors. This means that banks can undoubtedly borrow at incredibly low rates from us depositors, but it has also meant many constraints have been imposed on banks. A bank that is going to take risk with depositors' money (and ultimately with the government's guarantee) is today, very highly regulated. Understandably, there are controls over the way it can lend out money and manage its affairs.

So beyond the "conventional" banks with their FDIC regulations and depositor-insured accounts, what emerged was the so-called "shadow banking" market. Lessor A was really a shadow bank. In simple terms, these are lenders who make loans (or leases) but do *not* take retail deposits. Instead they are funded in the wholesale bank markets (Lessor A was funded by Banks B). Because they do not take retail deposits, they are not subject to the same restrictions as the regulated depositary institutions. Their costs of funds are naturally higher than depositary institutions, but they can also take incremental risks and generate potentially higher yields on their loans (compared to depositary institutions). And indeed, with depositary institutions being increasingly regulated, a growing number of people and companies have had to turn to the "shadow credit" market to have their finance requirements met. The market emerged and became increasingly large over a number of decades. It's not that different from the way alcohol sales went underground during Prohibition.

Unlike the illegal sale of bootlegged liquor, however, there's nothing in the "shadow banking" system that is outside the law. Despite its name, transactions are above board. It's just the liabilities of the shadow lenders are not insured like deposits. But there's a consequence to that: since they are not insured, the funding sources of "shadow lenders" are left vulnerable.

Hence, while retail deposit runs may be a thing of the past, wholesale funding runs are still very much with us. Indeed, the run in the 2007/8 credit crisis was really a wholesale (not retail deposit) run. In simple terms, concern developed that many wholesale-funded finance companies and investment banks had made bad loans or bought bad packages of loans—securitizations. So the banks funding those finance companies started pulling their lines in 2007/8. When the wholesale funders themselves panicked, it triggered the colossal crisis.

It's complicated. Many other authors have thoroughly analyzed the nature of the wholesale banking run in 2007/8, a feat that I won't attempt here. But you can see anyway, how the intrinsic vulnerability of chains of debt funded by debt never really disappeared from our system. Deposit insurance moved the risk out of the insured bank sector, but it just re-appeared in the shadow bank (non-insured lender) sector. And in fact it's still there today. Since the crisis, banks (depositary institutions) have been even more heavily regulated and become even more conservative. So again, mainstream banks are simply not meeting the credit requirements of many businesses.

And yet again these financing needs are already being readdressed by a newly revived, post-crisis "shadow banking" market. In fact in an article that I co-authored in 2014 with Dr Craig Zabala in *The Journal of Risk Finance*, we analyzed the re-emergence of that market—and see also Chapter 4 of this book.[1] Dr Zabala himself founded, leads, and is the largest shareholder in the Concorde Group that specializes in providing capital to mid-market private businesses, including by providing private credit in the shadow banking market. The aim of his business, in other words, is to provide financing to precisely those that are not being serviced by the mainstream banks/depositary institutions. In the firm's latest public filing, Dr Zabala specifically states that, "Regulatory and financial market change over the past 20-plus years, especially since 2007, have created a significant supply-demand imbalance in the availability of capital for 'Middle Market' companies, particularly for those with revenues and market capitalizations under $250 million."[2]

It is even fair to say most of the foreseeable innovation in the financial world is likely to come from mid-market shadow credit providers like Concorde Group. This is far from unprecedented. In the past, many similar entrepreneurial finance providers have acted outside of the mainstream banking market. One such well-known firm was Drexel Burnham Lambert that really created today's "high yield" bonds market. It was founded as a route to provide leverage for mid-sized, independent companies via new public bond markets (again, quite outside of the depositary banking system). Drexel, as the reader may well know, unfortunately got caught up in market euphoria in the 1980s, took the high-yield credit market too far and ultimately—under the leadership of the notorious Michael

Milken—misrepresented the nature of some of the risks.[3] The firm collapsed amid scandal, but the innovation of high-yield credit and the provision of credit to the under-banked middle market belly of the U.S. economy was a solid and important idea. It is precisely this type of lending that firms like Concorde Group want to pick up, albeit using sound underwriting principles that do not allow for the excesses of firms like Drexel. Indeed, as a gesture toward the innovative nature of Drexel (and with a view to revitalizing the brand), Dr Zabala and the Concorde Group bought the use of the Drexel name.

The denuded nature of credit for the U.S. middle market is so acute now that even some household financial names have been increasingly moving into the "shadow banking" space. They have, in other words, been following the strategies pioneered by firms like the Concorde Group. For example, both Goldman Sachs, a leading global investment bank, and KKR & Co. L.P., a leading global private equity firm, recently created new Business Development Companies to provide mid-market commercial credit facilities outside of the mainstream depositary bank system.

So the picture seems pretty clear. If you do de-risk the leverage provided by the mainstream banking system as deposit insurance did, then much of the required credit in the system inevitably moves elsewhere—to these "shadow credit" providers. And hence we can also see how the vulnerability associated with all that credit, all those chains of debt (and hence of bankruptcy) can never really be extinguished from the financial system. You can, of course, see those chains in action in our Lessor A restructuring story. The *risk* can be pushed around the system, but it's always sitting there, just below the surface, waiting for its moment. And once it's out of the bag, it rapidly transmits itself from one related borrower/lender to the next.

I am not saying banks should not be regulated and indeed I think deposit insurance, and the protection it provides to retail depositors, is very important. It is just we should not believe that these devices eradicated the gremlin in the machine: it merely moved risk to other areas within the machine.

The transmission of risk in this way—and the way we saw in our story— is also because of the unique logic of debt. Debt, interestingly enough, has a similar logical format to a philosophical syllogism. In simple terms a syllogism tells us that if $A = B$ and $B = C$, then it follows that $A = C$. Likewise, if A owes \$x to B, and B owes \$x to C, then economically (even if not legally) speaking, A effectively owes the \$x to C. And it is this economic "transitivity" that allows debt problems to spread from one entity to the next. Indeed, said "transitivity" is recognized in English banking law in the so-called banker's "right of offset." Under this right if bank A owes say $100 to bank B, but in another account bank B owes $70 to A, then the two accounts can be netted off to create one obligation from A to B of $30.

Having said all of that, systemic vulnerability associated with debt is even more basic than all of the above. It is not even a product of a chain of inter-linked debts. The use of any form of debt itself always makes us exposed to bankruptcy. Debt can be a very powerful tool for good. Many people could not acquire houses, or cars, or computer equipment for their businesses, or even start their businesses without debt. On top of it, the judicious use of debt allows us to leverage up our returns on capital investments.

But debt also creates a type of servitude that we have all felt, I'm sure, at one point or another. Indeed the technical banking phrase is that debt must be "serviced"—the interest and principal must be paid back or else we are going to be facing financial failure. This is a burden, and it also makes us vulnerable whenever we make a purchase using debt. Indeed, it is this vulnerability that is precisely why we can achieve higher returns on those investments that are levered: the debt has increased the risk profile of the deal.

Actually, it is instructive to realize that the concept of bankruptcy has no meaning at all without debt. Imagine if you can, a world in which no one buys anything using borrowed money, not even houses or cars. There are no pawn brokers. Nothing is leased, nor does anyone leave any bills unpaid as this too, is a large form of debt in our system. It's difficult even to conceive of a commercial society of any size functioning under such a wholly debt-free system. (In fact, it is clear from ancient Babylonian records that the earliest forms of debt were merely unpaid invoices,[4] and without that type of debt, commerce hardly emerges). But if, per-chance, such a commercial environment were to exist, perhaps in some alternative financial universe, no one could really could go bust at all. No one could go broke since no one would ever have spent more than they have or more than they have earned.

Take even our aircraft example. Imagine if Lessor A bought all its planes by paying in cash (i.e., entirely in equity) and had no other debts. The company wouldn't make much of a return, but even a collapse in aircraft values could not bankrupt them: they would just lose asset value, but without going "into the red."

Think also of the two technical definitions of bankruptcy used by insolvency professionals. One is balance-sheet type bankruptcy, a situation in which your liabilities exceed your assets. The other is illiquidity, when you cannot pay your debts as they fall due. Both definitions are only meaningful in the context of debt or liabilities. Indeed that's really why bankruptcy, at least on a personal level, can often be a product of greed—if you just stop buying things you cannot afford (i.e., buying them on credit) you cannot go bust. And that's the point. Debt, with its risk of default, creates the possibility of bankruptcy. And chains of debt multiply and convey those risks in complex ways.

Complexity is the other key theme in our restructuring story above—in particular, how it manifests itself today in the financial services industry. There has been a huge increase in complexity in our financial instruments and our financial infrastructure generally over the last 30 years. My tale of the aircraft lessor with its long and circular chain of financial backers is merely one cute example of this overly complex financial engineering. But increased complexity has led to its own set of critical issues.

The problem of excess complexity in modern finance is related also to the issue of the "systemic" risk associated with certain financial entities, although the two issues are separate. Systemically Important Financial Institutions (or SIFIs) refer to those critical institutions whose failure can trigger wider failure in the financial system as a whole. These were the institutions that, in some cases, received huge government assistance in the 2007/8 credit crisis to avoid wider-scale economic impacts. (Think of AIG, or Citigroup, or the Royal Bank of Scotland in the U.K.) Their unique requirement for such protection of course raises many controversial issues: while we sort of need to bail them out in times of crisis to avoid large scale economic damage, why should the taxpayer have to pick up the bill? (See also my comments on bank "living wills" in Chapter 10).

(As an aside, I worked with a small country's government in 2008/9 on a bailout—many hundreds of millions of dollars—of one of their banks. I was told by a then government cabinet member that he could not really understand why the government was being required to assist the relevant bank when, "If I stole one single shoe from a store I would have to go to prison." A very fair point. Though we had to remind the minister that bad investment decisions were different from stealing and anyway did he really want to live with the systemic consequences of choosing the non-bailout option?)

SIFIs need not be complex institutions, per se, but they are very large relative to the financial system as a whole, hence why they have a systemic impact. That said, great size usually *does* involve great complexity, certainly in today's finance world, and it is the complexity that I think creates the most interesting issues. If the problem with SIFIs were just size, then the solution might be a relatively easy one. Just break them up—i.e., have rules that restrict any one bank or finance company from having more than a certain percentage of the market share for a given financial service or product. These rules would be rather like anti-trust legislation used to break up monopolies. Indeed this is, and has been, contemplated by the regulators since the credit crisis. However, the sheer interconnected complexity of SIFIs and their various business lines makes these break-ups extremely difficult. So complexity *is* a core problem here.

We need to recall that, like it or not, over the last generation a great deal of brain power and intellectual talent was directed to the financial services industry, particularly in centers like New York and London. Certainly that may have negatively affected the talent flow to other industry sectors, to government, and to any number of professions. But I think it did something quite particular to finance also.

You see, it may be that finance is one of those subjects where excess intellectual energy generating unique complexity, is not actually too helpful. We mentioned in Chapter 5 that some argue there is no real innovation in finance at all since all finance is merely permutations on the basic concepts of debt and equity. I think this is an exaggeration, but certainly it seems true that creating financial infrastructures that involve just too many "epicycles" is not sustainable. Given also the intrinsically psychological nature of markets, maybe applying too much technical brain power to the finance industry really does lead to trouble. I would refer the reader to the story of Long-Term Capital Management, the failed $100 billion hedge fund lead by, among others, two Nobel Prize-winning economists.[5]

Still, I'm not sure it's quite as simple as that. I don't think the issue is really too much brain power per se. Nothing should really suffer in the long term from the exercise of human ingenuity. The issue seems more linked to the *wrong type* of ingenuity—that is, the creation of overly complex, ineffective innovation rather than clever but also effective solutions to financial problems. You can find the same in many fields.

The principle of Occam's razor in the natural sciences tells us the simpler solution is generally preferable to a more complex one. An oft-quoted example of this is the Copernican Revolution. Prior to Copernicus, many great minds were struggling with the data coming through in the 15th and 16th centuries from increasingly fine telescopic measurements of the movements of the heavenly bodies. In light of the new data, to sustain a geocentric view of the universe required using serious brain power to add more and more complex circular motions ("epicycles upon epicycles") to the traditional Ptolemaic model. Copernicus' straightforward solution of the earth rotating round the sun in an ellipse—a heliocentric system which achieved strong conformity with the data—was a good example of simplicity replacing the, by then, overly complex and plainly incorrect Ptolemaic system.[6]

And I do think something similar is a distinguishing feature between *clever and effective* financial innovation versus merely *clever* financial innovation, the latter of which can sometimes be quite damaging. The securitization revolution in the 2000s (discussed already in Chapter 5, "What is Financial Innovation?") is a good example here. The core concept of securitization is a fine and important development. Securitization is really all about what is called "non-recourse" finance. That is, it is often most efficient to finance a pool of receivables purely by reference to the cash flows from those receivables without being dependent on the credit of (i.e., without lending against or "recourse" to) the finance company or bank that originated those receivables. This is a clever idea and a sound one, but not an overly complex one. But the problem in the 2000s was that a great deal of human brain power, as well as computer time, was applied to the notion of securitizations such that the underlying pools of receivables to be financed became endlessly complex. Many different pools of different types of mortgages were mixed with student loans, mixed with auto loans, and mixed with pools of other securitizations. It was the same really with the innovations in the "high yield" bond market of the 1980s (referenced above). It was actually a very sound idea that is now an established part of the financial architecture; but at its inception it was just taken too far, with excess leverage applied to ever increasingly risky young businesses.

Remember also, there's no laboratory to test financial innovation (again see Chapter 5)—hence it can be hard to tell when such innovation is being applied effectively and when it is being abused. Hard, that is, until there's a big-time financial or market accident. So it is this type of excess financial complexity that I think is a challenge, not necessarily financial innovation per se.

That's perhaps what my tale of the bizarre aircraft finance restructuring is telling us also. By all means the finance world should, and must, innovate; but let's be conscious of innovating in a pragmatic and user-friendly fashion. It may be very hard for regulators to legislate for "effective" financial innovation versus ineffective innovation—and anyway, letting the legislators into this issue would no doubt just create even more detailed and unworkable regulatory minutiae. Still, endless chains of obscure debt linked to obscure debt does create the sort of vicious circularity we saw in my little restructuring tale.

This does not mean we should be throwing the baby out with the bath water; it does not mean we should, for example, end the business of aircraft leasing. But it does mean the modern finance industry really must develop a culture, as best it can, of pragmatic innovation versus merely clever innovation; a culture not hijacked by otherworldly geeks nor abused by rapacious brokers. And indeed, creating an innovative finance culture, embedded nevertheless in sensible and prudent real world credit solutions would, I think, go a long way toward rehabilitating the whole finance industry in the public consciousness.

But in finishing, we must still wonder why in the first place all that brain power did go into the finance industry in the Western world, hence creating all this financial complexity (and perhaps instability)? And why, specifically, over the last 20 or 30 years? Others have certainly tried to analyze this question too. But I believe it is a sure sign of the relative decline of the whole Western world, including the U.S. Relative decline has been a part of European life for over a century, but it is fairly new to Americans. Still, the U.S. share of global manufacturing value went from approximately 29% in 1970 to approximately 18% in 2010, with China's percentage going from less than 5% to nearly 20% in the same period. The U.S. saw particularly steep declines in the 2000s—coming down to the 2010 level from about 26% in 2000.[7] That's a large movement and is only one slice of an ongoing trend triggered by globalization.

The problem seems to be that when you have very little else to produce—because much of that production has gone to China or India—you really are only left to dabble in finance. Some small countries with absolutely no resources or manufacturing capability whatsoever do exactly this and make a go of it: think of Singapore, or Lichtenstein, or Bermuda or even Switzerland. These are countries that became small niche financial ser-vices-centered societies. But they can make it work precisely because they are such small, compact economies (. . . unlike the U.S.).

In one sense, in the 1990s and 2000s major economies—huge ones like the U.S. or merely large ones like the U.K.—tried to make exactly the same bet as the Singapores of the world. Excess financial complexity and the credit crisis, or the curious bankruptcy scenarios of our story, was to some extent the result. And unfortunately for the West, the issue of relative global economic decline is a potent topic, outweighing even many of the issues we've touched on in previous chapters. The issues addressed in this book are undoubtedly important ones for Western economies today—excesses of financial speculation versus excess of financial regulation; the risk associated with, but also the importance of, financial innovation; or extreme wealth inequalities versus the burden of excess taxation. That said, the juggernaut of about two and a half billion people industrializing in Asia probably puts all those other issues into the limelight.

Markets or no markets, taxation or no taxation, we're still facing once-in-a-century changes in other parts of the globe. Maybe the West will innovate its way out of relative decline, perhaps via new energy sources like fracking or via further technology revolutions. But that's a huge subject in itself, and we'll certainly have to leave that for another day.

EPILOGUE

"Finance is wholly different from the rest of the economy."
—**Alan Greenspan** (1926–)

We've experienced in this book a type of journey through stories and analyses of some basic concepts in the financial world. Hopefully we have tried to see these ideas from a slightly oblique angle, and this has given us a certain perspective on the concepts.

The core notions we have covered (be it "value" or "risk/uncertainty" or "contracts" or "ownership" or "financial instruments" or "taxation" or "fraud" or "regulation") are seemingly separate notions. Each appears quite discrete. But I hope you have noticed that certain ideas and philosophical themes keep recurring throughout the book. In fact, I believe there is really one stream of ideas that link most of the concepts in this book. This stream became even more apparent to me as I was writing about the individual topics that comprise each chapter. Linking them all is a single thread that in many ways connects much financial thinking, preoccupation, and dialogue.

So, as a last step, let's try to see what unifies all these separate financial notions. Let's do it again by reference to a final fiction. But rather than use a story, I'd like to describe a hypothetical game or simulation.

The game I want you to consider is a sort of gambling game. The players are kids in a computer gaming community where they're winning electronic chips instead of real money.

In these types of online games, there's often a ringleader, an older kid or one highly experienced in playing the game. (I've seen that when I watch my own boys play these games.) The ringleader kid we will call the Joker.

Now, in this game the Joker has the unique role of creating little online worlds. The Joker, for a cost (in chips), can seed whole simulated worlds with their own computer populations, societies, and economies. The computer then generates and runs these virtual worlds. Each of those worlds has its own peculiar social structure, and each has unique economic ways of subsistence.

The Joker kid, by putting game points into seeding a new computer society, effectively does something similar to capitalizing a business. With his game point payment, the Joker provides an initial injection of economic potential into each world—or, we might say, the potential for future economic growth, welfare and utility. The Joker is a bit like a venture or seed investor. His points go toward buying simulated natural resources, or food supplies, or intelligence and ingenuity, or any other resources which the computer-generated people in a given virtual world have the potential to exploit.

Now, like any investor, the Joker wants something in exchange for his "capital" injection. So he gets a strange security—a cyber financial instrument—in exchange for his economic capitalization of a given world. We will call this online security the Global Economic Mother of all securities (the GEM), and each one gives the Joker ownership of all virtual economic wealth in a given online world (after all, it is he who capitalized that world). We might think of the GEM as a magical, ancient cuneiform tablet that materializes on the screen with these global economic ownership rights etched, as if in a contract, into the stone. Think perhaps of magical-type objects sometime appearing in online adventure games.

In addition, the GEM tablets or stones themselves glow. The brightness with which they shine depends on a certain sense of "welfare." Each GEM tablet radiates a glow corresponding and proportionate to the level of economic well-being in a given virtual world. And from the glow of the stone, the Joker kid receives, over time, dividends in the form of new game points—effectively the dividend or profit that he receives for the ownership rights in the whole economy of an entire virtual computer world.

So that's the basic set-up. But of course when the Joker first capitalizes/ initiates a world, the glow of a given GEM is limited. Consider the earth as an example of a real-life global economy. Early in human existence, and for many millennia, economic growth and welfare was limited. People eked out a living by hunting and gathering, innovation was minimal, and much of the potential utility latent in the earth (and in the human brain) had not been exploited. However, over time, worlds develop just as the human economy has on our earth. With this development comes a growth in their total welfare—which includes technological, industrial, and economic welfare. The glow of the GEM for each advancing world grows brighter accordingly. And with each increase in brightness, more game point dividends are awarded to the player holding the GEM.

And I say "the player," for this is where the game really begins. You see, once the Joker has seeded any given world and hence originated a new GEM, he doesn't keep the GEM. Instead, he trades the GEM by selling it to one of the other kids playing on the online forum. For every single GEM, for each world, the Joker sells for value (for game points). And of course the kids who buy a given GEM stone can themselves trade them on to other kids. There's a whole, fairly liquid market for GEM stones among all the online players.

Naturally, the value of a particular GEM stone is associated with the likely economic growth prospects of a given world. A GEM providing ownership over a world that is highly undeveloped may be fairly cheap, and the glow (or dividend) from the stone will be limited. But if that world's economy develops, if the welfare of its little electronic homunculi advances, if its population grows and experiences higher living standards—well, naturally, the glow of the GEM stone increases. In that way the GEM stone provides more and more return for the kid holding the GEM. And as the glow of the GEM grows, the value, in the secondary market, of the GEM stone inevitably increases also.

Still, the kids have certain real challenges to face in playing the game. It is the computer's complex algorithms, not the kids that determine the economic growth of a given virtual world. There are some indicators for each simulated world of possible future economic prospects, but the kids don't really know *which* world is going to grow dynamically, or *when*, or by *how much*. On top of it, the kids will always be the usual mixed bunch of young humans—greedy and fearful and competitive.

They love to buy GEM stones they consider cheap. Each of the kids hopes to make a killing by seeing the price of the GEM stone increase as a global economy, represented by the stone, develops. It's always a gamble, but the upside can be huge. Timing is everything—and, remember, what are centuries in the real world are mere minutes or hours in these computer- simulated worlds. To take again the example of our earth, a great trade might have been to buy the earth's GEM stone in the late medieval period just before the Renaissance kicked in. If you held the earth's GEM stone for the next 500 years, you would have made a killing as economic production and welfare exploded like never before. An even shorter-term trade may have been to buy the earth GEM stone in, say, 1750, just before the advent of the industrial revolution, and to sell approximately 200 years later prior to the beginning of World War II. Another sweet trade. In fact, a really savvy child would have again bought back the earth's GEM shortly after the war—say in the early 1950s—and held it until today. This buyer would then have enjoyed, through the second half of the 20th century, the most explosive growth in human economic activity, welfare, and population in earth's history. In the game, the GEM would assume a brilliant glow, reflecting the soaring increase in dividends and value.

Of course, other deals can go less well. Buying an earth-like GEM stone in, say, 300 CE was not such a good trade. That date marked the tail end of the height of the Roman Empire, and if you were still sitting on the stone in say, 800 CE in the midst of the Dark Ages, the gleam of the GEM would be scarcely visible. (Rome had a population of about one million people at its height, but after its collapse, it was not until the 19th century that another city achieved that size.)

And there's a further sting to this game. Most worlds—certainly the earth—do seem gradually to improve in total economic welfare, even though this improvement may occur slowly over millennia, unevenly, and in fits and starts. So you would think a simple long-term hold strategy might be the best thing with these GEMs: a prudent young child would just buy one and sit on it for game-time millennia before seeing its glow reach full luminescence as its value rose.

But here's the catch: the Joker doesn't keep the game quite that simple. You see, the Joker periodically, and quite deliberately, destroys entire worlds. That's also part of his role in the game. It's great fun for the Joker player who, with a click of his mouse button, just snuffs out entire global economies, turning them into cyber dust. It certainly gives the game a unique twist. Some innocent child might be sitting on a fine GEM stone representing a world that has really advanced significantly, when quite suddenly, the Joker destroys that world entirely. Naturally, at that very moment the GEM stone goes black, and suddenly the owner of the stone finds he or she is holding a worthless electronic simulacra of a cuneiform-style tablet. You can imagine it must be quite a blow for your average child trying to have fun trading GEMs.

This aspect of the game is what really engages the players, especially the Joker. The GEMs are the electronic embodiment of hot potatoes—if you buy right, and at the right time, you can make a killing. But you do *not* want to be the last child holding the GEM when the music stops.

And on top of it all, the avaricious nature of young kids means some of them love to cheat. A holder of a given GEM typically has a bit more information about the underlying virtual economy represented by that GEM than anyone else. So in trying to sell a given GEM, kids are known to regularly exaggerate the performance of the underlying economies. They are not supposed to misrepresent in this way, but the little ones are quite unstoppable.

Some players also love trying to bribe the Joker himself—the Joker being the ultimate source of all authority in the game, the referee, the— "Government." Children may offer game points to the Joker if the Joker promises not to destroy a given world (and the Joker may, or may not, keep his promises). In other cases, kids look for tips from the Joker as they try to figure out which world he is about to destroy. That way, and with this "inside" knowledge, the child can "short" sell the GEM and make a killing from disaster. And, finally, there's the element of rumor. Sometimes, players hear "through the grapevine" that the Joker is about to destroy a particular world, and that suggestion itself can trigger collective panic among the fickle boys and girls. When they start selling the relevant GEM, its price (often quite unfairly) collapses.

The system does provide certain regulatory guidelines to try to prevent some of this mischief, and the Joker himself may impose specific rules on players. Players can, for example, be docked game points or even banned from the game for gross misrepresentations about a virtual economy underlying a given GEM. If you are caught trading off tips from the Joker about pending destruction of given economies, this too can result in a kid being suspended from the game (as well as the Joker being slung out and replaced). The makers of the game want, after all, for it to function in a vaguely fair fashion. Still, the rules are hard to implement. Trying to impose the strictest rules can gum up the whole game itself. Also, the Joker is often worn down by all the pranks.

And so there it is. If you didn't know about this game, well the high-roller geeky online kids call it—"shooting Geminos." It's an extraordinary game—a game of global economies.

I think the game largely speaks for itself, and I hereby copyright the idea if some computer-games house wants to make it into a real online play system! It's described as a kids' game, but of course finance is a much more serious business which, as we have discussed, can affect us all. Still, some of the players in finance certainly seem periodically to behave like kids. In any event, the game can help us link the threads of the financial themes of this book.

Understanding the game really starts with the GEM assets themselves. A GEM is not a global economy itself, it is a "representation" of that global economy. It gives the GEM holder ownership rights over the global economy, but the global economy is separate. Like GEMs, finance is all about these "representations" of economic realities—tokens or "fictions" that reflect the real world. (Financial instruments are themselves stories of sorts.) Financiers hold pieces of paper that give them rights over economic production, but they do not really do the economic production themselves (see Greenspan's quote at the beginning of this chapter). Indeed, that is why the whole finance industry is sometimes open to the accusation of being entirely parasitic on real economic activity. But the beginning of finance is to understand that it is itself about these representations, mirror images of real economics, as opposed to actual industry or agriculture itself. It is about buying stocks, or bonds, or options, or CDOs . . . or GEMs (and of course the closest real-world equivalent to GEMs are sovereign bonds).

Now these representative tokens of finance, financial contracts/ instruments (the GEMs in our game) have certain "values" linked to the performance of aspects of the real economy. And they are typically tradable rights since they are material, not moral, rights (think of our Faust story). Hence the finance world is consumed in understanding the value of these tokens/instruments. At the same time the value of the instruments (or of the GEMs) are dependent on the future performance of the underlying economy. Yet no one knows for sure, how that performance will pan out. Hence, we are also brought to the intrinsic "risk" and "uncertainty" in finance. Hence, also, why the value of the instruments/GEMs can fluctuate so much.

In this context of risk and value uncertainty, the buying and selling of the tokens/instruments represent a real opportunity to make serious money, but also to lose it all. Huge gains are sometimes the product of lucky bets and should perhaps be "taxed" to ensure a fairer distribution of profits among us all.

Meanwhile some businesses grow and grow, but they too have a life cycle and surely die—the Joker kills them all eventually. And every investor always frets about that prospect, even if it does not materialize. The corporate life cycle is, you might say, an economic form of entropy. So now we see that the trading of the GEM and other finance tokens or fictions is embedded in the human (and the children's) psychology of both "greed" and "fear." And while "greed" and "fear" can be real motivators, they are also the core of many of the moral inconsistencies we face in commercial life. These are emotions that drive us all into "Faustian"-type pacts, emotional conflicts that can undermine our ethical integrity in many ways.

We need to manage these psychological challenges everyday—and it's hard. Indeed, some people are tipped over the edge or are just fundamentally greedy (psychopathically so), and the result is "fraud," which is an unfortunate side effect of the GEM game or the game of trading in financial instruments.

And finally, it is to stop this type of fraud that the GEM game needs some rules and regulations. Certain constraints do need to be put on human (or childlike) behavior created by the financial or GEM game. Equally, though, the rules can become very cumbersome—sometimes so much so that the whole game comes to a standstill. At some point the kids can just lose interest in shooting Geminos entirely and flip to another online alternative. And this is a grave problem. For in spite of appearances, the game has great benefits in bringing needed capital to our (real or virtual) worlds. After all, it's only in exchange for newly-minted GEMs that the Joker injects initial economic capital or potential into a virtual economic environment. Likewise, the instruments of finance are ultimately critical in bringing needed capital to real-life economic activity.

So that's it—an inexorably-linked pattern, akin to the causal chain of the English nursery rhyme "The House that Jack Built." Again, it starts from the notion of finance as the use of representative fictions, *instruments* or tokens reflecting the real economy or real businesses; to these instruments being tradable at *values* that are changing because the economic future is *uncertain*; to the appeal to our *greed and fear* due to the possibility of making money off these valuation fluctuations; to the *moral failings* that this can engender; and hence finally to the *regulations* that are needed (within certain parameters) to stop total moral chaos.

That, I think, is the single flow of thought that unifies the stories in these chapters and the reason why these themes keep repeating themselves throughout the book.

These are philosophical or conceptual themes related to economics, but in fact are more particularly "finance" themes. It is "finance" since the ideas all originate from the notion of investing in a financial instrument, in a representative tool reflective of economic reality. It is finance since these are not stories of industrial production per se. It is finance since our book is a collection of fictions—fictions that somehow mirror, and occasionally distort, the underlying reality of all our economic lives.

END NOTES

CHAPTER 1

1. *Manias, Panics and Crashes – A History of Financial Crisis*, Sixth Edition, 2011, Charles P. Kindleberger and Robert Z. Aliber, pp. 43-44.
2. Likewise there can be as much as a 300–500 bps incremental yield premium (i.e. additional cost) on private debt as compared to publically listed, liquid debt for an identical issuer/creditor.
3. *Enquiries Concerning Human Understanding and Concerning the Principles of Morals*, 1777, David Hume.
4. *South Sea Bubble*, 1960, John Carswell, p. 120.
5. *Infectious Greed*, 2003, Frank Partnoy, p. 272.
6. *Inefficient Markets: An Introduction to Behavioural Finance*, 2000, Andrei Shleifer, Oxford University Press.
7. See, for example, George Soros' 2008 book, *The New Paradigm for Financial Markets* and his theory (based on his real life in the market) of "Reflexivity." In the book Soros, controversially, argues that the old market equilibrium paradigm must be replaced. According to his theory of Reflexivity, self-fulfilling investor participation in the capital markets and the herd behavior of investors may at times materially influence valuations.
8. See his latest book, *The Map and the Territory*.
9. *The Power of Gold*, 2000, Peter L. Bernstein, p. 370. Bernstein later quotes (p. 371) Robert Mundell, the Nobel Laureate in Economics, who wrote in the *Wall Street Journal*, Op-Ed page, December 10, 1999, "The main thing

we miss today is universal money, a standard of value, the link between the past and the future and the cement linking remote parts of the human race to another."

CHAPTER 2

1. *Speech on American Taxation*, 1774, Edmund Burke (1729–1797).
2. *Genesis Rabbah*, 89: 6, Julius Theodor (1849–1924).
3. *Against the Gods – The Remarkable Story of Risk*, 1998, Peter L. Bernstein, p. 15.
4. See *Macbeth*, Act 2, Scenes I and II.
5. *The (Mis)Behavior of Markets: A Fractal View of Risk, Ruin and Reward*, 2004, Benoit B. Mandelbrot and Richard L. Hudson.
6. *Ecclesiastes*, Chapter II, 8-11. Or see also *Matthew* 19:24, "It is easier for a camel to go through the eye of a needle, than a rich man to enter the kingdom of God".
7. *Tractates of Logical Philosophy*, 6.41, 1922, Ludwig Wittgenstein, translated from the German by C.K. Ogden.
8. See *The End of Eternity*, 1955, Isaac Asimov.
9. *Ibid* (note^{16}), 6.45.

CHAPTER 3

1. *The Cheyenne Way*, 1941, p. 237.
2. *Essays in Jurisprudence and Philosophy*, 1988, p. 94.
3. *Ibid*, p. 95.
4. *Wittgenstein on Rules and Private Language: An Elementary Exposition*, 1982, Saul A. Kripke.
5. *Philosophical Investigations*, 1953, Section 201.
6. *Law and the Modern Mind*, 1930.
7. See *Contractual Obligations v the Meaning of a Contract*.

CHAPTER 4

1. Since $\sqrt{-1}$ is defined as "i," hence $\sqrt{-3}$ is said to be 3i, and $i^2 = -1$.
2. See *Deuteronomy* 23: 19-20.
3. See *The Origins of Value: The Financial Innovations that Created Modern Capital Markets*, 2005, edited by William N. Goetzmann and K. Geert Rouwenhorst, Chapter 1 *The Invention of Interest; Sumerian Loans* by Marc Van De Mieroop, Oxford University Press.

4. See *The Origins of Value: The Financial Innovations that Created Modern Capital Markets*, 2005, edited by William N. Goetzmann and K. Geert Rouwenhorst, Chapter 7 *Fibonacci and the Financial Revolution* by William N. Goetzmann, Oxford University Press. Goetzmann also references *The Medieval Origins of the Financial Revolution: Usury, Rentes and Negotiability*, John H. Munro, The International History Review, 25 no. 3 (Sept 2003).
5. University of Pennsylvania Law School, 2004, Paper 49, Michael Knoll.
6. *Ha-Mishpat*, 1927, E.L Globus, p. 39.
7. *Babylonian Talmud, Baba Metzia*, 61b, 67a, et al.
8. Note also similar types of instrument were used in Italy (Venice and Genoa) in late medieval/early Renaissance days. Called "commenda" they involved one party investing capital and the other labor into a partnership (usually to finance a shipping voyage). See again note [4] above–ibid. Goetzmann also references *The Origins of the Commenda Contract*, John Pryor, Speculum 52, no. 1, 1977.
9. *Shadow Credit and the Private, Middle Market: Pre-Crisis and Post-Crisis Developments, Data Trends and Two Examples of Private, Non-bank Lending*, Dr Craig A. Zabala and Jeremy M. Josse, Journal of Risk Finance, Volume 15, Issue 3, 2014.
10. See the definition of *"Corporation"* in *The Devil's Dictionary*, 1911, Ambrose Bierce.

CHAPTER 5

1. See Chapter 2 in *Roman Shares* by Ulrike Malmendier, in *The Origins of Value: The Financial Innovations that Created Modern Capital Markets*, 2005, edited by William N. Goetzmann and K. Geert Rouwenhorst, Oxford University Press.
2. *The Ancient Roots of Modern Financial Innovation: The Early History of Regulatory Arbitrage*, June 8, 2004, Professor Michael Knoll, University of Pennsylvania Law School, Paper 49.

CHAPTER 6

1. Indeed this theme has been taken up in recent academic work—see *The Soul as Commodity: Materialism in Doctor Faustus*, 2013, Andrew Shifflett et al, Boydell & Brewer, pp. 21-30.
2. *The New Vote Buying: Empty Voting and Hidden (Morphable) Ownership*, 2006, Henry T. C. Hu & Bernard Black, 79 Southern California Law Review 811-908.

3. Article 18 of the *Declaration of the Rights of Man and Citizen from the Constitution of the Year 1*, 1793.
4. *Foundations of the Metaphysics of Morals*, 1785, Immanuel Kant.
5. *Economic and Philosophical Manuscripts, Alienated Labour*, 1844, Karl Marx.
6. *False Necessity – Anti-Necessitarian Social Theory in the Service of Radical Democracy*, 1987, Roberto Mangabeira Unger, p. 196.

CHAPTER 7

1. John Maynard Keynes (1965) [1930], *"The Classification of Money." A Treatise on Money*, Macmillan & Co Ltd. p. 7. "Fiat Money is Representative (or token) Money (i.e. something the intrinsic value of the material substance of which is divorced from its monetary face value)—now generally made of paper except in the case of small denominations—which is created and issued by the State, but is not convertible by law into anything other than itself, and has no fixed value in terms of an objective standard." Also N. Gregory Mankiw (September 29, 2008). *Principles of Economics*. p. 659. "Fiat money, such as paper dollars, is money without intrinsic value: It would be worthless if it were not used as money."
2. *The Ascent of Money: A Financial History of the World*, Niall Ferguson, 2008, pp. 30-31.
3. "For those who imagine the evolution of monetary systems as a linear progression from primitive commodity monies to gold and silver coinage and finally to purely nominal currencies like paper money, the early appearance of paper money in China in the eleventh century appears to be a glaring anomaly"—see *The Origins of Paper Money in China* by Richard von Glahn, Chapter 4 of *The Origins of Value: The Financial Innovations that Created Modern Capital Markets*, 2005, edited by William N. Goetzmann and K. Geert Rouwenhorst, Oxford University Press.
4. *The Power of Gold: The History of an Obsession*, Peter L. Bernstein, 2000.
5. In the Target store hacking, customer names, credit or debit card numbers, expiration dates and CVVs were involved in the information theft. (The CVV—the card verification value, also known as the security code—is the three or four-digit number typically requested by retailers when making purchases online or over the phone.) In California a class action suit against Target was brought and Robert Ahdoot, a lawyer for the plaintiffs, said he spoke to customers who claimed unauthorized ATM withdrawals had been made from their accounts. The CFO of Target ended up testifying before the Senate Judiciary Committee and Target is apparently spending $100m to upgrade to more advanced chip-based credit card technology.

6. *The Counter-Revolution in Monetary Theory*, Milton Friedman, 1970.
7. In *The Ascent of Money: A Financial History of the World*, Niall Ferguson, 2008, p. 107, quotes Keynes as saying this. See *The Economic Consequences of the Peace*, John Maynard Keynes, 1919, p. 78.
8. See 2011 *FDIC National Survey of Unbanked and Underbanked Households*, September 20, 2011, page 3 (FDIC study).
9. *Conjectures and Refutations*, Ch. 16, *Prediction and Prophecy in the Social Sciences*, VIII, p. 342.

CHAPTER 8

1. See Plato's *Timaeus* and *Critias*. Scheria and Ogygia were islands described in Homer's *Odyssey* that some have associated with Atlantis.
2. See *The Ascent of Money, A Financial History of the World*, 2008, Niall Ferguson, p. 86.
3. *Capital in the Twenty-First Century*, 2013, Thomas Piketty.
4. *A Theory of Optimal Inheritance Taxation*, Econometrica, Vol. 81, No. 5 (September 2013), 1851–1886, Thomas Piketty and Emmanuel Saez.
5. *The Social Contract and Discourses*, Chapter I, by Jean Jacques Rousseau, 1762.
6. *Ibid*, Chapter II.

CHAPTER 9

1. See the characters Iago in *Othello* and Richard III in *Richard III*, by William Shakespeare.
2. *Wall Street* was a 1987 American drama film, directed and co-written by Oliver Stone. In it a fundamentally twisted Wall Street investor (Gordon Gekko) lures a young broker Bud Fox into unlawful insider dealing.
3. See *Too Good to Be True*, by Erin Arvedkund; *Betrayal*, by Andrew Kirtzman; and *Madoff With the Money*, by Jerry Oppenheimer.
4. *Handbook of Psychopathy*, 2005, Christopher Patrick, Guilford Press.
5. *Amadeus* is a play by Peter Shaffer first performed in 1979 (later made into a movie in 1984) giving a semi-fictionalized account of the life of Mozart.
6. *The Economist*, May 31, 2014. Article pages 26–27, *Why thieves love America's health care system.*
7. Quoted in the *Wall Street Journal*, December 15, 2008.
8. *A framework for assessing the benefits of financial regulation, Repot prepared for the [UK] Financial Services Authority*, September 2006, Oxera.

CHAPTER 10

1. Thomas Hobbes famously described government as a "leviathan" in his 1651 book *Leviathan*.
2. According to the Office of Information and Regulatory Affairs, Office of Management and Budget, Executive Office of the President.
3. *The Consequences of Regulatory Accumulation and a Proposed Solution*, February 2014, Patrick A. McLaughlin and Richard Williams, Mercatus Center, George Mason University, No. 14-03.
4. *Federal Regulation and Aggregate Economic Growth, The Journal of Economic Growth*, June 2013 issue, John Dawson (Appalachian State University) and John Seater (North Carolina State University).
5. Per *Maine Banker*, the official publication of the Maine Bankers Association.
6. *How To Do Things with Rules*, 1987 edition, William Twining and David Miers, p. 147, (first published 1976).
7. In his article *How America Lost Its Way*, June 17, 2013, Niall Ferguson wrote, "We used to have the rule of law. Now it is tempting to say we have the rule of lawyers."
8. *The Rule of Nobody: Saving America from Dead Laws and Broken Government*, 2014, W.W. Norton, by Philip Howard.
9. See note [3] above.
10. *The Trial*, written by Franz Kafka between 1914 and 1915 and published in 1925.

CHAPTER 11

1. *Shadow Credit and the Private, Middle Market: Pre-Crisis and Post-Crisis Developments, Data Trends and Two Examples of Private, Non-bank Lending*, Craig A. Zabala and Jeremy M. Josse, *Journal of Risk Finance*, Volume 15, Issue 3, 2014.
2. Concorde Group, Inc. (May 21, 2014). *Addendum to the Confidential Memorandum*, dated March 8, 2010. Form D/A (filed March 27, 2013), U.S. Securities and Exchange Commission, File No 021-141436. See also the Concorde Group, Inc's website at: www.concorde-us.com. The firm describes itself as, "a holding company that provides high quality financial services to Middle Market businesses and investors. The Middle Market is defined as small and mid-sized public and private companies, aspiring and successful entrepreneurs and entrepreneurial companies, and venture companies with impressive track records and solid business models."
3. See, among other books, *Dangerous Dreamers: The Financial Innovators from Charles Merrill to Michael Milken*, 1993, Robert Sobel.

4. See *The Origins of Value: The Financial Innovations that Created Modern Capital Markets*, edited by William N. Goetzmann and K. Geert Rouwenhorst. See the chapter *The Invention of Interest – Sumerian Loans*, by Marc Van de Mieroop, p. 18.

5. *When Genius Failed: The Rise and Fall of Long-Term Capital Management*, 2000, Roger Lowenstein, Random House.

6. See, for example, such classics on scientific innovation as *The Sleepwalkers*, 1959, Arthur Koestler or *The Structure of Scientific Revolutions*, 1962, Thomas S. Kuhn.

7. See *The Data Mine*, (part of CQ Roll Call), April 23, 2012.

INDEX